Tomorrow's Parties

America and the Long 19th Century

GENERAL EDITORS
David Kazanjian, Elizabeth McHenry, and Priscilla Wald

Tomorrow's Parties

*Sex and the Untimely
in Nineteenth-Century America*

Peter Coviello

NEW YORK UNIVERSITY PRESS

New York and London

NEW YORK UNIVERSITY PRESS
New York and London
www.nyupress.org

A version of Chapter Two, entiteld "Whitman's Children," appeared in
PMLA, Vol. 128, No. 1, January 2013.

LIBRARY OF CONGRESS CATALOGING-IN-PUBLICATION DATA

Coviello, Peter.
Tomorrow's parties : sex and the untimely in nineteenth-century
America / Peter Coviello.
p. cm.—(America and the long 19th century)
Includes bibliographical references and index.
ISBN 978-0-8147-1740-0 (cl : alk. paper)
ISBN 978-0-8147-1741-7 (pb : alk. paper)
ISBN 978-0-8147-1742-4 (e)
ISBN 978-0-8147-9030-4 (e)
1. American literature—19th century—History and criticism.
2. Intimacy (Psychology) in literature.   3. Sex in literature.
4. Interpersonal relations in literature.   I. Title.
PS217.I52C69 2013
810.9'3538—dc23

2012035344

New York University Press books are printed on acid-free paper, and
their binding materials are chosen for strength and durability. We
strive to use environmentally responsible suppliers and materials to the
greatest extent possible in publishing our books.

Manufactured in the United States of America
c 10 9 8 7 6 5 4 3 2 1
p 10 9 8 7 6 5 4 3 2 1

To Anthony and Josephine Coviello

"There is nothing to do
For our liberation, except wait in the horror of it.

And I am lost without you."

—John Ashbery,
"They Dream Only of America"

Contents

Acknowledgments

A confession: the writing of this book was, if sometimes tiring, actually a great deal of fun. It is also true, though, that the period of its composition coincided, for me, with a lot of unforeseen, life-wide turmoil. To the people named here I want to say, first and above all, that the fact of this book existing, rather than not, is outrageously inadequate thanks to you. Your generosity, your brilliance, your unstinting care, and your heroic patience: these all deserve much, much more. Thank you for restoring the possibilities of joy.

For sustenance in Maine, intellectual, corporeal, and otherwise, deepest thanks to John Bisbee, Aviva Briefel, Tess Chakkalakal, Brock Clarke, Allison Cooper, Allen Delong, Dallas Dennery, Tim Diehl, Pamela Fletcher, Tim Foster, Paul Franco, David and Lesley Gordon, Cassie Jones, Aaron Kitch, Henry Laurence, Barry Mills, M. Katherine O'Grady, Steve and Heather Perkinson, Elizabeth Pritchard, Marilyn Reizbaum, José Ribas, Jen Scanlon, Kevin Wertheim, and Mark Wethli. Ann Kibbie held my hand through the worst of it—literally—and Frank and Susan Burroughs offered familial care for which there will never be enough thanks.

For their acuity, collegiality, and ongoing support I offer thanks to my colleagues in English—as well as Gay and Lesbian Studies and Africana Studies—at Bowdoin College. And thanks, too, to my students, whose eagerness and incisive curiosity have made my understanding of the books considered here sharper than it could otherwise have been.

And finally, there is the Bowdoin diaspora, who have for better than a decade now come through with astonishing quantities of love. Leah Chernikoff —and Larry Chernikoff and Allison Beck—Willing Davidson, David Diamond, Tasha Graff, Molly Hardy, Jared Hickman, Matt King, Abby Lord, Chad MacDermid, Frances Milliken, Caitlin Riley, and Nate Vinton: you are all an inspiration and a joy.

Speaking of Bowdoin, in May of 2010 I threw a shindig at the college called Tomorrow's Parties: A Queer Americanist Colloquium. The immense intellectual generosity of the participants not only made the weekend a delight, but galvanized the work of this book. Thanks to Katherine Biers, Elizabeth Freeman, Kara Keeling, Dana Luciano, Molly McGarry, Jordan Stein, and Pamela Thurschwell, as well as to our keynote speaker—who is also my inspiration and ongoing patron saint—Kathryn Bond Stockton. For their support over many years I am grateful as well to Ellis Hanson, Michael Moon, and Mark Seltzer.

Thank you also to Eric Zinner, Ciara McLaughlin, David Kazanjian, Elizabeth McHenry, Priscilla Wald, my readers, and everyone at NYU Press for their dedication to this project.

Much of *Tomorrow's Parties* was written while on leave in and around Chicago in 2009. For their hospitality during those months, often on an epic scale, I thank Jim Arndorfer, Judith Brown, Marcy Dinius, David and Andi Diamond, Kathy Flynn, Karen Gliwa, Ed Koziboski, Julia Rosenwinkel, Lanay Samuelson, Julia Stern, Wendy Wall, and Paula K. Wheeler. Whatever delights came to me then were curated, once more, by John Dorr, whose love built a floor beneath me—and walls, and windows, and rooms richly furnished—when I was sure there was none.

A magic similar to the sort worked by John and Karen—the magic of making the world habitable when it seems far otherwise—was made for me by those other friends of my youth, Sandy Zipp and Ilona Miko, and Mark Goble and Elisa Tamarkin, who somehow combined the gentlest care with the fiercest devotion. I do not know what to say of these depths of gratitude other than what I think you know: that even after twenty-plus years of confidences, tears, and mix-CDs, you are dearer to me now than ever.

Then, too, there is the extended posse of friends, colleagues, and karaoke co-conspirators in whose company so many of the best ideas of this book were germinated, and to whose example—of keen intelligence wedded to openheartedness—I have long aspired. With a song in my heart, I thank Katherine Biers, Mandy Berry, Sarah Blackwood, Hester Blum, Robert Chang, Jennifer Doyle, Stephanie DeGooyer, Elena Glasberg, Jody Greene, Glenn Hendler, Claire Jarvis, Katherine Lieber, Christopher Looby, Jackie Loss, Heather Love, Donal McQuillian, Sarah Mesle, José Muñoz, Eden Osucha, Masha Raskolnikov, Catherine Rice, Jordana Rosenberg, Caleb Smith, Gustavus Stadler, Pamela Thurschwell, Kyla Wazana Tompkins, Karen Tongson, and Ivy Wilson. Molly McGarry and Heather Lukes made a home for me, and a haven, in Los Angeles. Jasbir Puar transformed the El Quixote bar into our own private seminar on desire, loss, and hilarity. Jordan Stein talked through so much of this book he ought to be getting royalties, though his deeper contributions were to joy. And to Beth Freeman, my first-ever writing partner, and Dana Luciano, my best-ever life partner: you are the imagined audience for each and every one of the sentences that follow. Thank you for expanding the parameters of "love" for me, every day.

Skirting across all these categories, and infusing them all with her own exuberant charm, is Katie Swan, one-woman posse, giver of expansive care, the greatest thing about Maine, and quite a great deal besides. Love, gratitude, and then more love to you, Nurse Swan—and your little dog, too.

Contrary to what you may have seen on TV, belonging to an extended Italian family is actually a piece of inestimable good fortune. My family in Italy took me in when I most desperately needed it. Baci e la mia gratitudine alla famiglia a Napoli, Louisa and Mario Guerriera, and all of their nieces and nephews and children: Laura, Onofrio, Marilena, Enzo, Daniella, Tomasso, Rosaria, Gennaro, Paula, Fabbio, Vincenzo, Bianca, e mio fratello Roberto. Closer to home, but no less saving in their generosity and their care, are the Carcusas, the Carrieras, the Ciprianis, the Coviellos, and the Sterners. As Neil, Scott, and all my cousins know, and my beloved nephew Gio and brother John too, the world we inhabit is knit together by the astounding Scognamiglio sisters, Josephine, Louise, Diane, and Nettie. To them I can truthfully say: were it not for your several heroic interventions, I would not be here.

Sophie and Eliza D'Anieri, who are each day more beautiful, more hilarious, more formidable, and more inspiring than seems possible, have given to this book, and to my life, more than they know. I'll resist the temptation to talk to them about all their tomorrows, and say only this: girls, you are miracles of awesomeness. I am so proud of you, I am so grateful to you, and I love you so much.

Anthony and Josephine Coviello built a world around me, made of care and talk and an unbridled joyousness to which I always knew I could return, in exultation or in need. Dad, Mom: I am sorry for having put you through so difficult a time, though I know this is an apology you do not accept. Accept, instead, this small gesture of very great love.

Tomorrow's Parties

Introduction

The Unspeakable Past

Too Bleakly Stranded

In the summer of 1914, from his sanctuary at Lamb House in Rye, England, Henry James wrote a small letter he addressed to "Mrs. Fields." This was Annie Adams Fields, the widow of Boston publisher James Fields and, for nearly a quarter of a century, the intimate companion of another famed American writer, Sarah Orne Jewett, who had died in 1909. (Fields was herself to die, at age eighty, in January of 1915.) "Dear Mrs. Fields," James begins,

> I have left so many days unacknowledged the so beautiful & touching letter prompted by your generous appreciation of my volume of Notes. The reason is largely that even still the high pressure London of June & July is always at some big interrupting assault on one's time or one's preferences, & that I have been but within a few days able to break away from it & get down into these quieter conditions. The arrears of my correspondence—a very desperate quantity—have had more than ever to wait. It is meanwhile the sympathy of all old friends from far back like yourself, of "those who know," as Dante says, that is the reward of my attempt to reach back a little to the unspeakable past. I really like to think of those who know what I am talking about—& such readers are now of the fewest. We both have had friends all the way along, however; & I mustn't speak as if we were too bleakly stranded today. The only thing is, none the less, that almost nobody understands what we mean, do they?—we can say that to each other (and to Mrs. Bell & to Miss Howe) even if we can't say it to them. I think of you very faithfully & gratefully & tenderly, & am yours affectionately always Henry James[1]

Everything about this marks it as, distinctively, late James: the attenuated syntax, the gestures toward referents both obscure and strangely intensified, and not least the circulation of an only possibly implicit erotic content (flickering up there in the strange paired reference to the *Inferno* and to one or another variety of the unspeakable). Some of the referents are easy enough to trace. When James mentions Fields's "generous appreciation of my volume of Notes," for instance, he is referring to his collection of criticism, *Notes on Novelists with Some Other Notes*, published in 1914. More curiously, when James speaks of "those who know," he is quoting Dante's famous appellation for Aristotle ("Master of those who know"), which appears in Canto IV of the *Inferno* where Dante finds himself gazing, with mixed sorrow and reverence, upon the pre-Christian poets and philosophers, consigned to the outer edges of Hell but given there a place of sheltered honor.

It is a beguiling, if somewhat elusive, little letter. Ought we to read it as an essentially tender avowal of friendship and devotion? Or as chiefly melancholy? Does James intend it to be comic? Or merely wistful? And what of the small undercurrent of something sharper—something genial but, glancingly, ominous? The matter seems to pivot on what James calls, with characteristically rich suggestiveness, "the unspeakable past." A bit melancholically, he suggests to Mrs. Fields that he and she, now late in life, must labor against the impulse to think of themselves as "bleakly stranded," suffering the isolation that comes of inhabiting a world, or a vision of the world, that is comprehensible now only to "the fewest," and those numbers diminishing. And yet this is plainly also a kind of love letter, playful if mordant. James's affection, so vivid in the letter's companionable good-humor, travels too along the vein of James's sense of his and Mrs. Fields's mutual illegibility as citizens of the present, his winking insistence that they share in the possession of some now-occult, very possibly *damning*, knowledge. And if the wistfulness of James's sentences is any indication, their intimacy refreshes itself as well in the "sympathy" kindled by their mutual vulnerability to an odd kind of loss. It is as if, with a great lightness of touch, James enjoins Mrs. Fields to mourn with him the loss of nothing less than an entire world, a world in whose terms and horizons of knowledge friends might find one another, and be found.

Of course, James's ambivalent relationship to legibility—or perhaps we should say, the pleasure he is able to wring from a legibility that is always tenuous, partial, and covert—is no less evident here as well. All of this might induce us to ask: What "past" is it, precisely, that James imagines himself, Mrs. Fields, and their friends to share? Why is knowledge of that past offered both as a mark of potentially infernal condemnation—those who know, the letter reminds its recipient, dwell in Limbo—as well as a badge of proud distinction? And what is it, exactly, that makes this past, of all the possible and less manifestly Gothic things it could be, *unspeakable*? What rupture in historical continuity has unfolded between 1914 and some earlier time that leaves James and Mrs. Fields stranded, though not *too* bleakly?

Here is one way into the matter: "This is an event," writes classicist David Halperin, "whose impact and whose scope we are only now learning how to measure."[2] He refers here neither to the death of Socrates, nor to the dawning of print technology, nor for that matter to the attacks of September 11th, 2001. The "event" he has in mind is something more diffuse but, in its way, no less consequential, especially so in the lives of Annie Adams Fields (1834–1915), Sarah Orne Jewett (1849–1909), Henry James (1843–1916), and many another. He is speaking of what is sometimes called the "invention," at roughly the turn of the twentieth century, of homosexuality and its conceptual twin, heterosexuality, as distinct forms of being defined and differentiated by sexual object-choice. (Following the conventional scholarly wisdom, we could think of the Wilde trials of 1895, which James observed with stricken, horrified, plainly riveted interest, as one of the great watershed moments in the solidification, and public dissemination, of that invention.[3]) In these terms, we might read James's letter as the testimony of a man who lived through a long moment of singular upheaval and transformation: the movement (to put this in the most un-Jamesian starkness possible) from a time before the full emergence of modern sexuality as such, to a time after its surprisingly swift, decisive solidification. In its frank affection and obscure invocations, its enthusiasm and ambivalences, James's letter might seem to us a message from the outerlands of the modern regime of sexuality, proffered by a man accustomed to (if not wholly at ease in) earlier taxonomies of intimate life, and dissatisfied with those springing up around him. What he offers, from that curious vantage, is at once a nostalgia for the presexological past, an ambivalence about the current possibilities for legibility and illegibility both, and an insistence on the bare fact of rupture, of the present's ever-heightening dislocation from a past he understands himself and Mrs. Fields to share.

But to suggest that James lived, with impassioned ambivalence, in the aftermath of the emergence of modern "sexuality" as such is to raise all sorts of knotty questions. For instance: If the hetero/homo division we continue to live with today was "invented" little more than a hundred years ago, then what exactly did erotic life look like in that bygone era for which James expresses his melancholic nostalgia, *before* the hardening of such a distinction into the stuff of present-day common sense? How, and in what terms, were nineteenth-century subjects able to imagine the parameters of sexuality? To ask that most Jamesian of questions: What could be counted *as* sexuality? Was it a circumscribed set of bodily practices? A form of identification? A mode of relation? Was sexuality an aspect of one's identity? Or was it even something an individual could be said to possess? How did it consort with other coextensive and co-elaborated vectors of being, those at once embodied and legally consequential (such as one's race, one's gender)? And what, for that matter, did this great transformation feel like on the ground, to those who lived through the stages of its unfolding?

Tomorrow's Parties: Sex and the Untimely in Nineteenth-Century America is an examination of literary imaginings of sexuality across a long and unsettled passage in its American history, from the 1840s to the first years of the new century—the span, roughly, of James's life. As we shall see, this is a moment before it was assumed that every person and every intimacy could be assigned a hetero- or homosexuality, but in which the first stirrings of that great taxonomical division, the initial movements of coordination and solidification, could already be felt. In the chapters that follow I will consider in detail the work of authors whose places in the American history of sexuality range from the canonical to the improbable—from Walt Whitman, Herman Melville, and Harriet Jacobs to Sarah Orne Jewett, Frederick Douglass, Emily Dickinson, Henry David Thoreau, and Mormon founder and homegrown prophet Joseph Smith. Crucially, though, the book is concerned far less with intimated acts or practices (such as might gain an author entrée into a canon of queer or protoqueer literature, say) than with competing conceptions of the very *domain* of sexuality, of its habitable forms and extensions, that to contemporary eyes may seem extravagant, naïve, oblique, or even scarcely legible as "sex." I read these varied passions—relations that are friendly, but not chaste; carnal, but not matrimonial; filial, but not organized by the ties of family—as testaments to the imaginative labor of authors who, for fantastically disparate reasons, worried over the encroachment of a new regime of sexual specification, and so placed a countervailing emphasis on the erotic as a mode of being not yet encoded in the official vocabularies of the intimate. The intimacies they conjure do not parse altogether easily in the commonsense vocabulary of social and sexual relations whose swift ascendancy James puzzles over in his letter to Mrs. Fields. But it is exactly this resistance to easy legibility, even to the point of inscrutability, that makes these passions as beguiling, as bewildering, and as instructive, as they are.

Was Walt Whitman Gay?

Not long ago I edited and introduced a small book of prose Whitman published about his Civil War experiences and, because it was a Civil War–related undertaking, it afforded me the occasion to speak before far more general (as opposed to simply academic) audiences than I otherwise do. This was an almost uniform pleasure, a chance to introduce to groups more fluent in the details of Joshua Lawrence Chamberlain's flanking maneuver at Little Round Top some of the energizing insights of, among other things, queer studies. It did, however, bring home to me the less-than-immediate accessibility of a systematic account of this so vibrant period of transition. It is, as Foucault reminds us, the period in which the grafting of an age-old deployment of alliance onto a new, differently structured deployment of sexuality did so much to reconfigure the disposition of bodies, genders, perversities, and knowledges in what Foucault, with a somewhat breathless capaciousness, calls "the West." It witnessed, too, the rise of sexology, a new science of experts whose once-arcane terminology—hetero- and homosexuality, say—would gradually become the commonplace designations they remain.[4] All of these transformations in the meanings, parameters, and possibilities of sexuality in that period of such high upheaval make for a good deal of confusion of tongues between the texts of that era and the perfectly reasonably questions brought to them by a contemporary audience. For instance, the question that would come up on virtually every occasion was: "So, are you saying Walt Whitman was gay?"—a question posed sometimes querulously, sometimes encouragingly, but most often out of uninflected curiosity.

In a real sense, the desire to answer that question, thoroughly and precisely, to my own satisfaction and to that of my interlocutors, stands very near the origins of the book that follows.

The answer, after all, is not simple. What I said repeatedly, in a response that became honed with practice, was: yes and no. If you mean, did Whitman have what we would think of as sexual investments in and relations with people of the same gender, then the answer is, as far as I am concerned, yes. If you are asking, though, if Whitman was a gay man in most of the other senses that might be colloquially meant by the term—not least, did he have access to a sexually-rooted, taxonomically specific category with which to identify himself and others—then the answer is no.

Here, unsurprisingly, complications ensued. Inevitably, we would talk about what was described to me as "evidence"—"Where is your proof?" someone would ask. To which my answer began to come easily, typically in the form of another question: When we are considering sexual practices not legally or ecclesiastically sanctioned, what kind of proof suffices? (I also found myself saying repeatedly: when I tell you Walt Whitman had sexual contact with men, I do not imagine myself to be *accusing* him of anything, which is what makes me uneasy, in the first instance, with strict deference to languages of evidence and proof, vestigially prosecutorial as they are.[5]) My own interests lay less with thresholds of proof than with matters of time, history, and definition. Then, as now, I found myself much more fascinated by the messy misalignments—the uncoordinated points of partial overlap and unbridgeable disconnection—between the complex, modern senses of identity and affiliation that might be heard echoing in a commonplace term like "gay," on the one hand, and on the other Whitman's own experiences of erotic being and erotic life, as much as his writing seemed to me to gauge and explore them. To take one example: Whitman did not have to hand the same sort of far-flung network of allegiance and attachment that can come now from claiming the identity "gay."[6] Though there may indeed have been sexualized forms of affinity and mutuality in which Whitman happily partook—some of these would have been called "bohemia" or "sex-radicalism," though the form of erotic affiliation most precious to him was always "America"—the fact of his having had desirous contact with men was neither at the defining core of any of them, nor did it gain him admission into any of their sodalities. And this is part, though only part, of what it means to think of Whitman as a man inhabiting an intimate world differently structured than our own.

Of course, for many auditors, what I was delicately calling a world "differently structured" seemed more precisely to be a place of inhospitable ignorance, punitive silence, and haphazard psychic brutality, a world necessarily deforming, to men and women "like Whitman," in the kinds of loneliness and isolation it exacted as a matter of course. There is much to this position. Versions of it are repeated, in fact, with greater and lesser degrees of nuance and complexity, in not a few histories of nineteenth-century American sexuality, especially those that regard the eventual emergence of a publicly legible homosexuality as a necessary triumph, the first of the steps on the way to making a habitable queer *world*, as well as a vital queer politics that would fight to dismantle ignorance, shame, silence, and brutality.[7] (As for the loneliness of living a sexually nonnormative life in the mid- to late-nineteenth century, one does not struggle to unearth vivid testaments to suffering and grief, as any who have read Whitman's anguished notebooks, redacted at moments even by *himself*, can readily attest.) But there are pitfalls, too, in the reading of the past, even the sexual past, too strictly in the terms of a happily transcended, pre-enlightened "back then," and they are not only the dangers of a triumphalist presentism. We miss, above all, what I want to call the *earliness* of the erotic being of these writers. That earliness—in Whitman, James, Jewett, Thoreau, and a raft of others—meant not only that they were, in their erotic lives, consigned to what Christopher Nealon calls a "harrowing privacy," marooned and made mutually inaccessible by the lack of any usable language of self-nomination. What I mean to capture in the term "earliness" is instead the experience of sexuality as something in the crosshairs of a number of forms of knowledge and regulation *but not yet wholly captivated or made coordinate by them.*[8] Earliness, in this sense, might also play out in other, less dire ways. Here again an aspect of James's wistfulness in his letter to Mrs. Fields comes into focus. For to inhabit an erotic self in the twilit moment *before* the arrival or calcifying of the terms of sexual identity, as James did, might also be to enjoy a special kind of freedom—one threatened, to be sure by the encroachment of a variety of new regimes of sexual knowledge, but whose fragile, uncollapsed spaces of illegibility or definitional ambiguity left precious room for much besides suffering and loneliness: for invention, say, or teasing obliquity, or coy solicitation, as well as evasion, improvisation, and all the other vectors of extravagant imagining.

This extravagant imagining is what most preoccupies *Tomorrow's Parties*. As Thoreau wrote in *Walden*: "Extra vagance! it depends on how you are yarded."[9] In the chapters that follow, we will track the extravagances that flourish in the space of a not-yet-congealed sexual specificity as they wind through the tangles of James's syntax and the compressed obliquity of Dickinson's correspondence; in the inarticulate longings of *Walden*; through the expansive dreams of the power of consecrated matrimony as offered by escaped slaves, land-bound sailors, and homegrown American prophets; in communities of the childless and chaste; in the streets of Manhattan; in the locked rooms of the infirm; in the makeshift war hospitals of Washington, DC; and even out onto the tiny islands of coastal Maine. There, I will contend, in these repeated moments of indirection, obliquity, and untimeliness, the pursuit of systematic and detailed answers to simple questions—Was Walt Whitman gay?—brings us into sharp contact with impasses and dilemmas substantially more broad. Some of them cut to the quick of the conceptual underpinnings of a number of our critical practices. For instance: What exactly do we mean when, following in the tracks of Foucault, we speak of sex as "discourse," say, or of the "discursive constitution" of sex? What are the codes of legibility that allow us even to recognize something—a body, an act, an impression, a thought, a sentence—as sex, or sexually invested? What have those codes of legibility to do with what gets to count, not only as sex or sexuality or sexual identity, but as History as well?

Speaking of History: Wilde in the World

Speaking of history: The "event" that carries the most conventionally historical weight in *Tomorrow's Parties* (as protean, multiply determined, and blurred in its parameters as it is, as elementally without clearly defined origin or end) is the Wilde trials.[10] A preliminary word about my sense of that event, of its gravity and consequence and reach, might help clarify something of the quality of the "history" at stake in what follows. It is of course by now common to think of the Wilde trials as a moment of crystallization, when the disparate, scattered, and inchoate energies of previous decades of legal wrangling, psychological profiling, medical opinion, demographic scrutiny, pedagogical insistence, and economic consolidation achieved—seemingly in one swift movement—their coordinated and astoundingly well-publicized fulfillment.[11] Another way to put this has been to say, as Ed Cohen does in his crucial *Talk on the Wilde Side*, that the Wilde trials mark a special kind of culmination. They read, for Cohen, as the spectacular realization of the processes described in Foucault's *History of Sexuality, Volume 1*, in which, among other things, the homosexual is invented as a species, a category of being. Of course, even this crystallization left ample room for disorder and definitional incoherence—think only of the sharp conflict between lingering "inversion" models of homosexuality and the emergent minoritizing accounts of a distinctive homosexual identity, a conflict Sedgwick anatomizes so productively in

Epistemology of the Closet. Still, the mass proliferation of the image of Wilde as a type of man, and the supersaturation of that type with a host of legible—specifically sexual—signs and suggestions, revolutionized sexual life in Europe and America in a way no other single event, no publication or proclamation or act of law, had come near to doing. Many were the people on the ground who recognized as much: as W. D. Stead wrote to Edward Carpenter, the early, powerful advocate for the viability and vitality of gay male life, "A few more cases like Oscar Wilde's, and we should find the freedom of comradeship now possible to men seriously impaired to the permanent detriment of the race."[12] James's letter, as I read it, is at once an echo and a confirmation of Stead's trepidation.

But Cohen's work also suggests that what transpired in the Wilde trials was not only the playing out, in slow motion, of Foucault's famous dictum about the emergence of the homosexual as a species (though we can be certain that, in the spring of 1895, it felt rapid enough). What was at stake was something like the public emergence of "sexuality" as such, and what was achieved in the various legal proceedings was not merely a deducing of sex from exterior attributes, a specification of the telltale signs of male deviance, but rather a wider generalization of this deducing process. In their attentions to Wilde's body and history, his tastes and his imagination, they invented a broad and, as it would prove, almost infinitely adaptive *strategy* for the linking of a whole series of unconventionalities (in dress, gender behavior, manner, speech, relation to class, family, age, nation, and law) to the possibility of a specific *sexual* deviance. What was "invented" by such a strategy, in turn, was the idea of sexuality itself as a thing within us, a thing *belonging* to each of us, that somehow bound together all these seemingly unconnected, heterogeneous traits, fusing them into a notion of character that was defined, with new and exhaustive "depth," by sex. (This is part of what David Halperin means when he writes, in a passage to which we will return, that "modern" sexuality is distinguished by an "unprecedented *combination* of . . . previously uncorrelated conceptual entities" [emphasis added].[13]) By virtue of the vast media coverage attending them, the Wilde trials made spectacularly public not just the new character of the homosexual, not just the sudden vulnerability of all intimate same-sex relations to being read as deviant and degenerate, and not just the unresolvable incoherence of competing inversion and minoritized models of homosexuality. They accomplish, too—again, in an unprecedentedly mass-publicized way—the sweeping *coordination* of a range of once only marginally interlinked dispositions under the idea of sexuality.

Only one of the things that might fascinate a reader of mid- to late-nineteenth-century eroticism is the trajectory, the flux and errancy, of this movement toward coordination: such a "movement" might come most alive in its intermediate stages, its scattered moments of pausing and acceleration. If we take the Wilde trials to be a kind of culmination of this movement, these stages imply a mode of "history" that would be given shape by partial formulation, recalcitrance and yielding in unpredictable sequence, uneven emergences and submersions.[14] Precisely here, I think, is where the splendid, often exhilarating, sometimes bewildering extravagance of the literature of the period—Thoreau's insistent disappointment, Dickinson's wrought obliquity, Smith's interplanetary ambitions—comes into rich meaning. For to look at moments before this coordination is to look squarely at possibilities for the disaggregation, or staggered articulation, or differential emphasis, of one or more of these not-yet-coordinated vectors of being. It is to see something of the shape sex could take—errant, unlikely, not always legible *as* sex—before it quite became the sexuality we now know, or think we know.[15]

Errancy, Extravagance, Untimeliness: Notes on Method

If there is a strong emphasis in the chapters that follow on the errant and the unyarded, the extravagant and the untimely, it is in large part a measure of my desire to add my own voice to a broader conversation about queer sex, queer history, and their braidings around the question of temporality. Readers familiar with this work will have already heard its resonances here. In thinking about the in-between time of the regulated erotic body across the later nineteenth century, I am indebted to Dana Luciano's reading of what she calls "chronobiopolitics"—"the sexual arrangement of the time of life"—in *Arranging Grief*, which so deftly conjoins an interest in emerging modalities of biopower with questions of temporality. My worry over the curtailments, rather than the affordances, of the advent of modern sexual identity draws on Heather Love's accounts, in *Feeling Backward*, of those for whom the emergence of such an identity was the occasion for darker affects than those of liberation. And I am informed here, too, by the attunements to futures left dormant, or uncreated, that we find in Molly McGarry's work on spiritualism, Jose Muñoz's on Bloch and the "not yet," and Christopher Castiglia's on literature as counter-archive. Like Sharon Marcus, Bruce Burgett, Christopher Looby, and Jordan Stein,

I mean to attend most closely to styles of erotic being that may not rise to the level of "discourse" as it is traditionally understood, but are for that no less telling or worthy of explication. Perhaps above all I follow in the wake of Elizabeth Freeman's magnificent work on "erotohistoriography" and the drags of temporality—on the spaces of lag, delay, and suspension we find between a variety of styles of erotic being and their becoming legible as *form*.[16] All these works, whatever their other predilections, I take to be invaluable to the tasks at hand since they orient us, cumulatively, away from a sense of sex as that which is (as the phrase goes) "discursively constituted," and toward a differently calibrated regard for the styles of erotic being that exceed, or precede, or fall aslant of, or otherwise escape captivation by, the genres, codes, and forms of their immediate surroundings. Freeman's project of erotohistoriography "honors the way queer relations complexly exceed the present," and the attention to precisely that *otherwise* she and these other scholars have brought to such high articulacy has been particularly valuable for me in the effort to describe, with as much clarity as intricacy, the contours of a series of erotic possibilities that were not quite, not yet, legible in the terms of the century's impending sexual taxonomies.[17]

All of this is to say that I borrow from this ample and varied critical conversation, in the first instance, a prevailing trepidation about the fate of those extravagances of erotic imagining—a trepidation over the way the reach and variability of such extravagance, its expressive richness, can fall out a bit in certain modes of literary historicism. In this sense, the most basic aim of *Tomorrow's Parties* is counterhistorical and, you might say, restorative. The chapters that follow, addressed as they are to figures who occupy diverse places in the canon of sexually revelatory literatures, look to give a renewed sense of the vitality and breadth of imaginings of sex in the latter half of the American nineteenth century, even by so relatively narrow a range of figures as I consider here, and even by authors of whom it has long been presumed that "the sexual" was a matter of incidental or merely glancing concern. By pursuing detailed, comprehensive readings of a handful of authors and works, the book aims above all to provide a richer analytic vocabulary with which to describe the movements of sex in the long, last moments before it might have known itself as "sexuality" in its modern senses. Following, like so many of us, the trail blazed by Sedgwick, my hope is to try to tell "a story about sexuality that does not yet exist as a convention or an identity."[18]

Crucially, though, the work of the following chapters is not intended as a kind of exposé: the purpose is not to disclose in unforeseen places a suppressed or submerged sexual content. This is not, in other words, a project much invested in queering the nineteenth century because to do so—to turn "queer" into a transitive verb—seems to me to rely on a presumed knowledge of just what action "queering" would entail, just what it would mean to translate something not-yet-queer into something queer, or queerer. Indeed, one of what I take to be the high joys of this kind of work runs directly counter to such a presumption. I am thinking of the pleasures of unlikeliness, of errancy, and of surprise that follow from a readerly practice that takes seriously the idea that sex is not a pregiven quantity, a thing whose shape, form, and extent we know in advance.[19] They are the pleasures that come from never settling the question of what sex can prove to be or to have been, *or of what might prove to be sex.* In the book's final "Coda" I will discuss in greater detail some of the implications, theoretical as well as methodological, of such an approach to sex. Here I will say simply that the chapters that follow mean both to exemplify that readerly practice, and to explain the conceptual dividends we stand to receive from it, by looking in close detail at scenes from a long moment in which the questions of what sex could be, and what could be sex, were especially prominent.

On this point I do not wish to be misunderstood. Such hesitancy with respect to queering the sexual past does *not* require of us, in turn, a sweeping sort of anticredulity about sex before sexology: it does not require us to regard with an unbelieving wariness (which always borders on the dismissive) accounts of the passions of intimate relation in a time before the ascent of the categories of hetero and homo. The fact of these writers' untimeliness—of their enmeshment in a moment of transformation, of uncompleted transition—offers livelier possibilities. Indeed, what unites the unruly collection of authors gathered here, beyond anything else, is the uncanny persistence with which, despite their so divergent interests, they return in their works to an articulate sense of what I have been calling the *earliness* of sexuality: a sense, again, of sexuality as a realm of experience and expression as yet uncodified, not yet battened into place by the discourses in which it increasingly found itself located. To tell this story properly requires not discarding but leaning against, and perhaps thickening, some prevailing historicist models, and I want to address these briefly by clarifying some of the stakes of my own procedures.

First, we are by now accustomed to approaches to presexological expressions of desire that have difficulty escaping the inevitable presumption that, as worldly post-Victorians, we see more clearly, can describe more acutely, and simply *know* so much more than even the authors themselves about the true tenor of the longings that they hesitantly or indirectly portray in their work. If this is a methodologically untenable presumption, its effects are not, for that, either uniform or simple. Depending on the critic's inclination, this "knowledge" tends to cause the moments in question to be regarded in one of two ways: either with pleased certainty (*"This* is what's really happening here") or committed epistemological skepticism ("It is impossible now to say what, if anything, is happening here"). We can term these two options, for the sake of brevity, the anticipatory and the agnostic approach.

With respect first to the agnostic approach: readings that emphasize the intractable illegibility of the past—those that, we might say, side with James's point about the unspeakability of the dynamics of intimate life from across the divide of modern sexual categories—have the virtue of a certain refusal. They resist, in the first instance, the impulse to erode the distinctiveness of the past by rendering it in the terms and taxonomies of the present. We might think here of Caleb Crain's admonition about early nineteenth-century intimacy in his *American Sympathy*: "They dwelt in possibilities that we cannot help but reduce to prose."[20] He describes here a reduction that is in practice exceptionally difficult to resist, inasmuch as the taxonomies of sexual being that postdate the nineteenth century make up for us the very fabric of commonsense sexual knowledge.

My own divergence from the agnostic approach is not the queer-deconstructive one. Crain's resistance to anachronism—to the reading of the sexual past in contemporary terms—does not strike me in any meaningful sense as a commitment to the normative more generally, as has been suggested in critiques of historicist approaches that self-consciously guard against anachronism and the misplacement of specifically modern conceptions of sexuality. Resistances to sanctioned temporal modes, specific temporalizations of being-in-the-body, and of the life cycle more broadly, may indeed be hallmarks of queer sexualities past and present, as a wealth of new queer theorists have taught us to see.[21] It does not follow, though, that to embrace anachronism as a scholarly or historical mode is, of necessity, to be queer, nor that to attend to the specificity of a given moment's codes of sexual being (its "policing of borders," say, or its concern for structures of historical "propriety") is to side, methodologically, with the normalizing impulses of modernity. Such a reading depends on a series of more and less facile analogies between, say, sexual and evidentiary versions of "propriety." It is only according to the false cognates of analogical thinking, in other words, that the treatment of the past as *other* to ourselves in certain key respects might parse as a necessarily sexually normative or even colonizing move. One might think instead of the overlapping of historical frames more in the terms suggested by Freeman's erotohistoriography—that is, as a kind of *friction*, an always-erotic rubbing together of similarities and differences. Such an approach neither ontologizes difference—there is in it no refusal of what Carolyn Dinshaw calls the "touch across time" that queer work can enable—nor elides the fact of specific *differences*, themselves only loosely grasped in their abstraction as *différance*.[22]

So my divergences are not, or not precisely, in the broadly deconstructive vein. And yet the agnostic approach does, I think, broach other sorts of methodological worries, and these come into particularly sharp focus when the matter at hand is sexuality in the long moment just prior to the advent of its modern taxonomies. For the agnostic mode, despite its strengths, also threatens to understress the movements *toward* a consolidation of sexual ideology that were already afoot, and that could be felt in their encroachment from a number of vantages. (This uneasy sense of encroachment is, as we shall see, very much at the heart of Hawthorne's *The Blithedale Romance*.) To regard the presexological past too strictly as a site of Jamesian unspeakability and illegibility, in other words, is to miss the degree to which the emergence of modern sexuality was a movement, a slowly unfolding *process*, rather than an event, however decisively the massive publicity of the Wilde trials may have circulated and solidified that emergence. As agnostics, we run the risk of underreading late-century figures' *entanglement* in regimes of sexuality that were, though not crystallized, impending.[23]

On precisely this ground, the anticipatory reading of presexological intimacy clearly appeals. In works like Kathryn Kent's *Making Girls into Women*, Jonathan Ned Katz's *Love Stories*, Valerie Rohy's *Impossible Women*, and Annamarie Jagose's *Inconsequence*, strains of social and cultural life from the 1840s through the 1880s and '90s come into meaning as harbingers of a complex sort, as early iterations of what would eventually *come to be* aspects of gay and lesbian identity, or as sites in which a protoqueer identificatory impulse might find traction or shelter, to emerge more fully in a later, more viable moment. Here, too, there is much to admire, and much that is generative. We might appreciate particularly the way such work renders the nineteenth century less a blank canvas, best left unbesmirched by presentist speculation or historical coding of any sort, than a period of coming-to-be in which impulses and desires not yet authorized by commonly available languages or codes found some of their first vital life. So, for instance, in Kathryn Kent's work (like Lisa Moore's before her and, in somewhat more problematic ways, Lillian Faderman's before them), we see the affordances made, in the many rituals of the cult of female friendship and in "sentimental culture" more generally, for modes of protolesbian identification and affiliation.[24]

If in what follows I depart a bit from the anticipatory approach, it is not because I think it is implausible, inaccurate, or without wide uses and strong insights. But as a way of telling the story of nineteenth-century sexuality, it threatens a particular kind of narrowness. To read the sexually piquant moments of nineteenth-century American writing as finally anticipatory—as harbingers for the approach of, or as laying the groundwork for, a language of sexual identity and affiliation that would indeed arrive later—is to risk missing much of the story. It is to presume, for instance, that all roads lead to Rome: that in the realm of sexual being, all muted deviances and inarticulate errancies were preparatory, awaiting their redemption in a later moment. But what if the sexual possibilities dreamed into being in the era before sexology proved *not* to be amenable to the forms of sexual subjectivity and sexual specificity that would, in fact, arrive? What if the queerness any of these authors proposed, or yearned after, or otherwise intuited, fell somehow aslant of the languages of sexual specificity that were to come, with a newly legible homosexual identity in tow? What if what we find are not uncanny foretellings but, as Molly McGarry has it, ghosts of futures past?[25] We might notice, in this vein, that in his letter to Mrs. Fields James can hardly be said to revel in the pleasure of a newly acquired language of queer self-nomination. But this does not make him a homophobe, or a coward, or a man suffering a crippling inability to love (as a curiously popular vision of James now has it).[26] It may be, rather, that in their extravagance and errancy, their disappointment or dislocation—in their bracing untimeliness—many of these authors envision possibilities that the arrived future, whatever its other affordances, simply would not yield. Thus, James looks back with a curious kind of regret, not on what was gained but what was, for himself and Mrs. Fields and their friends, irrevocably lost.

It is worth reminding ourselves, in other words, that the appearance of what we might want to call queer identity, or modern homosexual identity, was not a fate fixed in the stars, and was not the target toward which all emergences were speeding, arrow-like, across the century. Part of what can make us unmindful of this fact, I think, is precisely a too rigid concentration on "discourse," on the discourses in which sex might have found itself spoken. This is why Jordan Stein worries over the current critical difficulty entailed in "collect[ing] into the history of sexuality versions of queerness that never accede to discourse." "The history of sexuality," he avers, "can and should be written in relation to texts and experiences *that fail to be represented at the manifest level of discourse*" (emphasis added).[27] He points here to a fundamental methodological problem, and works with great deftness to turn us away from what we might think of as commonplace Americanist misapprehensions, or slightly misbegotten applications, of the work of Michel Foucault.

To put the matter at its bluntest: *Tomorrow's Parties* is determinedly not an attempt to tell the story of nineteenth-century sexuality as a "history of discourses." I offer this demurral for a few basic reasons. First, as Stein intimates above, the telling of the history of sexuality as a history of discourse is a method Foucault's *History of Sexuality* neither exemplifies nor endorses, though we are often assured that it does. The misapprehension here, I think, is at once conceptual and practical. For Foucault, the emergence of a modern regime of sexuality is not only, and not primarily, a matter of sex finding itself located more and more in one or another sort of official, quasi-confessional, expert discourse. That is, instead, a *component* of a larger series of movements he wishes to trace. No one turns this point more forcefully than David Halperin, who, in *How to Do the History of Homosexuality*, writes,

> The history of sexuality, as Foucault conceived it, then, is not a history of the representations, categories, cultural articulations, or collective and individual expressions of some determinate entity called sexuality but an inquiry into the historical emergence of sexuality itself, an attempt to explain how it happened that in the eighteenth and nineteenth centuries sexuality gradually came into existence as a conjunction of strategies for ordering social relations, authorizing specialized knowledges, licensing expert interventions, intensifying bodily sensations, normalizing erotic behaviors, multiplying sexual perversions, policing personal expressions, crystallizing political resistances, motivating introspective utterances, and constructing human subjectivities.[28]

Or again, returning to the quote we saw earlier in relation to Wilde: "What historically distinguishes 'homosexuality' as a sexual classification," Halperin writes, endeavoring to specify what it is about the invention of "modern" sexuality that so fascinated Foucault, "is its unprecedented combination of at least three distinct and previously uncoordinated conceptual entities: (1) a psychiatric notion of a perverted or pathological *orientation* . . . (2) a psychoanalytic notion of same-sex *sexual object-choice* or desire . . . and (3) a sociological notion of *sexually deviant behavior*."[29] What is crucial here is Halperin's canny insistence that it is the "unprecedented combination" of these movements, their heretofore unaccomplished systematic coordination, that makes for what we now call sexuality. The regime of sexuality, in other words, is one of implantation and investment: an intensification of zones of the body, a making-vulnerable or making-sensitized, a saturation of personhood with proddings and incitements and solicitations. Much of this goes missing when we think of sex as discourse, or when we underread what Foucault means when he suggests sex is "discursively constituted."

In practice, this conceptual misapprehension translates into a reduction of Foucault's project—which is an account of the emergence of sexual subjectivity as such, as a vector of modern, individuating, post-Enlightenment power—into a flattening sort of contextualization: the reading of a text, or act, or person, or phenomenon, in carefully accomplished coordination with one of several kinds of discourse that are contemporaneous with it. But this is to imagine Foucault as a far more conventional sort of historian than he was. As was his writerly habit, Foucault in *The History of Sexuality* tells the story of the emergence of sexual subjectivity as a vector of modern power from, in essence, the perspective of power's own ideal of operational efficiency and coordination. But he does not offer that fantasy of perfected and fully systematized coordination and control as a conventional historical account of, say, the unfolding of social and private life across the mid- and late-nineteenth century. (I think of Lauren Berlant's trenchant observation: "Sovereignty is a fantasy misrecognized as an objective state."[30]) To turn Foucault's approach into a kind of discursive contextualization is to miss this fundamental distinction. More grievously still, for scholars of nineteenth-century sexuality at least, it is also a mode of approach that gives us less purchase than we might want on the loose ends, the remainders of the processes Foucault describes: on the experience of any of the soon-to-be coordinated intensifications of the regime of sexuality *in their separation from each other*, in a moment before their accomplished systematization. Among its other substantial pleasures, the literature of period, with its extravagances and errancies, helps us fill in that other, looser part of the story.[31]

The work of *Tomorrow's Parties* does not presume, then, that legal, medical, pedagogical, commercial, and/or religious languages addressing themselves to sex "produced" nineteenth-century American sexuality, additively or otherwise. Thinking of discourse as a master code for nineteenth-century sexuality makes especially little sense, after all, when we consider that so much of the imaginative efforts of the writers in question was precisely to *evade* such codification, to conceive erotic being in terms and in formulations other than the given. We could think here of what Sedgwick calls the "nonce taxonomies" of intimate relation in James, and of their articulation, as the codification of sexuality became more and more strict, in an ever-more-stylized syntax that prizes attenuation, indirection, and deferral far above clarity of reference;[32] or of that syntax's strange kinship with Emily Dickinson's own deployments of suspension and multiplicity in the service of a privacy at once obdurately guarded and passionately communicative;[33] or of what Perry Miller aptly enough thinks of as Thoreau's "perverse" insistence on ceaselessly translating his passionate attachments to his fellow men into states of frustration, disappointment, and, in his dreamier moments, expectancy;[34] or even of Whitman's own late-in-life boasts about his fecund heterosexuality, which we might read less as self-closeting defensiveness (he was in dialogue with John Addington Symonds who, with new-minted languages of sexual identity to hand, pressed him insistently on the specifically homoerotic meaning of his poems) than as an unwillingness to have the intimacies he had imagined and enacted redescribed in the falsifying terms of a rapidly solidifying latter-day sexual taxonomy.[35]

In all these cases, the matters of chief interest to the readings that follow—errancy, extravagance, untimeliness in imagining the domain of sexuality—are ill served by an approach that assumes too hastily that something called sexuality, in mid- and late-nineteenth-century America, is exhausted in the discourses that aimed to regulate and codify it.[36] They have seemed to me better served by a practice invested in detail, particularity, and unsystematizable variousness—all the specificities that literature proffers in such abundance, *and in whose explication close textual reading specializes.* "Philosophical poetics is historical," Simon Jarvis has recently reminded us, "insofar as it takes technique to be at once the way in which art thinks and the way in which the work of art most intimately registers historical experience."³⁷ Following this note (itself borrowed from a reading of Adorno's *Aesthetic Theory*), and following, too, my own understanding of "close reading as a way of doing history," *Tomorrow's Parties* unfolds in chapters built chiefly around the patient, ground-level explication of the way I take the works in questions to think: that is, around logics, shadings, and idiosyncrasies of literary form.³⁸ It seems only hospitable to mention in advance, then, that a lot of what might be thought of as the explicitly theoretical and critical contestation in what follows is embedded in chapters that themselves attend quite often to larger uninterrupted swaths of primary materials than is perhaps now customary. Not everyone likes this, I know. But I risk that mode of critical address in the conviction that it is by dwelling with texture, rhythm and pulse, accretion and dispersal—the specific atmospheres of a given work's language, which come clearest in long exposure—that we can best begin to articulate those more errant, more uncoded stories of sexual possibility that are the book's central preoccupation.

This brings us to one final hesitation with respect to anticipatory readings of nineteenth-century sexuality. The reading of the emergence of modern sexuality as part of a "history of discourses"—in which early discursive formulations of erotic being are read as premonitory signs of a mode of sexual personhood that *had not yet* but would later come into full realization—has the signal hazard of erasing not only the staggered or disarticulated components of modern sexuality, but also all the fantastic visions, excessive imaginings, and unforeclosed possibilities that *would not come to be*. As Kathryn Bond Stockton reminds us, in terms I find resonant for so many of the writers we will consider, "our futures grow sideways whenever they cannot be envisioned *as* futures."³⁹ Think again of James and his wistful, half-pained regard for a now-unspeakable past whose details seem to him escalatingly illegible to any but those who, like him, partook in the strange pleasures of a time freer than his present from captivation by languages at once potentially "validating" (offering recognition, legibility, an alternative to silence) and, to a man of James's temperament, potentially entrapping. What I am calling the persistent earliness of sexuality across the works to be considered—an earliness whose evaporation James could be said to mourn—brings into rich and articulate clarity the range, the unsystematizable variety of investments that might be sustained in relation to the late-century arrival of new languages of sexual specificity. They help us envision not only those languages' affordances (for queer self-nomination and mutual-recognition of the sort pioneered by a man like Symonds) but also, and I think more revealingly, all that might have been lost at the close of the nineteenth century, all the errant possibilities for imagining sex that have sunk into a kind of muteness with the advent of modern sexuality. The modern form of sexual subjectivity that solidified around James and his friends, in other words, was not the *only* possible or imaginable historical emergence; a preoccupation with something like "discourse," or with the discourses in which sex found itself spoken of, can obscure this fundamental premise. So the larger aim of *Tomorrow's Parties*, in its departures from practices of discursive contextualization, is less to make clear the routes by which presexological forms of intimate relation came to arrive at what we now recognize as modern habitations of sexuality than to trace, in as much detail as we can, the outlines of any number of broken-off, uncreated futures, futures that would not come to be.

Maps and Trajectories

In all these ways, *Tomorrow's Parties* means to set itself in conversation with emerging scholarship that addresses temporality: the temporality of social forms (as in Wai Chee Dimock's recent accounts of nation-time) and, most crucially for my purposes, new queer scholarship that has begun to address the interface between sex and time as a way to reapproach, and perhaps enliven, the question of sexual history.[40] Unsurprisingly, much of this work has drawn strength from an attentive return to the works, fortunes, and followers of the Frankfurt School—unsurprising because Benjamin and Adorno (and Nietzsche before them) had much to say in their own time about expectancy, disillusionment, and the staggered temporalities they took to be modernity's signature. As should by now be clear, my work here is informed by Benjamin's regard for history as, in Christopher Nealon's fine phrase, "a matrix of claiming," a scene of unfolding always vulnerable to the predations or reclamations of an unknowable future.[41] But in what follows, and particularly in the prevailing concern with nineteenth-century sexuality as a phenomenon not yet captivated by the forces circumscribing it, I am interested as much in the richness a writer like Adorno enables us to see in something like *waiting*, in the pause that bespeaks a yearning without a viable path toward its own fulfillment; a politics not resigned but forestalled; an unwillingness to cede to the terms of a given social world, even in the absence of usable alternatives to it; or a multiply-inflected cathexis of the bare possibility of an arrived future that might, if not redeem, at least alter the intractable terms of the present tense.[42] (All these possibilities seem to me to follow from Adorno's sense of Nietzsche, who would aver, "I write for a species... that does not yet exist."[43]) As the new work of queer Americanist scholars like Freeman, McGarry, Castiglia, Rohy, Stein, Luciano, Looby, and a range of others makes clear, these formulations can propel us toward a more intricate, less simplifying regard for dispositions, affects, and only marginally articulable *relations* to politics and to history—relations that, because of what Lauren Berlant calls the difficulty of their immediate "convertibility to politics" or to conventionally "political" terms, can be too hastily dismissed as simply "a failure to be politics."[44] Beyond this, a framework given some of its shape by a reading of Adorno may allow us to see, too, how investments in futurity might not always and everywhere amount to capitulation to the logic of reproductive heteronormativity— that is, to see in what terms an antireproductive futurity might come into articulacy (it is in just these terms that we will be interested in the roles of children and of childlessness in a writer like Jewett, for example) and what it might take of us, as critics, to read expressions of hesitancy, disillusionment, pausing, or waiting *away* from the stark dichotomies of optimistic and pessimistic, insufficiently political or insufficiently free from the captivations of the Symbolic, happy or sad, no-future or yes-future. The stories the writers assembled here endeavor to tell tend to inhabit neither end of these polarities without remainder, and so are ill perceived by an insistence on the gravity and priority of only one.

And, if we can listen to them, they tell us things that might be of critical value to us. *Tomorrow's Parties* aims to bring back into focus some of the visions and conceptions of sexual possibility that may have disappeared from view with the advent of modern taxonomies of sexuality. In doing so, it works to suggest less that the writers of the presexological past were innocent, or naïve, or hopelessly repressed, than that their renderings of the intimate may offer us a good deal more than we have yet acquired the skills to read, renderings that may open out in particular onto imaginings of sexuality as something other than we have come to know it: as something not reducible, for instance, to a set of practices, an aspect of identity, or a property of the self. In this sense, the final and broadest aim of the book is theoretical. For the sexuality that enlivens the work of James and Jewett, Whitman and Smith, Thoreau and Dickinson, and the others is notable not only for its nimble refusals to yield to the divisive sexual teleologies and the punishing languages of deviance that would arrive at the century's end. The varied passions on display in these writings also share a remarkable resistance to one of the more intractable inheritances from the advent of modern sexuality, which we might understand as, in essence, *the liberalization of sexuality*. They share a resistance, that is, to the turning of sex into another of the liberal self's secured properties, into something that each of us, alone, is understood to *have*. This is a resistance we might do well to consider closely, since that privatization of sex is so much a part of even our strongest critical languages about sexuality. By laboring to wrench sex away from not only punitive languages but from *possessive* understandings of sexuality—from a conception of sexuality as something isolable in individual persons—the writers of the American nineteenth century have an enormous amount to teach us here in the new millennium, where the energy and insight of two decades of dynamic queer scholarship has yielded to a national moment of astonishing hostility and intransigence, where signs of progress are forever being counterbalanced by further reactionary contractions. ("The limitations on this possessive understanding of homosexuality," writes Nealon, with an eye to precisely this inhospitable civic climate, "are only just becoming clear to us in the United States."[45]) In their very obliquity and seeming naiveté, the disparate authors who come together in *Tomorrow's Parties*, allergic as they are to the liberalization of sexuality, provide a fantastically rich resource for the articulation of sex away from its possessivist moorings, as something other than an accoutrement of the private self, and as something more like a mode of relation, a style of affiliation, even, for some, a blueprint for sociality: the "parties" of my title.

Tomorrow's Parties pursues these possibilities across three sections, each one emphasizing a different aspect of that extravagance of imagining we have begun to discuss here. Part 1, "Lost Futures," looks at Thoreau and Whitman, as well as Dickinson, to gauge a range of ambitions for and yearnings after a discursively uncaptivated sexuality; much of the attention here rests on imaginings of sexual possibility that, in the event, would *not* find ample room for themselves in the structures of sex that would harden into place at the century's end. Part 2, "To Speak of the Woe That Is in Marriage," takes up several derangements of sexuality's chief sanctioning institution. It looks at the improvised and unsanctified couplings found in Sarah Orne Jewett, and turns then to the spectacularly extravagant imaginings of the power of extradyadic intimacy we find in the late work of Mormon prophet Joseph Smith. Unfolding around the explication of a single, abidingly difficult question—What does the polygamist want?—this chapter sets Smith's vision of the inadequacy of monogamous marriage alongside Frederick Douglass's sense of what that same intimate form, once consecrated and state-sanctioned, might do for the former slave. The coda to part two stages a related dialogue between Herman Melville and Harriet Jacobs. Where the work on Smith and Douglass wonders how our sense of the history of sexuality might be altered by the specificities of American trajectories of *secularization* (which are so drastically different from those of the European context Foucault had in mind), the coda considers how deeply the presence of chattel slavery and its institutions might transform other key conceptual grounding points in Foucault's genealogy, the entanglement of sexuality with an older system of *alliance* not least among them. The third and final part, "Speech and Silence: Reckonings of the Queer Future," reads James's *The Bostonians* and Hawthorne's *The Blithedale Romance* as a kind of diptych, each representing the perils and attractions of an erotic unconventionality, a deviance willing to know and name itself as such. The book's conclusion, a coda to part three entitled "The Turn," looks at James's *The Turn of the Screw* to consider the efficacies and liabilities of an understanding of sexual history as ruptured by a climactic turn—around Wilde, around James, around Freud—at the very end of the nineteenth century.

As the introductory and concluding remarks about Wilde suggest, the story told in *Tomorrow's Parties* is a transnational one, though it is not in my rendering a story *about* transnationality. It borrows from what has been called the transnational turn in American studies, principally by taking as a given that American life and writing in the era was shaped by forces, as well as by fantasies, that extended well beyond national borders, and that anything offered as "American" was always already a collocation of tropes, languages, impulses, and imperatives of wide, multinational provenance. At the same time, the work here does at moments address itself to the question of America's historical peculiarity and to the differences the American context might make to conceptualizations of sexual history. Nor is the book uninterested in, or for that matter unbeguiled by, the question of American nationalism— not, again, the *idea* of American nationalism as such but nationalism as an unforeclosed question. This is to say that the readings assembled here aim to attune us as closely as possible to the different inflections given to the idea of nationness by the various authors in question. In what follows, in other words, I try to hew closely to the ways that, for someone like James, Americanness is inconceivable in the absence of a European counterreferent, while for a writer like Whitman an investment in, and fluctuating ambivalence toward, the idea of an American national distinctiveness prevails more forcefully; for still others (Joseph Smith, for instance), formulations of America and Americanness expand well beyond the parameters of virtually any theoretically standard articulations of the nation. As we shall see, for these many and divergent strands of nationalist imaginings—in particular for the concept of "this young nation" (as Thoreau put it in 1852) as an entity in a dynamic state of coming-to-be, imbued with expansive promise but capable of fulfillment only in a moment just over the horizon of present-tense articulability—sexuality proved both a sensitive register of anxiety and ambition, and an exquisitely responsive expressive vehicle.

Scholars of the history of sexuality, and of queer studies more generally, often find ourselves asking: What would it take to imagine sexuality differently? What would it mean, and what would it require, to disentangle the disparate elements of being, of experience and affect, sensuality and selfhood, bullied into lockstep coordination by the modern, postsexological regime of sexuality? If one of the most potent legacies of the Wilde trials is its invention (and massive circulation) of an almost infinitely adaptive strategy for the linking of a whole series of dispositions and comportments to the possibility of a specifically *sexual* deviance, how do we begin to think outside the terms of those solidified linkages? What does sex even look like if it is somehow removed from the idea of sexuality as a thing within us, a thing that somehow sweepingly binds together all these scattered attributes and fuses them into a definitive sense of who we are? What are the terms in which such alternate inhabitations of corporeality, desire, and their extensions might be lived, or imagined, or brought to articulacy? And what would the experience of those inhabitations feel like? What affects would they harness or align? How would we even begin to recognize as sexuality a mode of being that disaggregates those now-coordinated vectors of selfhood?

Luckily for us, the writings of mid- to late-nineteenth-century America address themselves to precisely these matters, and do so searchingly, eloquently, and variously. Their authors lived through a moment both before the great aggregation of elements we now call sexuality had taken solid hold, but in which the process of their initial, sometimes halting, sometimes swift and decisive, coordination was underway. And with differing emphases, enthusiasms, anxieties, and investments, they wrote about that experience. In many cases, they used it as a starting point for the most bracingly errant and extravagant imaginings of sex, sexual being, and much else besides. The challenge of course from here on the other side of the divide between ourselves and that unspeakable past is to read them, and so to leave them something other than too bleakly stranded. That is the prevailing ambition of the chapters that follow.

PART ONE

Lost Futures

1

Disappointment, or, Thoreau in Love

The revelations of nature are infinitely glorious & cheering—hinting to us of a remote future—of possibilities untold—but startlingly near to us some day we find a fellow man.
—Henry David Thoreau, *Journal*, 21 May 1851

People, Things

In the midst of the "Ponds" chapter of *Walden*, his much-polished opus of 1854, Henry David Thoreau offers up a wonderfully illustrative anecdote—wonderful because, though largely shorn of the leaning toward metaphor that characterizes so much of the rest of the book, the little passage nevertheless elegantly condenses many of the principal elements of Thoreau's style, his humor, and his genuine idiosyncrasy as both writer and thinker. "Once in winter, many years ago," Thoreau writes,

> when I had been cutting holes through the ice in order to catch pickerel, as I stepped ashore I tossed my axe back on to the ice, but, as if some evil genius had directed it, it slid four or five rods directly into one of the holes, where the water was twenty-five feet deep. Out of curiosity, I lay down on the ice and looked through the hole, until I saw the axe a little on one side, standing on its head, with its helve erect and gently swaying to and fro with the pulse of the pond; and there it might have stood erect and swaying till in the course of time the handle rotted off, if I had not disturbed it. Making another hole directly over it with an ice chisel which I had, and cutting down the longest birch which I could find in the neighborhood with my knife, I made a slip-noose, which I attached to its end, and, letting it down carefully, passed it over the knob of the handle, and drew it by a line along the birch, and so pulled the axe out again.[1]

If you are a reader at all susceptible to the charm of Thoreau's crafted *Walden* persona—to that admixture of wry amiability, occasional preachiness, and sometimes caustic irreverence—this is probably a moment you will find difficult to resist. Thoreau turns a scene of what appears to be commonplace irritation (his axe falls into an ice hole like a set of keys into a storm grate) into an occasion not for a burst of pointless rage but for something else: we are treated, instead, to a sudden deceleration and expansion of purpose, a swift movement beyond the merely practical and out toward the swervings, and the looser temporality, of what he calls "curiosity." Part of the charm of the passage, too, lies in its gentle self-deprecation, there in the deadpan invitation Thoreau extends to us to note the not-a-little-absurd figure he cuts, splayed face-first and nose-down on the ice. And more perhaps than any of this (beyond even the repeated figures of unperturbed "erection" we could surely remark upon), the passage underscores one of the most basic, most crucial elements of Thoreau's entire body of work: in his deft and unflustered engagement with knives, chisels, birch branches, pickerel, pond ice, fishing line, and axe helves, we see displayed again, in exquisite miniature, Thoreau's prodigious and articulate fluency with the world of *things*. Though an Emersonian in many inarguable respects, he is nevertheless demonstrably less interested in Nature as titanic system, or as vast unfolding metaphor, than as an array of small, complex, infinitely fascinating details—of particular surfaces and objects, of tangible things—even the least of which commands meticulous scrutiny and offers the possibility of nearly limitless revelation.

This is a Thoreau that we have come, by now, to know, a version of the author that is as legible in the popular imagination as in a range of scholarship.[2] But, as is perhaps appropriate to the man who left his cabin beside Walden Pond because "it seemed to me that I had several more lives to live, and could not spare any more time for that one" (*W*, 323), there are other Thoreaus as well, not all of them as renowned, or for that matter as cheering. Consider the very different tenor of this passage from the sole work that competes with *Walden* for ranking as his magnum opus, his *Journal*:

> Ah I yearn toward thee my friend, but I have not confidence in thee. We do not believe in the same God. I am not thou—Thou are not I. We trust each other today but we distrust tomorrow. Even when I meet thee unexpectedly I part from thee with disappointment. . . . I know a noble man; what is it hinders me from knowing him better? I know not how it is that our

distrust, our hate is stronger than our love. Here I have been on what the world would call friendly terms with one 14 years, have pleased my imagination sometimes with loving him—and yet our hate is stronger than our love. Why are we related—yet thus unsatisfactorily. We almost are a sore to one another.[3]

For those who have read little beyond *Walden*, the note of anguish here—of a frustration deepening into something painfully insoluble—may come as a surprise. Dismay and even rage (what Sharon Cameron, summarizing a whole tradition of Thoreau criticism, calls "rage at the social"[4]) are familiar enough features of *Walden*, to be sure, but this is something else again. And yet the note of bewildered and wearied heartsickness—Thoreau names it disappointment—is not at all uncommon in the journals, especially in those completed in the early 1850s, during Thoreau's last extended period of work on *Walden*, and also during a long moment of strain and dissatisfaction in his relation to Emerson.[5] The differences between the *Walden* persona and the Thoreau of the journals have been accounted for in a number of plausible ways—as, for instance, the differences between a published persona and a private self, or between a view of Nature that accommodates the demands of communicable legibility and a view that actively refuses such demand—and I have no wish to dispute these appraisals.[6] But we might frame the matter in differently suggestive ways by saying that if much of the lasting pleasure of *Walden* lies in Thoreau's splendid articulacy with the things of his world, what we find expressed most vividly in the journals is an ongoing consternation about just what kind of thing *other people* are. (As he writes memorably in December of 1851: "I do not know but a pine wood is as substantial and as memorable a fact as a friend. I am more sure to come away from it cheered" [*J*, 4:207–8].)[7] "A preoccupied attention is the only answer to the importunate frivolity of other people," Emerson had written rather imperiously in "Experience."[8] Thoreau, for his part, writes often like a man trying to convince himself of just that dictum, but whose attention keeps curving back toward the problem these frivolous creatures invoke, and are.

Much of what I want to do here is simply to introduce this other Thoreau, and along the way to think hard about this consternation of his, which shuttles in the work between anger and wistfulness, pained confusion and, at telling moments, a dreamy imaginative extravagance. My principal claim is that Thoreau was not just a man disappointed in others, as we are often told, but that he possessed what we might also think of as a kind of genius for disappointment. This is so to the degree that we understand his hallmark disappointment less as the sign of resignation, or surrender, or apathy, than as a particular kind of *yearning*—as, perhaps, a species of present-tense unhappiness that has neither forgotten joy nor abandoned its expectation.[9] Following several pathbreaking essays by Michael Warner, I want to suggest, too, that it is precisely this yearning, tuned as it so frequently is to the note of *expectancy*, that makes Thoreau so engaging and suggestive a figure in the American history of sexuality, and particularly in the history of sexuality as it unfolded across the middle of the nineteenth century, in that long, vexed moment before it was assumed every person and every intimacy could be assigned a hetero- or homosexuality, but in which the stirrings of that taxonomical division could already be felt in a number of quarters.[10] Thoreau's is a voice that speaks to us from before the apotheosis of those now commonsensical renderings of sexuality, and part of what is abidingly compelling about his work is how ill fitted it is, despite its expectant orientation toward the future, to the conceptual frameworks that in the decades after his death did in fact achieve broad currency.

The story Thoreau's work helps us to tell about this epoch of American sexual history is not, then, an overly familiar one. It is not the story of a monkish celibate who, out of fear or disgust or rigorous self-denial, fled from the debased modes of sexual being available to him. Nor is it quite the story of a man whose affinities and inchoate desires would later be codified, and come into more stable articulacy, as queer. It is, in other words, neither the story of a particular figure's place within a web of emerging sexual "discourses," nor the story of protoqueerness, of desires that anticipate forms of sexual specification yet to arrive. Important and even revelatory as those stories can be, Thoreau is perhaps more profitably understood as a figure who neither exemplifies his present nor anticipates the future but who, in his idiosyncratic conjugations of sexual being, suggests instead the outlines of a future that would not come to be.[11] Thoreau may strike us as so beguilingly strange a writer less because we can so easily read back into him a sexual bearing that he simply lacked the conceptual vocabulary to describe than because much of what looks like sex to him has, over time, dropped out from our commonsense understanding of where the perimeters of the sexual actually lie. And it is just this untimeliness in Thoreau—"untimely" in the sense borrowed most from Nietzsche[12]—that has made his odd visions of the very domain of sexuality, of its habitable forms and extensions, as nettling and intriguing as they are.

In what follows, then, I take Thoreau's famous dissatisfaction with his fellow men to be part of a career-wide effort to imagine the domain of sexuality itself in alternate terms—alternate not only to the encroaching hetero/homo division of gendered object-choice, but to the very vision of sexuality as, at base, another of the liberal self's secured properties. In this reading, Thoreau takes his place among many other writers of the American nineteenth century—figures ranging from Dickinson, Whitman, and Henry James to Frederick Douglass, Sarah Orne Jewett, and even Joseph Smith—who labor to wrench sex away from not only punitive languages but from *possessive* understandings of sexuality, from a conception of sexuality as something isolable in, and a property of, individual persons. For Thoreau this means, among other things, conceiving sexuality as a way of inhabiting a unique temporality, one that renders the body at once out of step with modernity's sped-up market time and exquisitely responsive to the call of an intuited but inarticulate future.

If it does nothing else, then, Thoreau's story usefully reminds us that the late-century arrival of identity-languages of sexuality—such that same-sex desire could, in the famous phrase, begin to speak its own name—was a development not without significant losses. In his yearning toward a future markedly out of step with the one that would actually arrive, Thoreau helps us begin to make legible some of the possibilities that may have dropped out from our visions of "the sexual" as such. In so doing, he helps us surrender, at least a bit, the faintly self-flattering tendency to regard the sexual past as essentially anticipatory: a version of the present in a moment before its (hermeneutic, ethical, political) fulfillment. It may not be that poor, priggish, prudish, conflicted Thoreau was unable to confront what we savvy moderns plainly see were sexual longings that he feared even to name. Rather, Thoreau may have envisioned sex in ways we ourselves have not learned, or have forgotten, how to see.

Vain Reality, Bodies Out of Time

Even schoolchildren know Thoreau was a bachelor, though they may know less well the vehemence of his bachelorhood. As he writes, not at all untypically, in his journal in November of 1851: "In the evening went to a party. It is a bad place to go." Why so? "These parties I think are a part of the machinery of modern society—that young people may be brought together to form marriage connections" (*J*, 4:185). That marriage is linked for Thoreau to the "machinery of modern society"—it is hard to know which of those words carries the greatest weight of Thoreau's contempt—speaks tersely enough of the depth of his resistance. The perhaps inchoate erotic potentialities of that bachelorhood, too, have not wanted for attention, of various calibrations. As Perry Miller observes, "what for long especially outraged commentators was the supposition that Thoreau flouted the highest, the most sacred, duty of masculinity: he was not interested in women!"[13] Readers of less-punitive inclination have been known to turn with particular determination to Thoreau's intriguingly puzzled affection for the French-Canadian woodchopper, Alek Therien, as the place in the work where the possibilities of a specifically queer reclamation of Thoreau appear most prominently and undeniably. Even here, though, the matter is hardly uncomplicated, since Thoreau's relation to Therien, as portrayed in the "Visitors" chapter of *Walden*, is, though plainly ardent, not at all transparent. The quality of that relation seems, rather, to range quite widely. At moments, Thoreau's enthusiasm for the young man—"A more simple and natural man it would be hard to find"—rises in pitch toward a striking affective intensity. "He was cast in the coarsest mold," Thoreau says, offering (as Henry Abelove notes) as detailed a description of anyone's physical figure as we find in *Walden*: "a stout but sluggish body, yet gracefully carried, with a thick sunburnt neck, dark bushy hair, and dull sleepy blue eyes, which were occasionally lit up with expression" (*W*, 145).[14] Then, too, there is the famous scene in which Thoreau prompts Therien to read aloud from the *Iliad* and he translates for him "Achilles's reproof" to his most intimate comrade Patroclus—a moment whose desiring resonances you need not be a credentialed classicist to parse: they are a good deal easier to sound than, say, the muddy bottom of Walden Pond.[15]

But these instances, however delectable they may be (and however purposefully we read Thoreau's deployment of them to have been), are crosscut in the "Visitors" chapter with passages very different in tenor. Compounded with, and to some degree confounding, this subtle eroticism are moments of almost clinical narrative detachment in which Therien emerges less as an object of seduction than of a naturalist's calculated scrutiny—as, in truth, a kind of specimen. "In him the animal man chiefly was developed," Thoreau succinctly informs us (*W*, 146). "There was," he avers, "a certain positive originality, however slight, to be detected in him, and I occasionally observed that he was thinking for himself and expressing his own opinion" (*W*, 150). The matter is not that Thoreau's enthusiasm wanes or buckles, but that the quality of his regard changes key, as it were, in fairly dramatic ways. When Thoreau writes, "I loved to sound him on the various reforms of the day, and he never failed to look at them in the most simple and practical light," the pleasure he expresses leans considerably more toward the anthropological (the joy of having found so intriguing an object) than when he recites suggestive verse (*W*, 148). I do not mean to suggest that these moments cancel the force of the more erotically piquant scenes. But they do, in their abrupt dilations and contractions of proximity to Therien, point to a certain uneasiness in Thoreau's regard for the young man. We see in these shifts and fractures of steady perspective not only the bafflement that Thoreau himself underscores, about how Therien can be so unspiritual yet so happy, but also a more poignant uncertainty as to just what register his affection can or ought to take. Over the course of the chapter, Thoreau seems to cast about for a mode of address that might be adequate to the idiosyncrasy of his feeling. He does not find one. Therien thus emerges as an object of curiosity in *Walden*, and in this he is like the other meticulously observed forms of wildlife. But he is also, evidently, an object of a different order, one for which Thoreau has no comparably stable or settled mode of address. If this is something of what love looks like in *Walden*—and I think it is—then that experience has at its center for Thoreau the practical problem we noted at the outset: the problem of just what kind of object other people are, and of what form of regard is proper to them.

What reads with respect to Therien as a kind of obliquity, or an instability of registers, often expresses itself more directly in the journals as pain. "It would give me such joy to know that a friend had come to see me," he confides, "and yet that is a pleasure I seldom if ever experience" (*J*, 4:217). Or again, in conclusion to the passage I quoted at the outset: "Ah I am afraid because thy relations are not my relations. Because I have experienced that in some respects we are strange to one another—strange as some wild creature. Ever and anon there will come the consciousness to mar our love— that change the theme but a hair's breadth & we are tragically strange to one another. We do not know what hinders us from coming together" (*J*, 4:137). "Who are the estranged?" Thoreau asks elsewhere: "Two friends explaining" (*J*, 4:213). These rather downhearted sentences in the journal echo something of the note struck some years earlier in Thoreau's first book, *A Week on the Concord and Merrimack Rivers*. There, in the "Wednesday" section, Thoreau had offered a long meditation on the possibilities and promises, mostly unrealized, of friendship. "There is on the earth no institution," Thoreau writes, "which Friendship has established." In fact, as he will aver only a few pages later, "To say that a man is your Friend, means commonly no more than this, that he is not your enemy." What Thoreau desires from his ideal friend is something different. In tones that, as in the journals, are half-pleading and half-imperious, Thoreau allows himself to imagine precisely how the "true and not despairing Friend will address his Friend." "This is what I would like," he says, "to be as intimate with you as our spirits are intimate—respecting you as I respect my ideal. Never to profane one another by word or action. *Between us, if necessary, let there be no acquaintance*" (emphasis added).[16]

The steady repetition of moments like this, across his wide-ranging writings, reminds us again that love is a special kind of problem for Thoreau. As these passages from the journals and *A Week* make so painfully plain, it is so in no small measure because the loved object is for him less an other than an embodied and externalized version of his own ideal self: he respects his beloved friend, he tells us, "as I respect my ideal." As he writes in his journals: "may I treat . . . my friends as my newly discovered self"; and later, "O my dear friends. . . . *I associate you with my ideal self*" (J, 3:312, emphasis added). But because his standard for this ideal is so exacting, his lovers, it appears, can only ever disappoint, can only ever remind him of the anguished distance between what he imagines could be and the pettiness, where people are concerned, of what is. It is this distance, this longing, that resonates with such plangency in the journals. So toxic to him, so debased are virtually all the available conditions of human contact—"modern society," language itself ("Silence is the ambrosial night in the intercourse of Friends," he writes in *A Week*)[17]—that again and again he yields to an imagining of love's flourishing that is difficult to separate from a sense of its total impossibility. Perry Miller, with dramatized distaste, recognizes as much when he writes that anyone who spends much time reading in the journals "must be impressed—indeed, appalled—not only by the obviously insatiable drive that brings Thoreau back, again and again, to 'friendship,' but by the monotony of his rhetorical devices for translating friendship into no friendship."[18]

But there are other ways of reading Thoreau's intimate frustrations. Consider Michael Warner's appraisals of Thoreau, and his insistence that Thoreau's persistent disappointments reflect, in the first instance, the typical dilemma of a specifically liberal market culture, with its emphasis upon an autonomy for the individual subject that is, in practice, unclearly separate from a marooned sort of self-enclosure. (This is, for Warner, a version of liberal individualism that Thoreau champions, in certain extreme ways even exemplifies, and yet by doing so renders intractably paradoxical.) But in Warner's reading, Thoreau's work shows too, and with an almost diagrammatic clarity, how for liberal culture what we might call the sexualization of gender difference—the turning of the genders into opposed but mutually complementary forms of autonomous subjectivity—would become increasingly crucial as a kind of solution for the knotty problem of otherness and its accessibility to the autonomous self. If in liberal culture "the other has become an inaccessible horizon because self includes all means of access to it," then gender difference emerges as something of a saving alibi, a way to imagine an accessible other. The name for this alibi, it transpires, is "love." Reading Thoreau in concert with Hegel, Warner argues that the mode of "love" that is set in motion to alleviate liberal individualism's self/other crisis is one that posits both gender difference as the signal mark of human alterity, and a neat complementarity of and between the genders, enacted in the mutual self-transcendence that is "love." Love between "opposed" genders in this way comes to stand as the *overcoming* of the elemental separation precipitated by the liberal conception of autonomous individuality. (Part of Warner's point here is that something like "heterosexuality"—a sexuality of differences and otherness—comes into salience long before its late-century juridico-medical "invention.") But as Warner also points out, *this is a solution Thoreau emphatically does not accept.* Indeed, he refuses it with a doggedness his later readers (Perry Miller among them) would find puzzling, unsatisfying, and downright perverse. As Thoreau states the matter succinctly in his journal: "What the difference is between man and woman, that they should be so attracted to one another I never saw adequately stated" (*J*, 2:245). Or again, from the same entry: "I love men with the same distinction that I love women— as if my friend were of some third sex" (*J*, 245). Unwilling to accede to the alibi of gender difference as a neat solution to liberalism's self/other crisis, Thoreau is left, where love is concerned, stranded, in possession of "desires for which he has no dignifying language."[19]

Warner's reading is a powerful one. We might inflect it a bit by noting, too, that the accessibility of a dignifying language is only part of the issue for Thoreau. Consider another of his acute, heartsick journal entries:

Does not the history of chivalry and Knight-errantry suggest or point to another relation to woman than leads to marriage—yet an elevating and all absorbing one—perchance transcending marriage? As yet men know not one another—nor does man know woman.

I am sure that the design of my maker—when he has brought me nearest to woman—was not the propagation of the species—but perchance the development of the affections—and something akin to the maturation of the species. Man is capable of a love of woman quite transcending marriage. (*J*, 3:211)

I am not sure this is Thoreau's dismissal of heterosexuality, though it might be. (For as meticulous and recondite a naturalist as Thoreau, this rejection of reproduction as the sine qua non of biological "design" is certainly striking.) But the passage is perhaps less crucially a reproval of heterosexuality than an injunction against the reduction of sex to propagation via marriage—an injunction, that is, against the *instrumentalization* of the mode of relation we now call sexuality. As readers of the bilious "Economy" section of *Walden* will recall, Thoreau takes great delight in rebuking the market imperative to transform the self into a tool of production, to establish an essentially instrumental self-relation.[20] Here in the journals, he carries that point to one of its unsettling, logical conclusions: he speaks directly against the making of sex into another of the liberal self's secured properties, one that might, like the self's other properties, be bartered or turned into a tool, a mere instrument of productivity. (As he writes rather more blisteringly at the end of an essay called "Chastity & Sensuality": "The only excuse for reproduction is improvement."[21]) In his emphasis on intimacies that, as Milette Shamir writes, are "based on physical distance rather than proximity, on concealment rather than revelation, on silence rather than speech," Thoreau refuses what he thinks of as the instrumentalization of sex in reproduction in favor of something other, some mode of relation he can only qualify with references to the antique past and the unwritten future.[22] What qualities define this love transcending marriage Thoreau does not say. But it will follow from a conception of sexuality as something quite other than one of the self's accumulated properties.

And Thoreau does undoubtedly believe that sex is susceptible to imagining in different terms—that, whatever its entanglement in "modern society" and its languages, sex nevertheless holds out the possibility of a realm of experience incompletely territorialized by market imperatives. What makes such a possibility most real to Thoreau is, again and again, his *body*—we might say, with Jane Bennett, the "vibrant matter" that is his body—and the thrilling way it brims over, on occasion, with intimations of an ampler fulfillment than the conditions of the present seem to allow.[23]

This is why Thoreau's insistent, recurring, heartsick disappointment, which often takes the form of articulate pain, just as often takes the form of articulate longing and, more precisely, of *expectancy*. As he writes in *A Week*, "There are passages of affection in our intercourse with mortal men and women, such as no prophecy had taught us to expect, which transcend our earthly life, and anticipate heaven for us."[24] Or as he exclaims in his journal, in still another passage that mixes disappointment with a future-directed longing: "O my dear friends I have not forgotten you *I will know you tomorrow*" (*J*, 3:312, emphasis added).

Or again, consider this dense and astonishing passage from the journals, also from July of 1851, and famously adapted and incorporated into *Walden*:

> Methinks my seasons revolve more slowly than those of nature, I am differently timed. I am—contented. The rapid revolution of nature even of nature in me—why should it hurry me. Let a man step to the music which he hears however measured. Is it important that I should mature as soon as an apple tree? Ye, as soon as an oak? May not my life in nature, in proportion as it is supernatural, be only the spring & infantile portion of my spirit's life shall I turn my spring to summer? May I not sacrifice a hasty & petty completeness here—to entireness there? If my curve is large—why bend it to a smaller circle? My spirits unfolding observes not the pace of nature. The society which I was made for is not here, shall I then substitute for the anticipation of that this poor reality. I would have the unmixed expectation of that than this reality.
>
> If life is a waiting—so be it. I will not be shipwrecked on a vain reality.
> (*J*, 3:313)

Here, then, is Thoreau's own parsing of Dana Luciano's chronobiopolitics of nineteenth-century life.[25] Thoreau's vision is of self, "society," and "nature" each moving propulsively forward at intriguingly varied and unsynchronized rates toward a future whose terms and possibilities are beyond the horizon of present-tense articulability. There is, in the place of anything definitive or realized—any "petty completeness" in the self— only "anticipation" and "expectation," whose pleasures are "unmixed," and so in contrast to the evidently mixed blessing of living in the temporal frame of the present, with its "vain reality." It is worth remembering, too, from his thoughts on the mere "propagation of the species," that Thoreau's futures are not tied to the order of reproduction ("Nature abhors repetition. Beasts merely propagate their kind."²⁶). Inasmuch as all this is so, we can begin to feel here—in the turn away from a strictly reproductive futurity as well as in that nod to friends whom he will know tomorrow—Thoreau's crucial sense, not only of love's futurity, but of what we might call the *earliness* of sexuality. The passage underscores the degree to which, in Thoreau's experiences, sex is as yet uncaptured by the discourses surrounding it; as such, it remains for him not merely a vehicle for disappointment but an exciting repository of unpredetermined futures.²⁷ The society he was made for is evidently not paced to modernity but to a time more slow, a time he does not posit in the preindustrial past but imagines as a fulfillment—he calls it, winningly, "entireness"—lying in wait just beyond the horizon of what the present can be and know.²⁸

When and if we think about what is queer in Thoreau, then, we might well be returned to this constellation of preoccupations: to Thoreau's impatience with the liberalization of sexuality and his refusals of the alibis of gender difference, yes, but also to his sense of his own desires as skewed into obliquity or inarticulacy perhaps most of all by the present tense, and what exists there. "Speak," Thoreau writes in his journal on Christmas Day in 1851, "though your thought presupposes the nonexistence of your hearers" (*J*, 4:224). (As Sharon Cameron shrewdly observes, though the journals pursue a rigorous "subversion of the human" as part of an ongoing naturalist project, Thoreau's writing there nevertheless "seems . . . to presume an audience, *albeit a posthumous one*" [emphasis added]).²⁹ We find him not just a man disappointed, but a man in possession of desires that are keyed, quite self-consciously, toward a futurity (pointedly outside the order of mere reproduction) where they might find for themselves new traction, new expansion, new significances. What his body intuits, Thoreau imagines a more hospitable future might allow him, somehow, to realize.

Only one of the ironies here is that the future toward which Thoreau so passionately yearned was not one that would come to be, at least not in iterations that would have been, for him, pronouncedly more habitable. For if we are correct in our reading of the depth and resolve of Thoreau's resistance to possessive renderings of sexuality—to visions of sex as another of the liberal self's disposable properties—then the language of self-apprehension that came to fruition later in the century could only have been a kind of anathema to him, and could only have provided him still another occasion for pained disappointment. Though it would indeed offer new possibilities for affirmative self-nomination, the emergent language of sexual specification would work in other ways as well: most pressingly, that language would also *solidify*, rather than disperse or dismantle, the very positing of something called sexuality as the self's most anxiously managed and tended-to property, something each of us is understood to *have*. This is indeed among the chief effects of the emergence of identity-languages around sex and sexual being, of the specification of individuals through sex. For to make sex into the root of identity is to render it a kind of Rosetta stone of selfhood that anchors and somehow coordinates so many disparate aspects of being. Identity-languages of sexual specification would not have gratified Thoreau, not least because of the comprehensive way they install sex as, precisely, the very least dispensable property in the self, another of the liberal individual's exploitable possessions.[30]

So if Thoreau resists the languages of love available to him—sex as reproduction, love as a complimentarity between "opposite" genders—it is not because he is, unluckily for him, situated in a moment before the full emergence of a language of specifically same-sex desire in which he might have found for himself greater room for self-validation. Indeed, it is hard to imagine Thoreau as the poster child for this vision of sexual history, which treats the late-century arrival of identity-languages of sex as the welcome occasion for same-sex love to speak, at last, on its own behalf. Perhaps the most articulate proponent of this vision is Jonathan Ned Katz. His *Love Stories: Sex between Men before Homosexuality* treats the later nineteenth century as a period of gradually intensifying courage and resolve, issuing finally toward the century's end in a politicized "going public" of love between men, anchored by figures like John Addington Symonds, James Mills Peirce, and Edward Carpenter. Thoreau's work suggests to me less that this account is implausible or even inaccurate than that its vision of the sexual past is worryingly partial. Whatever its very real strengths, this story tends nevertheless, in its emphasis on the attainment of affirmative languages of self-identification, to understress all that might have been lost in that attainment: to obscure, rather than illuminate, all that would *not* come to be, all the errant possibilities for sexual exchange and sexual being that the solidification of hetero and homo taxonomies would drive into inarticulacy or obsolescence. (Think again of W. D. Stead's letter to Carpenter, which we saw in the introduction: "A few more cases like Oscar Wilde's," he wrote, referring to the infamous 1895 trial, "and we should find the freedom of comradeship now possible to men seriously impaired to the permanent detriment of the race."[31]) A less private, less possessive rendering of sexuality itself is only one of those broken-off possibilities.

In this respect, Thoreau's writing provides special affordances to our own critical moment. In the first instance, it helps us forward in the project of beginning to imagine what it would be like to tell the story of nineteenth-century sexuality as something other than a "history of discourses."[32] For one unhappy byproduct of the discursive rendering of sexuality has been a persistent tendency toward teleology: a tendency (as we noted in the introduction) to imbue the end-of-century regime of sexual specification with a kind of a priori givenness, such that all varied and scattered discourses must be understood to conduce toward it, and all earlier figures must be seen to anticipate it. We miss so much, though, if we read Thoreau too strictly as an anticipatory figure, imagining him to be a writer of bracing protoqueerness who inhabits desires that language and history had not, as it were, caught up with but which, eventually, they would. What Thoreau most passionately desires from the future—not only an ideal friend but some less instrumental, less possessive rendering of sexuality itself—is not what the future had in store.

Critically, we continue to live with the consequences, many of them half-seen, of the exemplifying and anticipatory readings of midcentury sexuality. One of the most familiar has been the tendency to look back at erotically extravagant moments and to imagine how much *more* we know now than they did then: to think, that is, of how fluent with post-Freudian worldliness we are, how hypercompetent in the arts of discursive diagnosis and erotic detection. ("It never crossed their minds that there might have been a physical attraction or longing behind all this," biographer Robert D. Richardson Jr. assures us, in reference to a particularly homoerotic early poem of Thoreau's.[33]) But Thoreau's work, if we tend to it carefully, compels us to read those past moments with an eye toward all that the writers and thinkers of the naïvely pre-Freudian past might have known that we, perhaps, do not—to read, that is, with a keener interest in what forms of knowledge, imagination, and life are encoded even in their ripe silences, their inarticulacy, their apparent obliquity. His work raises the unsettling possibility that those antiquated, presexology writers, those citizens of a less enlightened time, might in fact know things we do not, or that we have over the course of time lost the ability to see clearly: about the parameters of sex, say; or about less private renderings of sexuality; or about modes of imagining the domain of the sexual that have perhaps sunken into a kind of illegibility, or muteness, in the aftermath of the calcification of the hetero/homo distinction. These are the other sorts of stories a historian of sexuality might, right now, be especially interested in telling. Thoreau does much to make them legible.

Sex, Sound

Back, then, for one concluding look at Thoreau. I have tried to show that part of what underscores the yearning that speaks through Thoreau's disappointment is a desire to articulate sexuality away from its possessivist moorings, as something perhaps not reducible to a set of practices, an aspect of identity, or a property of the self. I have suggested, too, that as such, sex comes into meaning for Thoreau as a realm of experience not wholly overcoded by market imperatives, one which thus offers the beguiling possibility of a more expansively satisfying bodily self-relation. We can think of this yearned-for corporeal otherwise as a freedom from capture by market instrumentalization, gender stricture, and, at its widest, from the nationalized whiteness that would do so much to fuse these imperatives into a nation-making biogenerativity. He wants a body unhooked from these simultaneous codings, in which racialization, sexualization, and liberalization all are densely interwoven as mutually-amplifying elements of optimized corporeality. To want sex as something other than a property in the self may be to chafe against these investments in the flesh.[34]

But how to imagine such a thing? What does a sexuality so constituted even look like? Would we know it if we saw it? On this front, I think it worth recalling that the most erotically satisfying moments in Thoreau's writing involve not Alek Therien, nor masturbation and its counter-part, chastity. The moments that tend most toward corporeal delight and sensual luxuriation refer, in fact, to none of these things. They are rooted, instead, in *sound*. "After a hard day's work," Thoreau writes in his journal,

> without a thought turning my very brain into a mere tool, only in the quiet
> of evening do I so far recover my senses as to hear the cricket which in
> fact has been chirping all day. In my better hours I am conscious of the
> influx of a serene & unquestionable wisdom which partly unfits and if I
> yielded to it more rememberingly would wholly unfit me for what is called
> the active business of life—for that furnishes nothing on which the eye of
> reason can rest. What is that other kind of life to which I am thus continu
> ally allured?—which alone I love? Is it a life for this world? . . . Are there

duties which necessarily interfere with the serene perception of truth? Are our serene moments mere foretastes of heaven joys gratuitously vouchsafed to us as a consolation—or simply a transient realization of what might be the whole tenor of our lives?

.... All the world goes by us & is reflected in our deeps. Such clarity! obtained by such pure means! by simple living—by honesty of purpose— we live & rejoice. I awoke into a music which no one about me heard— whom shall I thank for it? The luxury of wisdom! the luxury of virtue! are there any intemperate in these things? I feel my maker blessing me. To the sane man the very world is a musical instrument—The very touch affords an exquisite pleasure. (*J*, 3:274–75)

Almost exactly this motif, with the same underscoring of the body's sensual intuition of an ampler, as yet unformed constellation of itself, appears several months later in the journals, as Thoreau describes the after-effect of a dream:

And then again the instant that I awoke methought I was a musical instrument—from which I heard a strain die out—a bugle—or a clarionet—or a flute—my body was the organ and channel of melody as a flute is of the music that is breathed through it. My flesh sounded and vibrated still to the strain—& my nerves were the chords of the lyre. I awoke therefore to an infinite regret—to find myself not the thoroughfare of glorious & world-stirring inspirations—but a scuttle full of dirt—such a thoroughfare only as the street & the kennel—where perchance the wind may sometimes draw forth a strain of music from a straw. . . .

I heard that last strain or flourish as I woke played on my body as the instrument. Such I knew had been & might be again—and my regret arose from the consciousness how little like a musical instrument my body was now. (*J*, 4:155)

I am tempted to say that this exquisite carnal ravishment by sound is as graphic a scene of sex as we get in Thoreau's writing. For sound in Thoreau—not hearing, precisely, but the flesh-vibrating modulations of sound—induces a sensual responsiveness to the outer world that works abrupt and sweeping changes in the very organization of the corporeal self. As depicted here, sound belongs properly neither to the world nor to the listener, but is one particularly transforming mode of connection between them: "melody" passes through and inhabits the body, just as it passes through and inhabits the world outside the self. Not unlike Emerson's experience of vision, sound provides for a kind of contact that, in its instantaneously shaping movement through the body, is freer from captivation by the world's calcified forms of knowing and perceiving, less overcoded by all those misapprehending structures of connection, of mere "familiarity," with which Thoreau is so impatient. It is a type of phenomenon that confounds exterior and interior, and muddles, in an apparently quite delightful way, the borderlands of the self, projecting that self forward, if only momentarily, into future constellations that are as yet only dimly discernable: such episodes of sensual suffusion are for him "*foretastes of heaven*," reminders of what "might be again." Sound delights Thoreau in a way that makes him believe his body carries within it the possibilities of an ampler, richer, more sensually expansive future, a future not reducible to the doings of "the street and the kennel" but in which the body lives as a "thoroughfare of glorious & world-stirring inspirations." If we are right in calling these sex scenes, then sexuality for Thoreau is not something isolated in persons, not something apprehensible in the self alone, but is instead the name for what inheres between selves and the objects around them, for the current that connects and momentarily confounds them, and in doing so suggests back to the self nothing short of a revised template for being. That this does not, from many perspectives, look much like sex is, I think, much of the point.

Sad to say, this strain of what I think of as visionary sexual imagination is not (or not yet) among Thoreau's most potent legacies to the American literary tradition, although he is not without an authorial legacy having to do with sex. No account of Thoreau's place in a newly mapped history of American sexuality can afford to ignore the fact that, whatever else he did, Thoreau forged for many writers following him what we might call a style of masculinity—one that is probably familiar to anyone who has taught *Walden* to a room full of young people. Readers of the opening section of *Walden*, called "Economy," will no doubt remember the withering quality of Thoreau's regard for all forms of frippery, of material excess in living: for fancy food, clothes, household items or conveniences, all not strictly necessary things. His was, quite plainly, a brief against the superfluities of a newly burgeoning market economy. But as it proved in the event, Thoreau was not above making the familiar, off-hand, and not very thoughtful identification of that market and its excesses with women— was not above imagining women as *emblems* of that market—such that femininity might, by an unlovely twist of logic, come to represent, in itself, the excesses of a commodity culture that the self-reliant man must be on quick guard against. It almost goes without saying that there is about this something plainly *projective*. Just so, Thoreau, in his *Walden* persona, has incontestably bequeathed to many a young man wishing to be autonomous and independent the unlovely habit of projecting all manner of insecurities about the fragility of his own rugged self-possession onto a fantasized terrain of femininity and its improvident excesses—the habit, that is, of shoring up his own ever-embattled sense of solitary sufficiency through an invidious and demeaning comparison to proximate women, whom he may self-comfortingly imagine as, precisely, needy, wasteful, and unself-possessed. (This dynamic has had many literary inheritors, Hemingway being perhaps the least self-conscious in its deployment.[35]) Of course, as everyone knows—certainly as most grown-up women know—there is nothing needier than a man who needs to believe he is autonomous. Thoreau's solution to this dilemma not infrequently partakes of a misogyny that, whatever its complications, cannot be pretended away.

My claim here has been that Thoreau's writing provides us a fantastic resource for the understanding of sexuality as something quite other than we have come to know it—as, again, something not reducible to a set of practices, an aspect of identity, or a property of the self: all ways of thinking about sex that Thoreau's writing obdurately resists. And a related, if more implicit, claim has been that this imagining of sexuality away from its possessivist underpinnings is a particularly important theoretical move for us now, here at the crossroads of a number of accumulated impasses in both Americanist and queer studies. This has seemed to me important not only because of the field's need to move beyond a Foucault-inflected reading of sexual history as that which accumulates in "discourse"—that is, to move beyond the reduction of historicism to a kind of discursive contextualization—but also because that fashioning of sex as the property of individuals is a process now so thoroughly enmeshed in even our most incisive critical languages about sexuality that alternatives to it remain, as several scholars have recently noted, difficult to conceive. "The institutional framework of the lesbian and gay movement," Michael Warner writes, "predicated on identitarian thought, sees all politics as requiring a more consolidated gay identity and a form of life more fully conforming to the institutions of privacy."[36] Milette Shamir, in an especially keen reading of "depersonalized" intimacies and their logic in Thoreau, makes a closely related point when she writes, "Perhaps the fact that this [depersonalized] logic has been largely ignored is testimony to our own culture's, at times, monolithic understanding of intimacy as a capital exchange of affairs of the self."[37] Thoreau might help us to begin to articulate, and to test out, some less private visions of sexuality, to ends that may, or may not, prove useful.

As I hope has been equally clear, my claim is not that Thoreau is a kind of visionary whose bracing queerness somehow *excuses* the kinds of misogyny we find in his work or renders them superfluous. If I think neither that the misogyny of Thoreau's writings invalidates nor exhausts what is exciting about the work, it is because I remain convinced of the potential usefulness to us of that work, in ways that expand far beyond the perimeters of what Thoreau could have imagined even in his dreamiest moments on the banks and in the woods surrounding Walden Pond. I might be tempted to say that this mode of approach—finding in the work the seeds of a future beyond the horizon of its frame of articulation—is a kind of "reading-Thoreau-against-the-grain," in the Benjaminian model, but in truth it is not. The turning of disappointment into yearning, of dissatisfaction into an alert, responsive expectancy: these are precisely the inheritances from Thoreau that I have wished to bring into clearer relief. I would encourage us, in this at least, to be the followers he never wanted.

2

Whitman at War

Sex Is the Root of It All

In *The Better Angel*, a history of Walt Whitman's war years, Roy Morris Jr. recounts the story of an exchange of letters between the poet and one William H. Millis, a soldier Whitman had come to know in the hospitals through which he daily toured from late 1862 through 1864. Millis wrote to Whitman from his hospital ward in 1865, "I never will forget you so long as life should last. . . . I cant find words to tell you the love their is in me for you." And then, a decade later, Millis wrote once more: "Again I take the time & privilege of dropping a few lines to tell you that we have not forgotten you & want to hear from you. We have had a son borned since we heard from you & We call him Walter Whitman Millis in honor to you for Love for you."[1] Nor was Millis the only of Whitman's beloved charges to claim for his child so singular a lineage. There was also Benton H. Wilson, who in his letters liked to sign himself "your Loving Soldier Boy" and "as ever Your Boy Friend with Love." After some tense exchanges concerning his marriage—"I wrote to you a year and more ago that I was married but did not receive any reply so I did not know but you was displeased with it"—Wilson wrote cheerfully to the poet in 1868, "My little baby Walt is well & Bright as a new dollar."[2]

"The war of attempted secession," Whitman wrote some years after its conclusion, "has, of course, been the distinguishing event of my time."[3] This is hardly surprising. Decamping from his bohemian New York life in the winter of 1862, Whitman traveled to the Virginia front in search of his brother George, whose name he had read listed among the wounded. He found George alive and well, and nursing an only slightly wounded cheek. (He wrote home to his mother on December 29: "When I found dear brother George, and found that he was alive and well, O you may imagine how trifling all my little cares and difficulties seemed."[4]) There at the winter camp of the massive Army of the Potomac, he also found an entirely "new world," dense with horror and revelation: "I find deep things," he wrote to Emerson, "unrecked by current print or speech." "I now make fuller notes, or a sort of journal," he went on to say of the "memoranda of names, items, &c" he had begun to keep at the hospitals. "This thing I will record—it belongs to the time, and to all the States—(and perhaps it belongs to me)."[5]

That journal would later be shaped into Whitman's prose memoir *Memoranda During the War*, a work that gives vivid testament to what is, essentially, a simultaneous deformation and reconstitution. On the one hand, Whitman's once so exuberant faith in the limitless civic and national capacities of writing, of *his* writing, dies with those thousands of soldiers whose graves are marked, he keeps reminding us, "UNKNOWN."[6] Where once had been a poet who claimed of the American idiom that "it shall well nigh express the inexpressible," who with disarming bravado proclaimed the nation's poets to be more crucial than its presidents, there is in later writing a dolorous, refrain-like insistence on the point that, as he says in a heading added for *Specimen Days*, "the real war will never get in the books," Whitman's own included (*PP*, 25, 802). And yet, what finds strange replenishment in the war, even as Whitman's expressivist utopianism shatters and dissolves, is precisely his vision of sex. Or rather, there among soldiers and presidents, in hospital wards and streets and makeshift camps flooded by an unprecedentedly massive mobilization of far-flung Americans, Whitman discovers rich confirmation for what we might call his "Calamus" vision: a vision of desire as an adhesive, world-making power, uncontained by its partition into socially scripted limits or roles, which Whitman says finds its "openest expression" in his 1860 "Calamus" cluster of poems of urban anonymity and richly eroticized "manly attachment" (*PP*, 1035, 268). In the world of "Calamus," where passion kindles as much between the mutually-anonymous as between familiars and intimates, desire emerges not as the mode of relation solely proper to the marital bed but as the ground note of *all* human attachment and the force that is precious to Whitman not least for its capacity to bind together vast networks of virtual strangers into impassioned sodality.[7] "Passing stranger!," he writes in one of the "Calamus" poems, "You do not know how longingly I look upon you. . . . / You give me the pleasure of your eyes, face, flesh, as we pass, you take of my beard, breast, hands in return"—anticipating, with extraordinary uncanniness, the ardent, tender, intensely corporeal devotions with which he would attend, bed by bed, to the ranks of wounded soldiers he meets, and about whom he so lovingly narrates in *Memoranda*.[8]

As one of what had been Whitman's guiding premises founders in the war—about writing and its nation-making capacities—another, about sex and *its* unexpended capacities, solidifies.

Following in the vein of a number of fine readings of Whitman at war—especially those of Betsy Erkkila, Charley Shively, Robert Leigh Davis, Max Cavitch, and Michael Warner, who in different ways trace out the queer resonances of Whitman's hospital life[9]—I want to consider in detail how, under the peculiar pressures of the war, Whitman's vision of sex both transforms and, in curious ways, extends itself. For *Memoranda* and his other writings from the war do not simply replay the sexual-nationalist project of "Calamus," removing it from the streets of New York into the hospitals of Washington. Instead, they open that project out in new, stranger directions—directions suggested not least by that queer pairing of baby Walts with which we began. Confounding the roles of stranger, comrade, lover, and reader in the "Calamus" poetry, Whitman had labored to dislodge sex from its narrow enclosure in dyadic heterosexuality and the reproductive family, seeking instead to release sex into every register of sociability, to saturate the social field with the adhesive vibrancy of desire.[10] *Memoranda* finds Whitman once more performing the role of comrade-lover, to be sure (and mining silence, once more, as a vehicle for the ardent intimacies he shares with the strangers he meets in great number). But the war prompts in him a range of other sorts of *surrogacy*: he is self-consciously nurse to the men, but also confessor, sibling, and very often parent—mother no less than father, intimate companion no less than witness and scribe. All of these roles he inhabits without the least foreswearing of the erotic content of his attachments. The war discloses a Whitman laboring to restore carnality, in its world-making force, to *family*, and especially to parenthood: to modes of relation that by the time of the war were at once the most hallowed in a mass culture stamped so definitively by the dictates of sentimentality, and also the most rigorously sequestered from, and scrubbed clean of, the tumultuous life of desire. The men who made Whitman a kind of progenitor for their children did not do so without reason.

Of course, what comes to the fore on the national scene after the war is not quite the vibrantly carnal familial form Whitman labors to realize. And this too is telling. Borrowing from Max Cavitch's account of Whitman's elegiac ambitions as well as Warner's splendid reading of Whitman's style of "trembling before history" in the war writings, I want to suggest finally that, not unlike Thoreau, he is perhaps better understood not as a prophet of sex but as a man glimpsing, through the upheaval of the war, the lineaments of a future that would not quite come to pass.[11] The war, as we shall see, finds Whitman turning with prophetic anxiety toward an unwritten, pending future, and prompts in him, too, a complex, eroticized regard for that future as a kind of repository, one seeded with possibilities he intuits, out on the edges of consciousness and embodied experience in the war, but not quite articulable there. That future is something he is anxious to parent, and sex is very much on the scene of that imagined generation. And yet Whitman is instructive here, too, in showing us the ways an investment in futurity, even one routed through the idea of progeny, might not be as finally, necessarily homophobic, or as flatly normative, as we have come lately to believe. Walter Whitman Millis is one emblem, and a fit one, of the weird, harrowing style of queer generation Whitman begins to imagine in the war.

Whitman's Children

Writing, we could say, figures most prominently in the conceptual world of *Memoranda* as that which is no longer adequate: the thing that cannot accomplish what Whitman had once, in his undimmed enthusiasm, imagined it could. The idiom that can well nigh express the inexpressible finds itself confronted with a real war that, in the vast unassimilability of its carnage and suffering and loss, will never get into the books.[12] How curious, then, that the act that stands at the heart of Whitman's many ministrations in *Memoranda* is, precisely, writing. Of his very first visit among the wounded, he writes, "I went through the rooms, downstairs and up. Some of the men were dying. I had nothing to give at that visit, but wrote a few letters to folks home, mothers, &c" (*M*, 9). Or again, still early in his tours, "Visited Armory Square Hospital, went pretty thoroughly through Wards E and D. Supplied paper and envelopes to all who wish'd—as usual, found plenty of the men who needed those articles. Wrote letters" (*M*, 15). And then, under the heading "Letter Writing": "When eligible, I encourage the men to write, and myself, when call'd upon, write all sorts of letters for them, (including love letters, very tender ones)" (*M*, 14). More even than wound dressing, or wordless gazing, or kissing, writing anchors Whitman's sense of what care giving means, and is. And this, we might presume, sits rather oddly alongside assertions like, "Of scenes like these, I say, who writes—who e'er can write, the story?" and "No history, ever. . . . No formal General's report, nor print, nor book in the library, nor column in the paper, embalms the bravest" (*M*, 26).

But the striking abdications we find in these latter sentences are more circumspect than at first they might seem—only printed or "formal" writing is abjured—and themselves share time in *Memoranda* with differently calibrated claims and expectations. Whitman does offer strident admonitions about the collapse, in the war, of seemingly all representation. But these come to be qualified, finally, not only by their circumspection, but especially by his concluding insistence that the real war shall in fact be written, truthfully and wholly—though only, he avers, "*hundreds of years hence*" (*M*, 128, emphasis added). *Memoranda* ends on precisely this note of strange expectancy: "And the real History of the United States—starting from that great convulsive struggle for Unity, triumphantly concluded, and *the South* victorious, after all—is only to be written at the remove of hundreds, perhaps a thousand, years hence" (*M*, 133). Here Whitman emerges from bloodletting and chaos into an uncanny, we might say Benjaminian, faith in the capacity of the future to restore even the lost particularities of the war to a kind of historical fullness. Clearly, Whitman sees in the conditions of the present little in the way of frameworks or terms through which the war might be comprehended without remainder, or entered in its totality into history. (*Democratic Vistas*, with its alternation between visceral disgust and jubilant expectation, makes this plain.) And so, in gestures that graft onto genuine and expansive devastation not hopefulness, exactly, but something more like a straining refusal of resignation, Whitman turns once more toward the future: less the future that casts its shadow beguilingly back onto the present (such as we know from a poem like "Crossing Brooklyn Ferry") than a future that promises to invest this so cataclysmic war with significances and legibilities that it cannot, in the delimited frame of present tense, claim for itself.

How do we make sense of this other sort of oscillation in the war writing, this shuttling between heartsick despondency and a provisional, almost wholly speculative refusal of resignation? One way to begin to do so, I think, is to pay close attention for a moment less to its meta-authorial declarations than to the *scene* of writing in *Memoranda*, and to the revised purposes authorship finds for itself there. For the writing Whitman does by the bedsides of his wounded soldiers is not undertaken in the name of any bardic nationalism. When Whitman writes in the hospitals, he does so, as the above excerpts begin to suggest, on behalf of a different set of self-created roles. I want to pause over those roles, and in particular over the forms of surrogacy they underscore, since I think we can find there something of a key to Whitman's concluding turn to the unwritten future and its potentialities. My sense is that Whitman's intimation of an ampler future is tied to the emergence of a new kind of sexually-saturated sociability, one that the war, despite its so unrelenting heartbreak and fearful carnage, allows him to glimpse and, in certain respects, forces upon him.

Early on, Whitman works as a kind of Cyrano, less a surrogate than a conduit. The passage quoted earlier from "Letter Writing" continues:

> When eligible, I encourage the men to write, and myself, when call'd upon, write all sorts of letters for them, (including love letters, very tender ones). Almost as I reel off this memoranda, I write for a new patient to his wife.... Wants a telegraphic message sent to his wife, New Canaan, Ct. I agree to send the message—but to make things sure, I also sit down and write the wife a letter, and despatch it to the post-office immediately, as he fears she will come on, and he does not wish her to, as he will surely get well. (*M*, 14)

But this changes slightly as Whitman begins to observe the other caregivers, and particularly the women, in a way more emulative than anything else:

> In one case, the wife sat by the side of her husband, his sickness, typhoid fever, pretty bad. In another, by the side of her son—a mother—she told me she had seven children, and this was the youngest. (A fine, kind, healthy, gentle mother, good-looking, not very old, with a cap on her head, and dress'd like home—what a charm it gave to the whole Ward.) I liked the woman "nurse Ward E"—I noticed how she sat a long time by a poor fellow who just had, that morning, in addition to his other sickness, bad hemmorhage—she gently assisted him, reliev'd him of the blood, holding a cloth to his mouth, as he cough'd it up—he was so weak he could only just turn his head over on the pillow. (*M*, 15–16)

Whitman seems less to observe these women—these faintly angelic wives and nurses, now christened with blood—than to find in them a bearing, a whole style of relation to the wounded men, that he himself might learn to inhabit, and to fill with the particularity of his own investments.

This style of surrogacy comes to inflect all the bedside scenes Whitman narrates, where his attentions hover in their tenor between not only the comradely and the amorous, but the avuncular, the paternal, and—as these identificatory moments underline—the spousal and the maternal. Whitman's attachments to the men draw resonance from all these modes of intimate relation, which so conspicuously blend the presumptively chaste and the potentially amorous, while granting exclusive prominence finally to none. Indeed, in the letters written back *to* the poet, nothing speaks so vividly as the multiplicity—one is tempted to say the multitudinousness—that invests Whitman's surrogacy, a many-ness made plain not least in the array of endearments by which he was hailed: "Friend Walt," "Dear Comrad," "Dear Uncle," "Dr Frind and elder brother," "Dear brother and comrad," and of course, repeatedly, "Dear Father."[13] "You will allow me to call you Father wont you," Elijah Douglass Fox writes to Whitman in November of 1863: "I do not know that I told you that both of my parents were dead but it is true and now Walt you will be a second Father to me wont you, for my love for you is hardly less than my love for my natural parent. I have never before met with a man that I could love as I do you still there is nothing strange about it."[14] Or again, as if in answer to Fox's grading of parental care into some other unprecedented kind of love, there is this, from a letter to Whitman from the parents of Jimmy Stillwell, also from 1863: "and now Dear friend again I would ask you to see to him all you can and you hear things that would interest him and help to pass away the time O if i had wings like noah Dove how soon would i fly and Sit Down by his Side but you must be mother to him."[15]

Not for the first time in Whitman, we find the poet living out what we could call the logic of the *and*: father *and* mother *and* friend *and* lover *and* uncle *and* comrade, etc. (These scenes find an uncanny echo in Louisa May Alcott's 1863 *Hospital Sketches*, where nurse Tribulation Periwinkle observes of a stricken solider in her care, "now I knew that to him, as to so many, I was the poor substitute for mother, wife, or sister, and in his eyes no stranger"—though of course Whitman concedes nothing of the poverty of such substitutions.[16]) But what most comes into focus here is the very framework in which the practice of "surrogacy" has meaning for Whitman: if for Whitman to be a surrogate is to stand in for an absent, more familiar companion, it is also to do so *with a difference,* to inhabit that role in ways no less supplementary (we might say, metonymically) than strictly replicative. Surrogacy in this sense involves for the poet an unresolving, generative play of identity and difference, or multiplying *differences.*

Nowhere is the richness of this affective interplay more fully or more gorgeously realized than in the letter Whitman would write to the parents of a soldier named Erastus Haskell. The letter is not brief but is, in respect to the complexity and delicacy of the roles Whitman renders there for himself as well as his readers, worth quoting in full. Watch, in particular, for the letter's calibrated gradations of address—its initial attentiveness to the fate of Haskell's body, its turn toward his parents, then arrestingly *toward the dead boy himself*, and then back; and note, too, the shifting microclimates of tone, the suturings of journalistic to parental to amatory modes, that develop around those movements:

Washington August 10, 1863

Mr and Mrs Haskell,

Dear friends, I thought it would be soothing to you to have a few lines about the last days of your son Erastus Haskell of Company K, 141st New York Volunteers. I write in haste, & nothing of importance— only I thought any thing about Erastus would be welcome. From the time he came to Armory Square Hospital till he died, there was hardly a day but I was with him a portion of the time—if not during the day, then at night. I had no opportunity to do much, or any thing for him, as nothing was needed, only to wait the progress of his malady. I am only a friend, visiting the wounded & sick soldiers, (not connected with any society—or State.) From the first I felt that Erastus was in danger, or at least was much worse than they in the hospital supposed. As he made no complaint, they perhaps [thought him] not very bad—I told the [doctor of the ward] to look him over again—he was a much [sicker boy?] than he supposed, but he took it lightly, said, I know more about these fever cases than you do—the young man looks very sick, but I shall certainly bring him out of it all right. I have no doubt the doctor meant well & did his best—at any rate, about a week or so before Erastus died he got really alarmed & after that he & all the doctors tried to help him, but without avail—Maybe it would not have made any difference any how—I think Erastus was broken down, poor boy, before he came to the hospital here—I believe he came here about July 11th—Somehow I took to him, he was a quiet young man, behaved always correct & decent, said little—I used to sit on the side of his bed—I said once, You don't talk any, Erastus, you leave me to do all the talking—he only answered quietly, I was never much of a talker. The doctor wished every one to cheer him up very lively—I was always pleasant & cheerful with him, but did not feel to be very lively—Only once I tried to tell him some amusing narratives, but after a few moments I stopt, I saw that the effect was not good, & after that I never tried it again—I used to sit by the side of his bed, pretty silent, as that seemed most agreeable to him, & I felt it so too—he was generally opprest for breath, & with the heat, & I would fan him—occasionally he would want a drink—some days he dozed a good deal—sometimes when I would come in, he woke up, & I would lean down & kiss him, he would reach out his hand & pat my hair & beard a little, very friendly, as I sat on the bed & leaned over him.

Much of the time his breathing was hard, his throat worked—they tried to keep him up by giving him stimulants, milk-punch, wine &c— these perhaps affected him, for often his mind wandered somewhat—I would say, Erastus, don't you remember me, dear son?—can't you call me by name?—once he looked at me quite a while when I asked him, & he mentioned over in[audibly?] a name or two (one sounded like [Mr. Setchell]) & then, as his eyes closed, he said quite slow, as if to himself, I don't remember, I dont remember, I dont—it was quite pitiful—one thing was he could not talk very comfortably at any time, his throat & chest seemed stopped—I have no doubt at all he had some complaint besides the typhoid—In my limited talks with him, he told me about his brothers & sisters by name, & his parents, wished me to write his parents & send them & all his love—I think he told me about his brothers living in different places, one in New York City, if I recollect right—From what he told me, he must have been poorly enough for several months before he came to Armory Sq[uare] Hosp[ital]—the first week in July I think he told me he was miles from White House, on the peninsula—previous to that, for quite a long time, although he kept around, he was not at all well—couldn't do much—was in the band as a fifer I believe—While he lay sick here he had his fife laying on the little stand by his side—he once told me that if he got well he would play me a tune on it—but, he says, I am not much of a player yet.

I was very anxious he should be saved, & so were they all—he was well used by the attendants—poor boy, I can see him as I write—he was tanned & had a fine head of hair, & looked good in the face when he first came, & was in pretty good flesh too—(had his hair cut close about ten or twelve days before he died)—He never complained—but it looked pitiful to see him lying there, with such a look out of his eyes. He had large clear eyes, they seemed to talk better than words—I assure you I was attracted to him much—Many nights I sat in the hospital by his bedside till far in the night—The lights would be put out—yet I would sit there silently, hours, late, perhaps fanning him—he always liked to have me sit there, but never cared to talk—I shall never forget those nights, it was a curious & solemn scene, the sick & wounded lying around in their cots, just visible in the darkness, & this dear young man close at hand lying on what proved to be his death bed—I do not know his past life, but what I do know, & what I saw of him, he was a noble boy—I felt he was one I should get very much attached to. I think you have reason to be proud of such a son, & all his relatives have cause to treasure his memory.

I write you this letter, because I would do something at least in his memory—his fate was a hard one, to die so—He is one of the thousands of our unknown American young men in the ranks about whom there is no record or fame, no fuss made about their dying so unknown, but I find in them the real precious & royal ones of this land, giving themselves up, aye even their young & precious lives, in their country's cause—Poor dear son, though you were not my son, I felt to love you as a son, what short time I saw you sick & dying here—it is as well as it is, perhaps better—for who knows whether he is not better off, that patient & sweet young soul, to go, than we are to stay? So farewell, dear boy—it was my opportunity to be with you in your last rapid days of death—no chance as I have said to do any thing particular, for nothing [could be done—only you did not lay] here & die among strangers without having one at hand who loved you dearly, & to whom you gave your dying kiss—

Mr. and Mrs. Haskell, I have thus written rapidly whatever came up about Erastus, & now must close. Though we are strangers & shall probably never see each other, I send you & all Erastus' brothers and sisters my love—

Walt Whitman

I live when home, in Brooklyn, N Y. (in Portland avenue, 4th door north of Myrtle, my mother's residence.) My address here is care of Major Hapgood, paymaster U S A, cor 15th& F st, Washington D C.

In one respect, this is desire as a kind of historiography. Whitman begins by discounting any special role for himself, other than that of concerned caregiver and intimate observer: "I am only a friend," he writes, "visiting the wounded & sick soldiers, (not connected with any society—or State.)" And yet something like national history, and its sudden and to him painful inarticulability, is very much on his mind as well. We see this vividly in his remarks near the letter's close, where he writes of Erastus, "He is one of the thousands of our unknown American young men in the ranks about whom there is no record or fame, no fuss made about their dying so unknown, but I find in them the real precious & royal ones of this land, giving themselves up, aye even their young & precious lives, in their country's cause." Whitman strikes a half-despairing note here, familiar from so much of *Memoranda*, over what we might think of as the muteness of the war's archive: the inadmissibility, there, both of so great a volume of human loss and of the singular contours of *each* of the uncountable deaths that make up that volume.

If Whitman's writing here looks to push against such loss, it is in large measure through its meticulous, close-grained, and ineradicably carnal attention to the person Erastus Haskell was. Desire, that is, does a kind of historical *work* here: it works to preserve what Cavitch calls the "individuated mourning" that would be so troubled by the routinized statistical tallying of the war's mass carnage.[17] The letter is, in this vein, a small miracle of delicacy and tact. So seamless are its slight shifts of register, and so simultaneously gentle and yet unguardedly frank is the voice guiding it, that Whitman's descriptions and declarations—"he was tanned & had a fine head of hair, & looked good in the face when he first came, & was in pretty good flesh too"; "I assure you I was attracted to him much"—seem neither affrontive offerings to grieving parents, nor the least coy about the desire that invests them. Whitman proceeds here as if under the tacit presumption that the boy's parents share with him, in an untroubled way, the conviction that any less than fully carnal attentiveness, any memorialization of the young man that excludes his erotic body, would be finally falsifying, a further surrendering of the now-lost but infinitely rich *particularity* of Erastus Haskell. Or, to put this another way, for Whitman the erotic body carries particularity, carries the vanished specificity of this young soldier, like nothing else at all. And so it is to that body he turns in his effort to stanch, even if momentarily, the torrent of loss this one death occasions, and to preserve some small but telling remnant of this one man's singular personhood for what he calls the country's "record." Hence, his dilation, in a letter to the dead young man's parents, over a beauty that is no less "noble" for being, also, carnal.

But there is much else besides memorialization at work here, and the invocation of the carnal body as perhaps the richest index of a of dead soldier's ineluctably singular personhood. Consider again the audience for this writing: the parents of a child killed at war, hopelessly far from them, their care, and their capacity to intervene. In some respects, Whitman appears to comfort the Haskells by, in effect, becoming them. He reassures them, first, that their son did not die without an intimate, loving presence near to hand—though in that same gesture he also, however gently, supplants them. But the dialectics of surrogacy and supplement grows stranger still at the end of the letter, where the address abruptly turns *to* Erastus, and where Whitman writes an achingly tender love letter to the boy, for whom his own grieving parents are now, themselves, surrogates. Do we imagine the Haskells to be pleased, or moved, or discomfited by this peroration, or by the quality of attention it describes? For if Whitman's care is, again, emulative—if his exacting, bodily-rooted, gazing, tender, worried, and unwavering quality of affectionate care for the boy delineates his fluency in the role of surrogate parent—that gaze marks, too, the muted, delicately rendered but unforesworn desirousness that invests it. Whitman is parental here but he enjoys too the freedom, as a surrogate, from any of the prohibitions that might be imagined to come with that office.

Here again is another of the war's strange revelations. In what I have called his tact, Whitman essentially intimates, and then elaborates upon, an imagined affinity between himself and the Haskells, a common desire to mourn Erastus in the grain of a flesh that he tacitly assumes they, as parents, knew and cherished down to its least corporeal details. Parenting, Whitman seems here to assume, is no less carnally-invested an activity than, for instance, nursing. As Whitman understands them, both combine a scrupulous attentiveness of bodily care with modes of attachment from which elements of desire can no more be excised than those of tenderness or worry or hope. In the scenes reenacted in hospital after hospital, he glimpses in all a new thing: the possibility of a *familial* relation no less infused with the vibrant life of desire than the love of comrades had been.

Family itself—that bastion of middle-class propriety and sentimental enshrinement—opens itself up in the war to new carnal dimensions. (Or, if not new, newly explicable: as others have noted, Whitman's own familial relations, particularly with his mother and his siblings, provided him a rich enough training ground for these discoveries and elaborations.[18]) That it should be the Civil War, of all things, that brings the need for this recasting of familial structure into relief for Whitman is in at least one respect not surprising. It scarcely needs underscoring that the governing trope for understanding the sectional conflict boiling over the nation was that of a nuclear family turned violently against itself: brother vs. brother, a house divided, etc. And so Whitman takes to the field in the way he best knows how: just as he had earlier labored to make citizenship itself a state of erotic relatedness, he now lays the groundwork for a national mending at the root of which is a scripting of familial life as enlivened and solidified by the desire that traverses it. It makes a splendid kind of sense, then, that Whitman should find himself so strangely hailed after the war by the young men he loved—hailed as namesake, grandparent, but also species of father *and* mother to children who carry his name into the unwritten future. With its inescapable figures of familiar rupture, the war clarifies for Whitman what a carnally saturated family might look like, and broaches, too, the prospect of a mode of generation that is sexual though not quite normatively hetero-, nor for that matter normatively reproductive.

We might think of this other war project as something like the *eroticization of the sentimental family*, though that formulation, recalling as it does both the Freudian family and Foucault's accounts of its appearance, misappraises something of the idiosyncrasy of Whitman's investments. And it gives us, too, a misleading sense of Whitman as a kind of prophet, or harbinger of new emergences. (The sexualized familial form Whitman feels as a live possibility in the war looks, after all, only very little like the rivalrous, sex-stricken ensemble Freud would describe, the family that becomes, in Foucault's words, "the crystal in the deployment of sexuality."[19]) Whitman's relation to time is stranger and denser than the merely prophetic. If it does nothing else, his letter to the parents of Erastus Haskell, which so conspicuously conjoins the tasks of surrogacy with those of a kind of archive making, reminds us of how the prospect of this style of sociability, and in particular this familial structure stripped of its sexual prohibitions, might give ballast to Whitman's expectancy, his emphatic hopes for a moment, hundreds-of-years-hence, that will offer ampler room for meaning to the war he keeps insisting cannot, in the present tense, get into the books. His own queer progeny might read as one measure of this future's dawning possibility.

We are of course well equipped, today, with the means to diagnose the epistemological and ideological blindnesses this sort of explicitly familial futurism risks. Lee Edelman's is only the very strongest of the works that instruct us, carefully and exhaustively, in how such turns in Whitman back him away, in crucial respects, from the more radical intimations of his war writing (about the intimacy of sex and negativity, say, that a specifically nonreproductive queer sexuality renders unmaskable).[20] We have learned, that is, to regard with suspicion visions of a future tied to the order of generation, of what Judith Halberstam calls the "time of inheritance": a "generational time" organized around biological repro- duction and its presumptive sexual logics.[21] Without discounting these kinds of inquiry, I will say nevertheless that it may be possible to approach Whitman, and a range of writers who share his moment, at a different angle. Whitman's war, I think, invites us to wonder if there might not be some slender gap, an other-than-seamless overlap, between reproduc- tive futurism and an investment in the future as such—to wonder, say, if a future can be something you parent, with and through sex, but not heterosexual reproduction. Such an orientation might indeed be in cer- tain senses delimited by disavowals of the death drive—just as Edelman suggests—in which homophobia is often an indispensable element. But it might suggest as well something of the errancy, the "sideways growth" Kathryn Bond Stockton identifies with and in queer childhoods, though in the context of Whitman we would need to stretch Stockton's sense of sideways growth so that it frames not a single, bounded lifetime but sev- eral of them, bundled into series.[22] What in some readings might look sus- piciously like generational time, marked by the pairing of children and futurity, Whitman might think of instead as a kind of *seriality*, something "replicative but not procreative," as Elizabeth Freeman has it.[23] He helps us make room for visions of sociality and its possibilities that are not tuned to the notes of queer negation and the shattering force of the death drive, but are not for that simply liberal, simply redemptive, simply normative, simply not-queer.[24] Like Thoreau, Whitman harbors visions of sex and its possible futures more idiosyncratic than such parsings quite allow. And in his glimpsed hope for the emergence of a specifically carnal family, one neither captivated by sentimental propriety nor splintered by unavowable sexual rivalry, he takes his place alongside Thoreau as still another writer who imagined a future for sex that would not quite come to be.

No, No, No

"'Tho' always unmarried," Whitman wrote in a letter of 1890, "I have had six children—two are dead—One living southern grandchild, fine boy, who writes me occasionally."[25] So did he punctuate a nearly twenty-year- old correspondence with John Addington Symonds, who had pressed him, in more and more exacting terms, on the question of whether or not the comradeship envisioned in "Calamus" was a relation that might include what he called "ardent and *physical* intimacies." As Michael Robertson neatly summarizes the famous exchange, "Never have two sentences spurred so many biographers to such futile investigations."[26]

There is certainly a winking disingenuousness in Whitman's so forceful refusal of Symonds—"My first instinct," he tells his young companion Horace Traubel of the letters, "is violently reactionary—is strong and brutal for no, no, no"—though we go not much further than Symonds himself in recognizing in his response something to do less with timidity, or for that matter a sudden want of erotic nerve, than with a committed, even flirty, evasiveness.[27] (Symonds would write to Edward Carpenter of his impression that Whitman "wanted to obviate the 'damnable inferences' about himself by asserting his paternity," reminding us that Whitman's "answer" was itself designed to be disbelieved, even by its immediate recipient.[28]) Eve Sedgwick notes aptly that a series of disconnects separates British men like Symonds (and Carpenter and Oscar Wilde) from the poet across the Atlantic. She writes:

> Even assuming that what Symonds was "driving at" was in fact, as genital behavior, also something Whitman had been driving at in his poetry, still the cultural slippage of the Atlantic crossing meant that the sexual-ideological packages sent by the Kosmic American were very different from the ones unpacked by the cosmopolitan Englishman. The most important differences lay in the assumed class contexts in which the sexual ideology was viewed, and in the standing of women—both of "femininity" and of actual women—in the two visions.[29]

For Sedgwick, Whitman's "no, no, no" is the mark not of some underprocessed internalized homophobia but of the steep difficulty of *translation*—a translation rooted, for her, in a crossing of continents and classes.

And yet these may not be the only, or the most crucial, differences at play here. To my ears, Whitman's refusal speaks most emphatically to the point to which his writings, as well as Thoreau's, have returned us again and again in their entanglements with expectancy: that of the arrival, at the end of the century, of a mode of conceptualizing sexuality that would not redeem their earlier visions so much as fall aslant of them. For what Symonds offers Whitman, with an eagerness for comment and confirmation, is one model of what would later be called modern homosexual identity in its nascent form. Symonds was after all an especially keen student of German sexology—"His discovery of the German sexologists had a revelatory effect upon Symonds," Robertson notes[30]—and it was from Karl Heinrich Ulrichs that he gleaned his preferred conceptual framework for men who desire men, which was that of *sexual inversion*. Ardent reader and impassioned devotee of Whitman that he was, Symonds brings to the poet a reading of his work adapted to the specific medical language that had proved to himself, and to many men following him, so useful and even liberating, so much a linchpin for the discovery first of a defense, and then a community, and then a larger-scale *politics*, rooted in same-sex desire. If Symonds's badgering approach to his idolized Whitman can seem at times like an interrogation, it can also, from different angles, look like the awkward proffering of a gift.

And Whitman, as we know, was having none of it: no, no, no. But we can see, too, at this juncture how his refusal, which seems so plainly disingenuous, might be tied less to his own fear of, say, the making-public of the physical love of men for men than to a distrust of the distortion his own erotics suffer in their translation into Symonds's taxonomies. A sexually-saturated national citizenry, a public life dense with anonymous amorous commerce, a family form made vibrant and binding through carnal exchange: none of these modes of imagining desire and its force squares easily with "sexual inversion" or the forms of identity that might follow from it. In the violence of his repudiation, then, we might see not only the mark of the class misrecognition Sedgwick describes, but of time's unspooling, of the dawning of a future that does not quite square with the vision Whitman had of it.

So perhaps Whitman's famous reference to his children and the achieved masculine potency they represent is not solely the dodge it seems to be and that Symonds himself suspected. Perhaps his disingenuousness is itself more playful than defensive or, for that matter, deceitful. *Perhaps he does, after all, have children in mind*—even if only obliquely, and even if not the ones for whom biographers long have hunted.[31] Think again of the baby Walts with which we began, those namesakes from the great and terrible war. These children, if we imagine them to be the progeny ghosting somewhere around Whitman's winking invocation, are not emblems of hetero-virility. They are not the mark of his timidity or his shame. They are instead the evidence of a species of specifically queer generation: a whole style of queer world-making, and indeed queer future-making. That future, every day nearer to Whitman at the century's end, might have seemed to him to have a little less room for such errant styles than once he had hoped it might.

Coda

A Little Destiny

"The only excuse for reproduction," wrote Henry David Thoreau, "is improvement." "Beasts merely propagate their kind."[1] This moment, from "Chastity & Sensuality," suggests I think not the sexual squeamishness often attributed to him, but rather an insistence on sex as something other than an isolable property in the self, to be turned to use, instrumentalized and profited from like any other aspect of being organized by a market-inflected possessive individualism.[2] Though he would himself feel notably little of Thoreau's uneasiness before the prospect of the bestial, Whitman, too, dreams of a kind of generation that is erotic and vibrantly corporeal, and yet not reducible to mere biology or brute reproduction. For both authors, sex comes into meaning not as a manipulable possession, and still less as the self-saturating, deeply characterizing trait it would gradually become. (It is precisely this deepening conceptual conflict between such nonpossessive imaginings of sex and its gradual institutional emergence as something quite different that we hear in the sharpness of Whitman's exchange with the insistent Symonds.) Instead, for each of the authors, sex names a special mode of experience, a conjugation of the self whose effects are at once exhilarating and disconcerting—exhilarating for its clarifying derangements of the ordinary course of bodily existence, and disconcerting for the way it troubles the very premises of personhood, especially as they are anchored in liberal, possessivist terms. Together, Whitman and Thoreau strive to envision sex not as *yours* or *mine*, not a property or set of tools, but something else: a style of relation, a unique vector of the body's being in the world. Even through their divergent enthusiasms and anxieties, they suggest the possibility of an unloosening of sex from, among other things, the market-based logics of liberal individualism and individual productivity in which it found itself, and that the dawning of a hetero/homo distinction would only further ratify.

If this unloosening made both writers untimely, it tuned them, too, again in differently inflected ways, to the call of an intuited future, a yet-to-dawn moment whose arrival might convert the only marginally legible errancies of their present tense into more viable possibilities. They were, of course, far from the only writers, and far from the only American writers, to address themselves to unripened futures.[3] By way of conclusion to this section, I want now to look briefly at one of their queerer bedfellows: Emily Dickinson. Reading her in concert with the vexed expectancy of Thoreau, or the extravagant death-haunted imaginings of Whitman, one cannot much avoid the sense that, whatever her unlikeliness, Dickinson knows intimately of what they speak. She knows, that is, what it is to feel misrecognized by prevailing imaginings of sanctified ardor and devotion; what it means to balance between a hunger for articulacy and the expansive permissions of silence; and above all how it feels to yearn, with sometimes painful intensity, for another time, a removal from the clockwork of the present tense into some freer, ampler moment. She knows the queer yearning for what Dana Luciano, in a splendid phrase, calls "an otherwise that is not necessarily elsewhere."[4]

And yet, along with all these so striking commonalities, there are also divergences among the three that are not merely differences of emphasis. So I want to turn to Dickinson now as a complicating kind of counterexample, one who vexes the visions of sex and futurity we have observed so far, but without disowning them. Looking at a few passages from her letters to Susan Gilbert, I mean to suggest that among the things Dickinson's writing can make luminously clear for us is just how differently the prospect of futurity might be experienced by men and women, however intently both might be turned away from the moorings of dyadic heterosexuality. Dickinson's futures are not Whitman's, and they are not Thoreau's. Given the many other congruities that cross them, her unlikeness, at least in this respect, reminds us both how powerful a difference gender might make for the sexual politics of futurity, and what forms that difference might take.

The young Emily Dickinson, in her extraordinary letters to her beloved Susan Huntington Gilbert—who would later marry Dickinson's brother Austin and become Susan Dickinson—can sound a lot like the young Thoreau: impassioned, in possession of a talent for figure and a seemingly inexhaustible lexical playfulness, and very often finding in silence an ampler field for intimate avowal than in the constraints of speech. Consider the movements of her effusive letter from 11 June 1852.

I have but one thought, Susie, this afternoon of June, and that
of you, and I have one prayer, only; dear Susie, that is for you.
That you and I in hand as we e'en do in heart, might ramble
away as children, among the woods and fields, and forget these
many fears, and these sorrowing cares, and each become a
child again – I would it were so, Susie, and when I look
around me and find myself alone, I sigh for you again; little
sigh, and vain sigh, which will not bring you home.

I need you more and more, and the great world grows wider,
and dear ones fewer and fewer, every day that you stay away –
I miss my biggest heart; my own goes wandering round, and
calls for Susie – Friends are too dear to sunder, Oh they are far
too few, and how soon they will go away where you and I
cannot find them, dont let us forget these things, for their
remembrance now will save us many an anguish when it is too
late to love them! Susie, forgive me Darling, for every word I
say – my heart is full of you, none other than you in my
thoughts, yet when I seek to say to you something not for the
world, words fail me; If you were here, and Oh that you
were, my Susie, we need not talk at all, our eyes would
whisper for us, and your hand fast in mine, we would not ask
for language.⁵

"Silence," Thoreau had written, striking his own queer note, "is the
ambrosial night in the intercourse of Friends."⁶ Here Dickinson, devel-
oping what would become a theme in her correspondence with "Susie,"
desires to say to her "something not for the world," but finds too limited
a resource in the words they might exchange. In a series of sentences that
make ardor precious by counterposing it to the unpredictable swiftness of
mortal separation, she insists instead on the kinds of communion, at once
soulful and bodily (of eyes and hands), of which she and Gilbert might
avail themselves, in relation to which mere language is at once inadequate
and unnecessary, a thing not longed for.

It is by now a commonplace to read Dickinson's early letters as predictive,
early iterations of aesthetic and artistic problems she would later more fully
engage.⁷ That makes a kind of sense here, though what might later be called
"aesthetic choices" emerge more directly, in this letter, as pressing problems
of intimate life. Think of the derangements of conventional language we so

associate with Dickinson's singular practice: her rigorous disassembly of the sentence; her proliferation of syntactic possibility through punctuational ambiguity and suspension; her resistance to standardization at virtually all levels of writing, from her careful fashioning of fascicles to her hypertext-like inclusion of multiple alternative versions down to her expansion of the field of writing to include material scraps like pictures and leaves.[8] All of this we might understand to be anticipated here. But these stylistic practices are prefigured less as an artist's struggle with her recalcitrant medium than as part of a differently calibrated *need*—the need to communicate to Susan Gilbert, to *say* something to "Susie" "not for the world." Whatever thing not for the world Dickinson wishes to say to Gilbert, she implies, it will not be uttered in the world's language.

Nor will it be quite in the world's time. In the figures of longing for her friend, there is also a kind of temporal displacement of the sort we might recall from Thoreau. It is in this instance a yearning for a return to what she marks as the grieflessness of childhood—a removal, per-haps, from a present so scored for Dickinson by the prospect of a death that makes every future read as "too late" for love. Precisely these con-joined displacements—out of language, out of time—recur insistently in the correspondence, as Dickinson endeavors to carve out some viable ground for her and Gilbert's attachment. Indeed, I think one strong way to frame the decades-long outflowing of writings to "Susie" is to under-stand them as the extended parsing of what is, for Dickinson, a bedevil-ing, sometimes anguishing, question. Over the years it takes on different shapes and inflections, different urgencies and opacities, but always it is there: *Where might we love one another? Where can* two women love one another? Where can two nineteenth-century American women be pres-ent to one another in the full breadth of their devotion, their need, and their ardor?

Because Dickinson is Dickinson, the answer to which she most persis-tently returns is, of course, *eternity*. In death, that is, we arrive not at the unbreachable separation the young Dickinson had learned to fear, but at a communion otherwise inaccessible. "Sister," she writes in December 1865,

> We both are
> Women, and there
> is a Will of God –
> Could the Dying
> confide Death,

> there would be no
> Dead – Wedlock
> is shyer than Death. (*OMC*, 137)

"*Wedlock / is shyer than Death*," Dickinson writes, insinuating that whatever privileges, worldly secrets, or occult knowledges "Wedlock" might bestow, its revelations are more delimited, more circumspect, than those conferred by the strange grace of death. Marriage figures here as, in essence, a second-order sort of confidence. The death that in Dickinson so pervades life, in other words, may be one key to the "otherwise that is not necessarily elsewhere."

The heralding of death as the space and time of love's richest flourishing invests Dickinson's expectancy with a particular mordancy, which we will consider in more detail shortly. But not all of Dickinson's efforts to find for herself and Gilbert some place beyond the confinements of what she calls in another letter "this dim real"—by which she means the world in Gilbert's absence—are quite so anchored in mortal inevitability (*OMC*, 45).⁹ Her letter of October 1851, so bedazzling for its deft punning on the names, titles, and characters of the works she and "Susie" had in their separation been enjoying, does more than effuse. The letter, whose theme is communion in absence, also makes a kind of case for writing itself:

> I wept a tear here, Susie – on purpose for <u>you</u> – because this
> "sweet silver moon" smiles in on me and Vinnie, and then it
> goes so far before it gets to you – and then you never told me
> if there <u>was</u> any moon in Baltimore – and how do <u>I</u> know
> Susie – that you see her sweet face at all? She looks like a fairy
> tonight, sailing around the sky in a little silver gondola with
> stars for gondoliers. I asked her to let me ride a little while
> ago – and told her I would <u>get out</u> when she got as far as
> Baltimore, but she only smiled to herself and went sailing on. . . .
>
> It is such an evening Susie, as you and I would walk and have
> such pleasant musings, if you were only here – perhaps we
> would have a "Reverie" after the form of "Ik Marvel," indeed
> I do not know why it wouldn't be just as charming as of that
> lonely Bachelor, smoking his cigar – and it would be far more
> profitable as "Marvel" <u>only</u> marvelled, and you and I would
> <u>try</u> to make a little destiny to have for our own. Do you know

that charming man is dreaming <u>again</u>, and will wake pretty
soon – so the papers say, with <u>another</u> Reverie – more
beautiful than the first?

Dont you hope he will live as long as you and I do – and keep
on having dreams and writing them to us – what a charming
old man he'll be, and how I envy his grandchildren, little
"Bella" and "Paul"! We will be willing to die Susie – when such
as <u>he</u> have gone, for there will be none left to interpret
these lives of our's. (*OMC*, 8–9)

As Virginia Jackson reminds us in her exemplary reading of the letter, "Ik
Marvel" is the author of the popular *Reveries of a Bachelor* of 1851, and
it is on the model of his "lonely" bachelorhood, or in a careful derangement of that model, that Dickinson, in a heartbreaking phrase, hopes that
she and Gilbert might "*try* to make a little destiny to have for our own."
Marvel figures here as an interpreter of their lives outside of matrimony,
but also as a kind of curator of them, the secret-keeper around whom they
can convene in mutual explication. Dickinson intimates to Gilbert that it
is only here, in the more winning time of writing, writing to one another
and writing about writing, that this other bachelor life together might be,
finally, *habitable*: it is here, in epistles that, like the extravagant figures
that populate them, collapse space, suture the temporalities of composition and reception, mingle presence and absence, that their little destiny
lives, lives *as* writing and its interpretation. If Dickinson often resists the
constraints of speech, and if, as Jackson argues, she resists the corralling
of this letter to her "Susie" into coding as "literature," this is not because
of some incurable sense of writing as suspect, duplicitous, or elementally
inadequate. She also understands writing to carve out from the "dim real"
a different sort of space, in time and out of it, attached to the material
embodiments of the world but not wholly constrained by them.[10] What
they have together in writing, in what opens in written correspondence
between them, is a special kind of displacement in which they are afforded
an oblique but, to Dickinson, real and cherishable presence to and with
one another. It is there, and only there, that she and Gilbert can conspire
to make a little destiny to have for their own.

That destiny, though, is from the first not without its sorrows, and
they are not only those of mediation. As her letters make achingly
clear, Dickinson did not need Freud to instruct her in the lesson that,

whatever its lacerations, grief is among the greatest of all preservers. "To miss you, Sue," she writes to the woman now fifteen years married to her brother,

> is power.
> The stimulus
> of Loss makes
> most Possession
> mean.
> To live lasts
> always, but to
> love is firmer
> than to live.
> No Heart that
> broke but further
> went than
> Immortality. (*OMC*, 181)

Brokenheartedness—what she calls "the stimulus of Loss"—makes love immortal, and makes things possessed at once richer in significance (they *mean*) but also insufficiently consoling (they *are* mean). Or again, as Dickinson writes in a letter that, on first blush, might seem a straightforward memento mori admonition, but reads just as plausibly as a far more pointed, far more heartsick reminder to Gilbert of how deeply Dickinson once believed in her devotion:

> To lose what we
> never owned
> might seem an
> eccentric Bereavement
> but Presumption
> has its' Affliction
> as actually as
> Claim –
>
> Emily. (*OMC*, 200)

The letters after Gilbert's marriage to Austin often read as a turning over of just this "Presumption"—the presumption that she owned Susie's

devotion—and just this "eccentric Bereavement," a parsing of the affliction of a love both cherished and lost, and cherished still *as* the affliction
of loss. As she wrote years earlier, "Your—Riches—taught me—Poverty!"
(*OMC*, 105). Where can two women live out their passion and devotion to
one another? Here is one answer: within the sustaining grief, the eccentric
bereavement, of the one for the loss of the other.

Even before Gilbert's marriage, though, there is a disquiet in
Dickinson's yearning for that queer otherwise—call it an anticipated
afflictedness—far different from what we have yet seen. Where for
Thoreau the present tense is enlivened, despite its cruel and comprehensive disappointments, by an intuited futurity, for the young Dickinson,
dreaming of that little destiny, the future is itself the peril. Some
moments are teasing and flirtatious. Here is how, in April of 1852, she
imagines marriage and motherhood:

> I do think it's wonderful, Susie, that our hearts dont break,
> every day, when I think of all the whiskers, and all the gallant
> men, but I guess I'm made with nothing but a hard heart of
> stone, for it dont break any, and dear Susie, if mine is stony,
> your's is stone, upon stone, for you never yield any, where I
> seem quite beflown. Are we going to ossify always, say, Susie –
> how will it be? When I see the Popes and the Polloks, and the
> John-Milton Browns, I think we are liable, but I dont know! I
> am glad there's a big future waiting for me and you. (*OMC*, 21)

All the world's whiskers, though they may auger the prospect of a big
future—a future of pregnancy—here figure more pertinently as an occasion for teasing, wordplay, and the sustaining of flirtation between the two
women, the one stony and the other beflown. It is the two of them who
emerge finally as more together, more conjoined, than any others ("a big
future . . . for me and you").

But there are far darker surmises as well. Here is Dickinson only a few
months later, in a letter worth quoting at some length:

> Mattie was here last evening, and we sat on the
> front door stone, and talked about life and love, and whispered
> our childish fancies about such blissful things – the evening
> was gone so soon, and I walked home with Mattie beneath the
> silent moon, and wished for you, and Heaven. You did not

come, Darling, but a bit of Heaven did, or so it <u>seemed</u> to us, as we walked side by side and wondered of that great blessedness which may be our's sometime, is granted now, to some. This union, my dear Susie, by which two lives are one, this sweet and strange adoption wherein we can but look, and are not yet admitted, how it can fill the heart, and make it gang wildly beating, how it will take <u>us</u> one day, and make us all it's own, and we shall not run away from it, but lie still and be happy!

You and I have been strangely silent upon this subject, Susie, we have often touched upon it, and as quickly fled away, as children shut their eyes when the sun is too bright for them. I have always hoped to know if you had no dear fancy, illumining all your life, no one of whom you murmured in the faithful ear of night – and at whose side in fancy, you walked the livelong day; and when you come home, Susie, we must speak of these things.

How dull our lives must seem to the bride, and the plighted maiden, whose days are fed with gold, and who gather pearls every evening; but to the <u>wife</u>, Susie, sometimes the <u>wife forgotten</u>, our lives perhaps seem dearer than all others in the world; you have seen flowers at morning, <u>satisfied</u> with the dew, and those same sweet flowers at noon with their heads bowed in anguish before the mighty sun; think you these thirsty blossoms will <u>now</u> need naught but – <u>dew</u>? No, they will cry for sunlight, and pine for the burning noon, tho' it scorches them, scathes them; they have got through with peace – they know that the man of noon, is <u>mightier</u> than the morning and their life is henceforth to him. Oh, Susie, it is dangerous, and it is all too dear, these simple trusting spirits, and the spirits mightier, which we cannot resist! It does so rend me, Susie, the thought of it when it comes, that I tremble lest at sometime I, too, am yielded up.

Susie, you will forgive me my amatory strain – it has been a very long one, and if this saucy page did not here bind and fetter me, I might have had no end. (*OMC*, 30–31)

What begins as a love letter of "childish fancies" that looks to trade intimate confidences and secrets of some "dear fancy" devolves into a meditation upon the "anguish" to which any entanglement in the world of adult sexual exchange seems poised to bring to Dickinson and her friend. "It does so rend me, Susie," Dickinson writes, "the thought of it when it comes, that I tremble lest at sometime I, too, am yielded up." This is a "trembling before history" different from what we saw in Whitman, a terror-struck sense of limitless vulnerability to a future as "dangerous" for them as it is apparently unopposable (a thing they "cannot resist").[11] The scene of romantic pleasure yields almost before it can be completed to a vision of marriage as, for the wife, an unhappy combination of neglect on the one hand, and on the other a quality of attention that scorches and starves. According to Dickinson's extended metaphor, to be subject to the heat of a husband is (in a way that might recall, even as it inverts, Bradstreet's "A Letter to Her Husband, Absent upon Public Employment") to be held fast in one's life-wide powerlessness ("their life is henceforth to him"). It is to be thrown back with fondness and sorrow upon an unbetrothed past: a "morning," which is Dickinson and Gilbert's present tense, that she figures not as anticipatory at all but as the disappearing moment of life's most vital satisfactions, known chiefly in sad retrospect.

The transformation of the "dull lives" of the unplighted into the scene of what Dickinson invokes as life's most precious pleasures is striking, not least in the stridency of tone Dickinson herself notes, as she chastises herself for her "amatory strain." And yet that shift is anticipated by the strange meditation that precedes it. Walking beneath the moon, Dickinson "wished for you, and Heaven," and turns then to consideration of "that great blessedness which may be our's sometime." Dickinson had been talking "about life and love," and is contemplating that "union . . . by which two lives are one," and so appears to be thinking, here on paper to "Susie," about love and about marriage. But at no moment is it clear how we might pry apart the vision of connubial love as "blessedness" from the invocations of an afterworld, of "Heaven," that surround it. Is the happiness Dickinson scripts here, "this sweet and strange adoption wherein we can but look, and are not yet admitted," that of the marital bed or the grave? Is the joy that, she says, "will take *us* one day," and in which they will "lie still and be happy," that of the bride "whose days are fed with gold"? Or is it does it accord more with what she calls elsewhere "The Overtakelessness / of Those / Who have accom— / plished Death" (*OMC*, 125–26)? As Dickinson figures it in her so amatory letter, the achieved communion of death, which may look a lot like that of matrimony, is also far, far preferable to it, far less asphyxiating and less anguished. (Or, to put it another way, the more fully it can be imagined as a species of death, the *less* anguishing the prospect of matrimony appears.) Dickinson suggests, too, that for women like her and Gilbert their inevitabilities, those of mortality and matrimony, are more or less equivalent.

For Dickinson's dream of "an otherwise that is not necessarily elsewhere," then, the uncreated future cannot quite be the scene of expansion and reclamation, of inarticulacy emerging at last as pleasure, that it is, in their differing ways, for Thoreau and Whitman. "Eternity" makes possible some of these transactions, and to the degree that it does we can perhaps understand Dickinson as practicing a variety of the queer spiritualism that Luciano, theorizing that nineteenth-century "otherwise that is not necessarily elsewhere," has in mind. Dickinson's is, we might say, an investment in an afterworld that is eroticized inasmuch as the pleasures of intimacy, ardor, and devotion which are otherwise available to her only as retrospection, or possibilities frozen in the alembic of an unyielding grief, figure there as viable *satisfactions*, as communions with the beloved no longer unattainable. As for the nonotherworldly future: that, it seems, promises considerably less, even to so relatively comfortably situated (because white, because propertied, because middle-class) a daughter of New England as Dickinson. For her, the less promising but only barely less inevitable eventuality is marriage, and the estrangements, perils, conditions, and confinements that come with it. As she makes clear to Gilbert, her freedom to decline both of those coming futures felt, to her, minimal, if extant at all. And in this, of course, she was not alone. So I want to turn, in the section that follows, to different visions of marriage—that emblem of futurity more fearsome to the young Dickinson than death—to understand more precisely how, for some, imaginings of sex might find in the conceptual framework of marriage not only a form of dire confinement but also surprising possibilities for extravagance, errancy, and upheavals reaching far, far beyond the couple form.

But these were not Dickinson's imaginings (Dickinson who remained, with her "Title—Divine / The Wife—Without— / the Sign"). Her letters offer different clarities. In certain respects, the point she brings us to is a simple one: in the nineteenth century—no less than today—the conceptual territorializing of the self that accomplishes the yoking of sex to reproduction, of pleasure to biology, plays itself out in consequentially divergent ways, and with consequentially divergent force, on and across bodies differently coded according to gender. Setting the queer visions of futurity of men like Whitman and Thoreau beside those of a woman like Dickinson brings some of those divergences into relief. The young and anxiously unmarried Dickinson, if her letters are any indication, experiences precious little looseness in the ligaturing of desire to brute biology, or in the social machinery that sees to their strict conjoining in matrimony; what room for errancy and extravagance she does carve out comes, as we have seen, largely under the cover of an unextinguishable grief or an eroticized longing, less for Gilbert than for the Eternity that will, at last, bring them together, completely and without distortion. To imagine sex as irreducible to biology, and a thing outside the strict containments of the liberal possessivist self, is a rich and, as I hope Thoreau and Whitman have shown us, immensely generative project. But the freedom, the *room* to imagine sex in such terms was also, of course, a kind of privilege. To say as much is not, I think, to denigrate the labor of imagination we see in what I have called the untimely imagining of sex and sexual possibility. But it is to recall that this was an undertaking whose plausibilities were, like much else in nineteenth-century American life, unequally distributed.

PART TWO

To Speak of the Woe That Is in Marriage

3

Islanded

Jewett and the Uncompanioned Life

"History," Frederic Jameson tells us, in the famous phrase, "is what hurts."[1] It is, as theoretical pronouncements go, near on to indisputable, and not any less so in the case of women in the nineteenth century, ensnared as they must be (as Dickinson has already suggested to us) in the workings of a marriage plot not typically written for their benefit. For women ill-at-home in those workings, the pains come in particular intensities. Loneliness, isolation, a certain out-of-timeness, a pervasive sense of one's own illegibility, or even impossibility, to and in the given world: no one would dispute that these are high among the inheritances of, for instance, sexually nonnormative women, even those sheltered by privileges of race and station, and even before the advent of modern sexual taxonomies gave legal and medical point to the pathologization of women straying too far afield of the trajectories of matrimonial life. Sarah Orne Jewett, a writer to whom the phrase *the female world of love and ritual* clings like a badge of uncertain distinction, would seem to confirm as much.[2] Her portraits of widowed, jilted, unmarried, and otherwise (to use one of her favorite adjectives) uncompanioned women gravitate conspicuously toward heartbreak and, in a word, hurt—toward what Heather Love, in a recent reading of "loneliness and impossibility as lived experience" in Jewett's fiction, calls "the feelings of loss, disappointment, and longing that are *internal* to female worlds of love and ritual."[3] If for Jameson history is what hurts because, as Christopher Nealon writes, "history" is "the name we give to the impossibility of reconciling personal life with the movements of a total system," then the particular quality of irreconcilability Jewett seems to want to describe is of the sort Dickinson intimated: that of a woman who fears there is little in the available range of intimate forms and structures to give coherence, heft, or permanence to the force and quality of her life's investment in other women.[4] She writes, then, about the intricacies of the feeling of being dislocated from worlds that appear more easily habitable to others: of being, as often as not, unnoticed, inaccessible, unviable.

Love's is an especially strong corrective to idealized readings of the intimate world of women that is so often Jewett's milieu. Those accounts, she observes, tend both to under-read the privileges that sustain that world (as critics like Richard Brodhead, Elizabeth Ammons, and others have insisted) and, most consequentially, to misapprehend the hurt that at all points underlies it.[5] And though Love's admonitory reading seems to me timely and incisive, still I hope in the chapter that follows to show that Jewett's work does something a bit different. The story I find there is one that falls intriguingly aslant of both idealized visions of autonomous female domestic bliss *and* of the historical primacy of the hurt that Jameson discusses and Love underscores. Reading Jewett's work, we can find ourselves confronted with a question at once simple on the face of it but of real theoretical consequence, especially to critical endeavors built around the telling of the history of sexuality: *What if history does something other, or something more, than hurt?* What if wounding is not the only register for the experience of being in history, or the aptest, even for women for whom enmeshment in the marriage plot may indeed be an exercise in a kind of masochism?[6] What would it require "to recognize that history is not *only* what hurts," as Dana Luciano writes, "but what may also, given time, be rendered (pleasurably) otherwise"?[7]

With its striking generic and formal peculiarities—its resistance, for instance, to the narrative armature of the marriage plot—Jewett's work can plausibly seem an intimate meditation on the refusal of the lived world to conform to the generic demands of either tragedy or comedy. But in Jewett's hands these resistances and inflections, these attentions to the messy inextricability of joy and sorrow, amount to something else as well. She offers, I want to suggest, a reading of being in history that tracks the terrible force of its distortions and captivations even as it adroitly resists the idea that our captivation by something called "history" is remainderless, or that what remains is merely residual and so inconsequential. In *The Country of the Pointed Firs*, the book of linked stories I want to examine in detail here, she portrays a collection of people who, by virtue of accident no less than agency, stand in widely differing relations to the ordering forms of the world. Among the most forceful of these, of course, are the imperatives of reproductive coupledom. Without minimizing or even qualifying the varieties of heartbreak that afflict its inhabitants,

Jewett nevertheless envisions a world we might find remarkable not least for its being, as lived, only loosely ligatured by the imposed destinies of heterosexuality. Dunnet Landing, Jewett's fictional Maine town, is not untouched by those destinies, not at all. But it is, in ways I want to suggest are telling, conspicuously unpredetermined by them.

What flourishes in that space of nondetermining constraint is the subject of the chapter that follows. Working in the vein of critics like Love, Judith Fetterley and Marjorie Pryse, Kate McCullough, and Sharon Marcus, I want to look closely at the kinds of sociality Jewett figures with such tenderness: at the forms of love that come to thrive within a social structure not wholly overcoded by matrimony; at *Firs'* fascination with what it calls recluses and strayaways, whose hurts and errancies are unreclaimable even within that looser sociability; and at the ways the narrator's intimacies with the world of women by whom she is surrounded—with Mrs. Todd in particular, her "enchantress"[8]—sponsor, too, a curious affinity for *men*, a kind of queer kinship across gender and typically located on the margins of the marriage plot.[9] Throughout the book, Jewett insists that this is a vanishing sociality, an almost antique world of "elaborate conventionalities" and permissions that is, to the narrative's manifest dismay, modernizing by the moment (*Firs*, 5). Curiously, her persistent register of that modernity's encroachment is, as we shall see, its *normalizing* force, its flattening out of an eccentricity that is never far from, though not quite reducible to, erotic errancy. She writes in all from the far edge of precisely the moment whose disappearance Henry James would lament in his letter to Jewett's longtime intimate companion, Annie Fields.

Throughout these readings of affinity and seclusion, queer kinship and a curious kind of extrahuman object-love, I want to keep in focus the way Jewett's work might provide us with a salutary historiographic model. There is, as I have been suggesting, need of one. For all the sophistication Jameson brings to it, the history-as-hurt model, in one or another of its iterations, is by now familiar: it stands behind the reading of history (typically in concert with a Foucault-inflected interest in "power") as the name of our necessary, necessarily disfiguring, entrapment, as the constraint that produces us. That model is of course immensely enabling—the early and galvanizing years of queer theory are among the things it enabled. But it is also, as I have tried to show, a method that leaves much out of the telling of the story of sexuality, particularly as it unfolds across the late nineteenth century. It can leave us ill-equipped, as Jordan Stein notes, to understand as capaciously as we might like, or to understand as sex *at all*, all that fails to appear as or in "discourse" and yet might not *not* be sex. (Hence his desire to "collect into the history of sexuality versions of queerness that never accede to discourse.")[10]) And it might leave us to wonder, along with Sharon Marcus, "what remains to be seen if we proceed without Oedipus, without castration, without the male traffic in women, without homophobia and homosexual panic" as the default premises.[11] Jewett can be especially instructive for us as we try to imagine how to tell the history of sexuality otherwise, in ways that sacrifice neither the vibrancy of certain strands of life unscripted by marriage nor the anguish that so often prevails in those queer outerlands—as we try to take seriously, that is, Elizabeth Freeman's trenchant reminder that "history is not only what hurts but what arouses, kindles, whets, or itches."[12] As I suggest in the conclusion to this chapter, Jewett also helps us to grapple with one of what I take to be the most suggestive, ongoingly vexing questions in queer scholarship, framed splendidly by Luciano in her Derridean-inflected meditation on queer spectrality in the American nineteenth century: How is it that we can we get, historiographically speaking, pleasure and justice to hold space together in the same room, on the same page, in the same body?[13]

Love Unbound

What does it mean to fall in love not with another person but with a scene of sociability? In what terms, and according to what figures of intimate relation, might that love know itself? And what is it about that sociability that makes it, in the first place, the object of so idiosyncratic a form of desire?

In its opening moments, *The Country of the Pointed Firs* orients itself around precisely these questions. Here is the opening story, "The Return," in its entirety:

> There was something about the coast town of Dunnet which made it seem more attractive than other maritime villages of eastern Maine. Perhaps it was the simple fact of acquaintance with that neighborhood which made it so attaching, and gave such interest to the rocky shore and dark woods, and the few houses which seemed to be securely wedged and tree-nailed in among the ledges by the Landing. These houses made the most of their seaward view, and there was a gayety and determined floweriness in their bits of garden ground; the small-paned high windows in the peaks of their steep gables were like knowing eyes that watched the harbor and the far

sea-line beyond, or looked northward all along the shore and its back-
ground of spruces and balsam firs. When one really knows a village like
this and its surroundings, it is like becoming acquainted with a single person. The process of falling in love at first sight is as final as it is swift in such
a case, but the growth of true friendship may be a lifelong affair.

After a first brief visit made two or three summers before in the course
of a yachting cruise, a lover of Dunnet Landing returned to find the
unchanged shores of the pointed firs, the same quaintness of the village
with its elaborate conventionalities; all that mixture of remoteness, and
childish certainty of being the centre of civilization of which her affectionate dreams had told. One evening in June, a single passenger landed upon
the steamboat wharf. The tide was high, there was a fine crowd of specta-
tors, and the younger portion of the company followed her with subdued
excitement up the narrow street of the salt-aired, white-clapboarded little
town. (*Firs*, 5)

This book is a love story: that is what, cumulatively, the opening strains suggest. But what *kind* of love story? In advance of any of its yet-to-be narrated
residents, Dunnet Landing itself figures, in a curious adjectival neologism,
as "attaching," which we might provisionally take to mean something like
"conducive to the forming of attachments to itself." According to the first
figure Jewett offers, such an attachment to a neighborhood—to a special
geology as well as to its equally idiosyncratic social forms—works on the
model of intimacy between persons: "It is like becoming acquainted with a
single person." Fair enough: this, then, is our love story, that of a person for
a place, set on the model of a person for a person.

But that conventional figure gets curiouser and curiouser the more
we look at it. We notice, first, a doubleness in Jewett's reading of Dunnet
Landing as like "a single person," a phrase that finds an echo in the next
paragraph's reference to the narrator herself as a "single person." In both
instances the manifest meaning of the phrase—one person, not more—
holds space with the suggestion of a different possibility: that the attaching town is like a "single person" insofar as "single" means something
more like uncoupled or uncompanioned. In *that* sense, "single" gathers in
implications of solitude and isolation (such as we soon will see embodied
in figures like poor Joanna and Elijah Tilley) but also, perhaps, of a kind
of freedom: a freedom, in singleness, from the bounds of couplehood or,
more pointedly, marriage. Sleeping in the language of the opening passage,
in other words, is an intimation that the central story of the book might

be best conceptualized in terms of the kinds of love available to a person unconstrained by the plottings of matrimonial life. Or again: the idiosyncratic kind of love that the book wishes to narrate is not precisely the love of couples, as convention might invite us to suspect, but is instead one of the possibilities for ardor that flourishes, like the single person, *outside* of the territorialization of intimate life by the strictures of the marriage plot.

If these figures provide one set of analogues for the attaching love of a given place around which *Firs* will be built, the final sentence of the first paragraph overlays them with another, differently qualifying set of terms: "The process of falling in love at first sight is as final as it is swift in such a case, but the growth of true friendship may be a lifelong affair." In one sense, the conventional polarities get reversed here: "friendship" is not the poor cousin to "love" but, in this account, what supersedes it. (And whatever chastening of the amatory element of love we might hear in the word is itself qualified by the ever-so-slightly suggestive resonance of the word "affair.") With uninsistent delicacy, that narrative "tact" with which she is so identified, Jewett puts us on notice here with respect to two points.[14] The first is that the love plots of *Firs* are likely to unfold under other-than-traditional rubrics—it is, quite pointedly, *not* marriage that makes for the consummation of love at first sight. The second is that this distance from marriage plots ought not to suggest to us any circumscription, or for that matter any diminishment, of the life of the passions. Jewett's narrator begins the book by staking her claim in Dunnet Landing as one who loves it—"a lover of Dunnet Landing"—and also, a shade more roguishly, as one who goes there *to be* a special kind of lover. She is a lover of Dunnet Landing in all senses: an enthusiast, a woman living out her passions there, a person whose *role* there is that of a lover.

The opening vignette, then, invites us to read *Firs* as a story of the deterritorialization of "love"—of its fracturing into unpredicted assemblages, which fail to parse particularly easily into marriage-based taxonomies of intimate relation but are not, for that, wanting in ardor, durability, or intensity.[15] It will be a story about how love, once it is removed from its overcoding by marriage, can look like a range of other, stranger things. There is every reason to follow Faderman, Donovan, Fetterley, Pryse, Love, and others in thinking of the work that emerges as, accordingly, a lesbian story—or, more precisely, to say that one among those assemblages involves the domestic intimacies, and kindled love, between women that would read with relative stability as lesbian, according to taxonomies only barely not shaped into place around the scene of Jewett's writing.[16] Almiry Todd's relation with the narrator is of course the place in the book where this aspect of the plot is most vividly realized, and one hardly struggles to trace its lineaments. It is there in the admiration each woman offers, in differing but similarly muted forms, with respect to the other ("I'd stand right here an' say it to anybody," is Mrs. Todd's disarming version [*Firs*, 8]); in the narrator's moments of jealous pique, as well as Mrs. Todd's; and perhaps most suggestively in the way that, even at the end of "William's Wedding"—the final story added in to posthumous editions of *Firs*, perhaps to make it better conform to the contours of a traditional work of fiction by involving its conclusion in, inevitably, a marriage—the pairing with which Jewett chooses to leave the reader is not that of the aged William and his bride but of the narrator and Mrs. Todd, joined in intimate, companionable silence: "We went home together up the hill, and Mrs. Todd said nothing more; but we held each other's hands all the way" (*Firs*, 256).

Even before Mrs. Todd's own painful entanglements with marriage become clear (she loved a man who would not marry her and married a man she thought kind but did not love), her very occupation, in its witchy resonances, gives point to her peculiar status in the matrimonially ordered world. (Elizabeth Ammons calls her, not at all implausibly, Jewett's "white witch."[17]) Of her "queer little garden" the narrator writes:

> At one side of this herb plot were other growths of a rustic pharmacopoeia, great treasures and rarities among the commoner herbs. There were some strange and pungent odors that roused a dim sense and remembrance of something in the forgotten past. . . . With most remedies the purchaser was allowed to depart unadmonished from the kitchen, Mrs. Todd being a wise saver of steps; but with certain vials she gave cautions, standing in the doorway, and there were other doses which had to be accompanied on their healing way as far as the gate, while she muttered long chapters of directions, and kept up an air of secrecy and importance to the last. It may not have been only the common ails of humanity with which she tried to cope; it seemed sometimes as if love and hate and jealousy and adverse winds at sea might also find their proper remedies among the curious wild-looking plants in Mrs. Todd's garden. (*Firs*, 6–7)

Bill Brown is certainly correct to note that, "If there is one occupation and preoccupation that makes the sketches cohere as a novel, just as it solidifies the relationship between the narrator and Mrs. Todd, it is the gathering of plants."[18] But if one of the ghostlier implications of the passage above is that Mrs. Todd, in her secretive dealings with women stricken by the ailments of love, provides an abortifacient, then she stands, too, less as a figure detached from or untouched by heterosexuality and its entanglements than one who, having suffered her own sorrows, looks to heal other women of its more debilitating effects.[19] In her garden so conspicuously open to the paths of the social world, she emblematizes precisely the special sociability the narrator loves, which figures here as above all else *curative* in its aims and intentions.

In all these ways, *Firs* can profitably be understood as a kind of lesbian fiction, appearing in the last moments in which its intimations might yet be known otherwise. But if this is lesbian or protolesbian fiction, then much of what's striking about it is the breadth and variety of *other* loves it includes—and includes with an irreducible heterogeneity—as figural analogues, extensions, rivals, and kin to the love between women. The lesbian plot, for which the female world of love and ritual has served as a kind of critical template, takes its place among a series of other assemblages of intimate life that interest Jewett, inasmuch as they, too, grow more and more possible as affect becomes unloosed from its strict territorialization by marriage. We might in these terms begin to stretch Pryse's notion of Jewett's "transitivity" (which she understands to mark Jewett's resistance to the sorts of categorization that "1990s critics attempt to impose on her work in the name of historicism") to include the whole unruly range of intimacies and passions to which an uncompanioned life appears to give rise.[20] An improvised love between women is *one* form that unloosening can take, but there are others.

For instance: In what relation to the intimacies between women do we understand the proliferating love of nonhuman objects—plants, livestock, pets—that so fascinates the narrative? Mrs. Todd's "queer little garden" is only the first site of this curiously vectored love, with Almiry herself figuring not as a cultivator or enthusiast but "an *ardent lover* of herbs" (*Firs*, 6). Think, too, of the small note struck in the midst of the outing to Green Island, where Mrs. Todd and her widowed mother discuss the "likeliness" of cats:

> "Why, this ain't that kitten I saw when I was out last, the one that I said didn't appear likely?" exclaimed Mrs. Todd as we went our way.
>
> "That's the one, Almiry," said her mother. "She always had a likely look to me, an' she's right after her business. I never see such a mouser for one of her age. . . . She's a real understandin' little help, this kitten is. I picked her

from among five Miss Augusta Pennell had over to Burnt Island," said the old woman, trudging along with the kitten close at her skirts. "Augusta, she says to me, 'Why, Mis' Blackett, you've took the homeliest;' an', says I, 'I've got the smartest; I'm satisfied.'"

"I'd trust nobody sooner 'n you to pick out a kitten, mother," said the daughter handsomely, and we went on in peace and harmony. (*Firs*, 31)

Mrs. Blackett's expertise in the selection of kittens, so much a testament to the New England hardihood and practicality the book celebrates, emerges also as something else. Set alongside her daughter's ardent love of herbs, Mrs. Blackett's investments here can begin to seem less an emblem of her domestic fluency and more a point about, strangely, passion: an intimation of the routes an unexpended ardor might take, of some of the ways "love" might reassemble itself, in a world so conspicuously unstructured by the affective patterning of married life. And Mrs. Blackett is far from the only example.

Something of the intricacy of this unbinding of affect comes perhaps clearest in the case of poor Joanna, the narrative's quintessential recluse. Brokenhearted and inconsolable, she takes herself to Shell-heap Island to live in penitential solitude. When Mrs. Todd and her friend Mrs. Fosdick consider how Joanna endured her companionlessness ("Joanna was one that loved her friends" [*Firs*, 55]), they make a kind of refrain, half mournful and half conciliatory, of the fact of her attachment to, of all things, her hens. "'There was her hens,' suggested Mrs. Fosdick, after reviewing the melancholy situation. 'She never wanted the sheep after that first season. There wa'n't no proper pasture for sheep after the June grass was past, and she ascertained the fact and couldn't bear to see them suffer; but the chickens done well'" (*Firs*, 55). And then, a moment later, once more: "'There was the hens,' repeated Mrs. Fosdick kindly. 'I expect she soon came to makin' folks o' them'" (*Firs*, 55). In their soothing refrain, Mrs. Fosdick and Mrs. Todd share an unspoken knowledge, an understanding of the entanglement of grief and the love of an object-world. Making folks of hens or of kittens, tending herbs and gardens with a lover-like ardor: I take these scenes to exemplify for the narrative the unpredictable rerouting of affect, in this case out onto the proximate object-world, that the de-centering of matrimonial intimate structures can effect. Alongside the love between women that kindles at Dunnet Landing, where unruptured normative families take up virtually no stage time, is this multifaceted ardor for the world of *things*: flowers and herbs, hens and kittens.

Bill Brown is only one of several critics to take special note of Jewett's arresting attention to things, what he calls her "materialist epistemology." He reads her "fixation on the artifactual record of human history" in relation to contemporaneous developments in the fields of anthropology, ethnology, and museology, whose projects of knowledge accumulation through objects, their study, and their arrangement, were shifting in important ways around the scene of Jewett's writing.[21] But Jewett also seems to be asking, in these recurring figures, a differently inflected set of questions, less concerned with anthropology or ethnography than the strange intertwining of the object-world with, again, the life of the passions. Each scene of engagement with the nonhuman world of things raises the question: Who knows what objects a person's ardor, once unbound, might transform? Who knows how the ordinary things of the world might find themselves reconfigured by the force of a love unloosed?[22] It would be an underreading, I think, to imagine this pervasive form of object-love to be solely compensatory, to think of each object as a makeshift substitute for more desired but prohibited or inaccessible possibilities. The love of nonhuman objects is not necessarily the mark of a *want* of human love-objects, nor is it necessarily "a kind of fetishism, in which objects come to stand for the missing parts of people, and by extension, for parts of missing people," as Valerie Rohy puts it in her rich account of anachronism and queer desire in Jewett.[23] That counterloving may measure less as a desolation of affect than the *release* of it. Mrs. Fosdick and Mrs. Todd speak not solely mournfully of Joanna.

Still, neither can we ignore the yearning behind this all, the great hunger for consolation that, as Mrs. Todd and Mrs. Fosdick also imply, the devotion to such objects expresses. Joanna, Mrs. Todd, and her widowed mother all have suffered losses and disappointments within the world of heterosexual relations, though again, the object-loves they pursue may register something other than the loss of those specific husbands and lovers. In the strong terms of Love's account, the displacement of passion onto the nonhuman object-world, whatever its pleasures or its consolations, would have to read as an emblem less of any specifiable loss than of the *pain*, inescapable and debilitating, that comes to women living a life outside of the protections and legitimacies of normative intimate life. That hunger for consolation, which drives Joanna to her hens and Almiry Todd to her herbs, responds on this account to a sorrow, a daily immersion in what Love calls "the context of social exclusion and denigration" that is the lot of the uncompanioned women.[24] What I have called the looseness of the sexual ordering of Jewett's imagined world, the looseness that sponsors the gathering of passion into unexpected forms and assemblages, reads in Love's framework as a world less open than systematically excluding, and anguishing to those left on the exterior of its embrace. For the excluded, Love writes, quoting Mary Daly's 1978 *Gyn/Ecology: The Metaethics of Radical Feminism*, the journey "is *rough*."[25]

It may be precisely that. In emphasizing what I take to be a more Deleuzian diffusion of affect in Jewett's Dunnet Landing, I do not mean to gainsay the sorrow. Even here, though, the matter is not clear-cut. For the pain of loneliness and disappointment to which Love draws our attention proves also to be the very ground of a whole series of attachments that, once more, do not come particularly clear in the terms of either anguished lesbian exclusion or consoling female homosociality. The narrator's own attachments run, we might say, a queerer course. In many ways, the narrator herself is the ideal, note-for-note match for Mrs. Almiry Todd. The one more worldly and the other more domestically proficient, Mrs. Todd and the narrator come together especially seamlessly in the way both exemplify the kinds of productivity, affective and material both, of which women are capable when freed from the toils of reproduction. Childless Mrs. Todd makes a cottage industry of her medicinal herb garden, while the narrator, a writer by profession, accomplishes her labors inside a schoolhouse emptied for the summer of its children—as elegant and concise a figure as one could wish for of the possibilities for creativity to which women might have access in the absence of offspring. And yet the narrator's quick-kindling intimacy with Mrs. Todd, whatever its primacy in the book and however richly it figures the possibilities of Dunnet Landing's special sociability, is far from her only avowed attachment.

Fast upon her enchantment by Mrs. Todd, the narrator makes the acquaintance of the strange Captain Littlepage, who visits her in her schoolhouse and embarks, in a way that at first unsettles her, on a story of a shipwreck and of a ghostly population of "fog-shaped men" (*Firs*, 22) encountered at the northern edge of the known world. "They all believed 'twas a kind of waiting-place between this world 'an the next," he says portentously (*Firs*, 22). At several moments in their interview we are invited to watch as the narrator's disquiet around Littlepage, which she makes clear might easily deepen into real fear, softens, diffusing itself into something more like sympathy and even tenderness. In each instance, what makes for that softening of regard is an upwelling sense of the captain's loneliness, and of the misunderstanding to which she imagines he must habitually be subject as a man ill-at-home in the comforts of the world in which he finds himself. At the outset of their encounter, the narrator recalls what she's been told of Littlepage and his "spells," and endeavors to square it with the man before her:

> There was something quite charming in his appearance: it was a face thin and delicate with refinement, but worn into appealing lines, as if he had suffered from loneliness and misapprehension. He looked, with his careful precision of dress, as if he were the object of cherishing care on the part of elderly unmarried sisters, but I knew Mari' Harris to be a very common-place, inelegant person, who would have no such standards; it was plain that the captain was his own attentive valet. (*Firs*, 14–15)

What charms in his appearance, and renders it for this narrator "appealing," is suffering: the "loneliness and misapprehension" his appearance broadcasts. In his fastidious aspect, she reads, too, the evidence that he plays for himself the care-giving role of (in a rich phrase) "elderly unmarried sisters"—a striking figure, balanced delicately between suggestions of loneliness, scrupulousness, and a lived-out mixing of gender roles on the margins of the marriage market. As the captain waxes more alarmingly grandiose, the narrator recalls exactly these sufferings of his to soothe herself: "Now we were approaching dangerous ground," she says, "*but a sudden sense of his sufferings at the hands of the ignorant came to my help*, and I asked to hear more with all the deference I really felt" (*Firs*, 16, emphasis added). Even in the fleeting glimpse she catches of Littlepage on the way to the jubilant Bowden reunion, the narrator finds herself drawn inexorably toward his lonely misplacement in the world: "There was a patient look on the old man's face, as if the world were a great mistake and he had nobody with whom to speak his own language or find companionship" (*Firs*, 70).

The matter is not only that Captain Littlepage emerges here as another version of the uncompanioned life, another of what the narrative will call, with tender deference to their eccentricity, "strayaway folks" (*Firs*, 81). More telling, I think, is the quiet tenacity of the narrator's own identification with him, an identification in which quite as much is implied about the narrator herself as is revealed about the captain. In his intriguing account of how the book's exhibit-like tableaux push toward the erasure of "secular and spiritual futurity," Brown suggests that the narrator herself "seems to possess no past," but I think this misses the mark.[26] For one of the things made legible by her striking tenderness toward the captain is, precisely, a past, one that seems only to confirm Love's claims about the primacy of hurt in the book. Beneath the narrator's lover-like ardor for the sociality of Dunnet Landing there is, evidently, suffering: a private experience of loneliness and misapprehension that shows itself less in any of her declarations or guarded self-descriptions than in the movements of her identifications. From her tenderness toward the misunderstood captain, that is, we can trace the outlines of her own unnarrated estrangement. At the same time, what that narratively occluded but implied exposure to misapprehension creates is not more loneliness but its reverse: it is affect, sympathy, *kinship*. The narrator's unnarrated but implied past sponsors in this instance a sort of queer kinship *across* gender, one that binds her to Littlepage on the ground of his eccentricity, its incommunicability, and his suffering.

The narrator's attachments to strayaway men—her queer affinities—themselves extend beyond the person of the captain. Consider her interactions with Mrs. Todd's unmarried brother William, whom she meets on their day trip to Green Island, where he resides with his widowed mother. Everything about the narrator's encounter with William is ghosted by the possibility of courtship, made vivid not merely by the presence of two conspicuously unmarried new acquaintances but by the fact that the house itself, as Mrs. Todd unexpectedly announces, was the scene of her own wedding. And yet so much of the content of the chapters on Green Island is made up of the diffusion of exactly that matrimonial possibility, and its reemergence in some different, considerably more uncoded, narrative register. William, who, as his mother says, "ain't disposed to be very social with the ladies" (*Firs*, 34), at last joins the women, and the narrator observes:

> He was about sixty, and not young-looking for his years, yet so undying is the spirit of youth, and bashfulness has such a power of survival, that I felt all the time as if one must try to make the occasion easy for some one who was young and new to the affairs of social life. He asked politely if I would like to go up to the great ledge while dinner was getting ready; so, not without a deep sense of pleasure, and a delighted look of surprise from the two hostesses, we started, William and I, as if both of us felt much younger than we looked. Such was the innocence and simplicity of the moment that when I heard Mrs. Todd laughing behind us in the kitchen I laughed too, but William did not even blush. I think he was a little deaf, and he stepped along before me most businesslike and intent upon his errand. (*Firs*, 36)

The laughter here marks both the romantic resonance of William's gesture and, it would seem, the utter incongruity of any such implication with respect to these two people, as well as the *sweetness* of that incongruity. And while it is not only laughter that diffuses the ambient narrative drive toward heterosexual coupling—tears do as well: the chapters contain Mrs. Todd's most painful self-recriminations about her own marriage to a good man she knew she did not love—that diffusion clears room for an affection that, like so many of Jewett's delicately rendered intimacies, is scarcely nameable in any easily available narrative terms (except perhaps under the deliberately capacious rubric of "friends"). That friendship figures as another of the narrator's queer affinities, in this instance for a man shaped, like Captain Littlepage, by a harrowing isolation, as well as a lived gender fluidity to which the narrative once more draws our attention. "William has been son an' daughter both," Mrs. Blackett says to her daughter, "since you was married off the island" (*Firs*, 33).

The suffering to which Love's reading of Jewett's writing returns us is, in these ways, hard to disentangle from the very visions of improvised, habitable sociality her essay means to complicate and critique. The pains of the one fuel the very attachments that sustain the other. But neither, as we have begun to see, is that scene of attachments the preserve of an exclusively female homosociality. Jewett's is without question a world in which pain, misapprehension, and loneliness prevail; the history to which its inhabitants are subject, particularly inasmuch as its legibilities are yoked to the marriage plot, *hurts*. Think only of Captain Littlepage, patiently awaiting the dawning of a world that might relieve him of the lonely misrecognitions he suffers in the world he inhabits, the world that feels to him as though it "were a great mistake" (*Firs*, 70). And yet hurt, exclusion, and misapprehension are not, for Jewett, the end of the story. There is for her a world that travels beneath the codes and structures of matrimonial life, one that is actually held in place by the modes of suffering—of loneliness and misapprehension—by which its inhabitants recognize, know, and, as Jewett suggests, come to sustain one another. To suffer in Jewett's world is not only to live in unredeemed isolation. It is also, paradoxically, to be opened to different affinities and allegiances, different modes of love. As Jewett stages them, these modes of love include an especially vibrant ardor between women, but also a style of kinship that travels across gender to embrace men as well.

The passionate world beneath the marriage plot, its intricacy and its expansiveness, is Jewett's great subject. As the encounter between the narrator and William on the island has shown us, the exploration of that world presents her with a formal, narrative problem as much as any other kind. Her distinctive narrative style—one that moves by implication more than explicitness, tracks stillness rather than concussive drama, invests in small gestures its greatest quantities of emotional force, and veers so self-consciously wide of the narrative tensions and trajectories of dyadic coupling—is part of an effort to capture the richness of a life, and a sociability, that fails to cohere around traditional templates of narrative development, but does not want for intensity, passion, grandeur, and drama because of that. What she finds there is not a world untethered to matrimony, to heterosexual coupling, or to their pains—or for that matter to the stratifications of class that marriage both enforces and solidifies, as the once-jilted Mrs. Todd well knows[27]—but a sociability not wholly in their grip. She narrates, in turn, the proliferation of love to which even that partial unloosening of the strictures of the marriage plot seems to give rise, making a story of the extension of affect into unpredicted precincts and often unnameable combinations (between women and women, men and women, the human and the nonhuman worlds). To be "a lover of Dunnet Landing," that provincial New England outpost, is in *Firs* to live in the errancies and extravagances of attachment that the unjoining of affect from its overcoding by the marriage plot makes possible, and to know the multitude of ways a small world might be knit into coherence, *habitable coherence*, in other than strictly hetero-familial terms. If "spinster" remains the nearest name for the idiosyncratic affective patterns of that life, the fault is hardly Jewett's.

Strayaways: Sociability and Queer Antisociality

The Country of the Pointed Firs was initially published in installments in the *Atlantic Monthly* in 1896, and was released that year as a book, with two concluding stories added. The dates alone make it hard not to read Dunnet Landing in relation to those forms of erotic sociability over whose strain and possible disappearance, in the wake of the Wilde trials, we have already seen several writers, several *men*, worry. To quote once more W. D. Stead's letter to Edward Carpenter: "A few more cases like Oscar Wilde's and we should find the freedom of comradeship now possible to men seriously impaired to the permanent detriment of the race."[28] That *Firs* continually points to the fragility, the *historical* fragility, of the sociability of Dunnet Landing, and that its characters fret explicitly about the flattening, normalizing force of the modernity gradually overtaking them, reminds us that it was not only the patriarchal world of male intimacy that the newly crystallizing sexual order threatened to disrupt. At stake in the homogenizing drive of modernity, for Jewett, is the fate of a wider queer sociability.

I want to turn in a moment to Jewett's vision of the historical vulnerability of that sociability. But there is more to be said about Dunnet Landing. For the scene that the narrator finds so attaching, stitched together as it is with varied and eccentric affective ties, is not, as Jewett understands it, a world habitable to all. This is not because she has an especially clear-eyed, especially critical, view of the racial exclusivity of that world, or of the privileged class position from which she narrates it. The 1990s saw a vigorous, often caustic dressing-down of Jewett for just these failures of perspective and for the complicities they were understood to imply.[29] Her hesitations about the sociality of Dunnet Landing are, indeed, not these. But those hesitations are nevertheless not without interest or intricacy. We have noted already the queer kinship that anchors the narrator's tenderness toward strayaways like Captain Littlepage and William (and, we might add, the eccentric Sant Bowden, whom she encounters at the reunion), and have marked, too, the occluded aspects of the narrator's own lived experience to which these affinities give subtle testament. But however capacious the homebuilt kinship system Jewett describes, at the expansive extrafamilial Bowden "family" reunion and elsewhere, her narrative attention returns again and again to those unhoused even by that looser sociability, who find there little in the way of shelter or sustenance. Alongside its account of the queer assemblages of affect that shape themselves beneath the impositions of matrimonial life, that is, is a story gripped by the fates of the unconsoled. For some critics, that intensity of attention to recluses and isolates has read as a kind of nightmare countervision of spinsterhood, Jewett's depiction of the terror that undergirds the freedom of being uncompanioned.[30] Jewett's recluses may not be that, precisely. They are more beloved, I think, than such an account quite allows. But they do provide another way into the questions of being in history, and in sexual history particularly, that preoccupy the book.

Poor Joanna, living out her days on the grimly named Shell-heap Island, alone but for the consoling company of her hens, embodies as fully as any figure in *Firs* the desolate sorrow, and the unredeemed pain, that Love suggests ought to counterbalance our too idealizing readings of the comforting homosocial world of Jewett's coastal Maine. There is without question something in the insistence, as well as the blunt finality, of Joanna's self-seclusion that troubles the promise of a curative sociality in which the whole of the book is so invested. That promise—of a sociability that somehow makes a woman's wounding in the world of heterosexual entanglement other than disfiguring and unendurable—is not simply Jewett's, or the narrator's. Both the urgency of such a promise, and the force of Joanna's disruption, come perhaps clearest in Mrs. Todd's recollection of her encounter with Joanna, at the end of a trip she and a young minister had made to persuade her to return to the fold of communal life.

> "I didn't move at first, but I'd held out just as long as I could," said Mrs. Todd, whose voice trembled a little. "When Joanna returned from the door, an' I could see that man's stupid back departin' among the wild rose bushes, I just ran to her an' caught her in my arms. I wasn't so big as I be now, and she was older than me, but I hugged her tight, just as if she was a child. 'Oh, Joanna dear,' I says, 'won't you come ashore an' live 'long o' me at the Landin', or go over to Green Island to mother's when winter comes? Nobody shall trouble you an' mother finds it hard bein' alone. I can't bear to leave you here'—and I burst right out crying. I'd had my own trials, young as I was, an' she knew it. Oh, I did entreat her; yes, I entreated Joanna." (*Firs*, 60)

Joanna's grand admission subsequent to this—that in doubting the providence of God she has committed "the unpardonable sin," that hereafter she lives without hope, committedly alone—seems to take up most of the narrative space. But the greater drama here, I think, lives in Mrs. Todd's response. It is Mrs. Todd's vehemence, her impassioned entreaty, that ties Joanna's fate back into the fabric of the larger world the book means to portray. "I'd had my own trials," Mrs. Todd says of her jilting by a wellborn lover, "an' she knew it." In one respect, Joanna's choice to remove herself from all other people is anguishing to Mrs. Todd because it reminds her of what she will later more fully recognize as the unscrupulousness, even the cruelty, of her own response to heartbreak. Mrs. Todd, who like Joanna loved a man who would not love her back, has by the time of this interview married Joanna's cousin, Nathan Todd, for whom she did not feel the passion of her first love. ("There's more women likes to be loved than there is of those that loves," she says with lacerating self-recrimination [*Firs*, 40].) Joanna's refusal of this comfort—the solace of a consolation-prize husband, a reentry into the world of normative intimacy—lands on Mrs. Todd as a complex kind of rebuke.

It is complex, and not simply shaming, because Mrs. Todd's desire here is not just for Joanna's company, but for her companionship *within* her new marriage. "Come ashore an' live 'long o' me at the Landin'," she says. She longs to create, within the scene of her marriage, precisely the curative world of female intimacy she will as a grown woman both embody and, as it were, bottle and dispense to other love-afflicted women in the form of herbs grown in the queer little garden that, as the narrator early on observes, opened her house out to the passing world and made it a place notable for "*its complete lack of seclusion*" (*Firs*, 6, emphasis added). Joanna's inconsolable grief sets a limit on the reparative power of that world. In her sudden, striking desperation on the island with Joanna we see just how deeply Mrs. Todd, even this early on, needs to believe in it.

Joanna disquiets the narrative emphasis on the remediating work of Dunnet Landing's special sociability by the comprehensiveness of her refusal to be solaced by it. That world continues to regard her, even in her reclusion, with what Mrs. Todd and Mrs. Fosdick understand to have been respect and care. "I expect that if it had been in these days, such a person would be plagued to death with idle folks," Mrs. Todd observes. "As it was, nobody trespassed on her; all the folks about the bay respected her an' her feelings" (*Firs*, 61). But whatever the real feeling with which Joanna is thought of, her relation to Dunnet Landing is neither reparative nor sustaining. She is in this respect strange kin not only to companionless Captain Littlepage but to the brokenhearted widower Elijah Tilley as well. (Despite the town's many efforts at condolence, Elijah concludes, "I can't git over the losin' of her no way nor no how. Yes, ma'am, that's just how it seems to me" [*Firs*, 94].) Jewett's steady reference to these figures seems to me to underscore her sense that even the looser sociability of a place like Dunnet Landing, which so sustains the narrator who arrives there burdened with her own unspecified but implied experiences with "loneliness and misapprehension," is not *remainderless* in its embrace. This is why Brown would write that "the force of Joanna's story . . . lies in its attention to the human suffering and endurance that is neither regional nor national, that is neither rural nor cosmopolitan, that is irreducible to being Anglo-American or Native American, and for which there is no concrete evidence."[31] Particularly for the brokenhearted, there is, it seems, no guarantee of amelioration in the social world. Some losses are intractable.

But the narrative's sympathy for Joanna, which rises toward a kind of reverence, suggests something more than Jewett's respect for the depth of this pain, or its illegibility. The tenderness of her treatment of Joanna, echoing that of the people of Dunnet Landing, clears room, too, for the more deeply complicating notion that some people are more themselves, find for themselves a greater breadth of being, outside of *any* sodality, no matter how capacious or consoling. Indeed, this is another of the narrative's understandings of what it is to be queer, a crucial counterstrain to its imagining of what it is to be among the special "strange" and "strayaway" folks of the world. In the terms of this counternarrative, it is to know your own affective history, your own "endless regret or secret happiness" as the narrator has it (*Firs*, 65), to lie beyond the possibility of recuperation by, or legibility within, any sociability whatsoever. It is to be not temperamentally but elementally *antisocial*, in the way critics like Leo Bersani and Lee Edelman have made especially vivid for us.[32] Jewett's word for this state of being is a fine one: "islanded" (*Firs*, 65).

To say as much—to say that some people are most wholly themselves outside the embrace of any sociability, or with Brown that Jewett's great strength lies in her "intimation of all the peculiarities, islanded beyond the reach of anthropology and history"[33]—is to suggest that the recurring vision of uncompanioned, islanded life is for Jewett not solely the stuff of nightmares. Despite how deeply it troubles Mrs. Todd, even Joanna's solitude comes to us framed by references to how altogether *cherishable* her strangeness is. Coming in sight of Shell-heap Island after hearing the tale of poor Joanna, the narrator observes, "There is something in the fact of a hermitage that cannot fail to touch the imagination; the recluses are a sad kindred, but they are never commonplace" (*Firs*, 63). Joanna figures here as among what Christopher Nealon, riffing on Gertrude Stein, calls "the luckily strange people in America."[34] She is strange and seemingly unlucky in her sorrows, but Jewett's narrator, possessed perhaps by something of Mrs. Todd's own desire not to allow Joanna's refusal of curative sociability to go uncontested, returns to Joanna both the full-hearted ardor she failed to secure in her lonely life, and the aspect of an unexampled kind of valor:

> Later generations will know less and less of Joanna herself, but there are paths trodden to the shrines of solitude the world over,—the world cannot forget them, try as it may; the feet of the young find them out because of curiosity and dim foreboding; while the old bring hearts full of remembrance. This plain anchorite had been one of those whom sorrow made too lonely to brave the sight of men, too timid to front the simple world she knew, yet valiant enough to live alone with her poor insistent human nature and the calms and passions of the sea and sky. (*Firs*, 64–65)

If Joanna is Jewett's "tragic spinster," her vision of "spinsterhood turned grotesque," she allows us to glimpse as well just what it is that queer heroism might look like in Jewett's fictional cosmology: it is made up of endurance, ardent-heartedness, and valor in face of comprehensive misapprehension.[35]

Whatever the heroism of Joanna's antisociality, though, Jewett nevertheless cannot resist the impulse to return her to something like community. The young and the old of the world, she insists, "cannot forget" Joanna: recluses are a "sad kindred" to one another, and also to succeeding generations of secret sufferers. The narrator goes on, imagining Joanna gazing back from her hermitage onto the mainland, "dim and dreamlike in the August haze": "There was the world, and here was she with eternity well begun. In the life of each of us, I said to myself, there is a place remote and islanded, and given to endless regret or secret happiness; we are each the uncompanioned hermit and recluse of an hour or a day; we understand our fellows of the cell to whatever age of history they may belong" (*Firs*, 65). In a way that refracts and perhaps redeploys Mrs. Todd's own impassioned need for Joanna not to rebuke the healing power of the social, the narrator herself works to inflect Joanna's solitude by making it the cornerstone of a kind of kinship that begins with other recluses (the "sad kindred"), reaches out to the young and old of succeeding generations, and concludes in a gesture as widely inclusive as it could possibly be: "we are each the uncompanioned hermit and recluse of an hour." One way to understand this gesture, this transformation of singleness and solitude into affinity, is as a kind of capitulation. It is, we might say, a moment that makes Jewett and Mrs. Todd unsettlingly alike in the urgency of their need to believe in the restorative powers of attachment, and of a sociality shaped with sufficient tenderness and breadth to make healing room even for those wounded beyond the hope of reparation. What threatens to be eroded in that gesture, of course, is the other strand of queerness the book sometimes embraces, the hallmark of which is a disruptive ill-at-homeness in the legibility of any sociability, any anthropology or history, any signifying system. It is, we could say, a capitulation of the power of the illegible, of the unassimilable, of the negative—a power identified so vigorously by Lee Edelman with the death drive—to the lesser comforts of sociality.[36]

Such a reading has its clarities, though this is not to say we therefore ought to arraign Jewett for a failure of queer conviction or nerve. That arraignment may depend on a series of tenuous equivalencies. I am not sure, for instance, that the longing for Joanna to achieve a posthumous legibility, an emplacement in history, is *identical* to the sacrificing of the unassimilability of the death-drive to the heteronormative reductions of the symbolic order. The longing for history may be, in small but important ways, a different thing, and not as easily reduced to an insufficiency of queer radicality or resolve. The sodality built around Joanna has, after all, a curiously vaporous present-tense existence, at least for her. The imagined gaze toward a dim and dreamlike mainland is the slender filament along which it is strung; its terms are secret and wordless, a feeling without name, and only approximation (loneliness, sorrow, disappointment, and the "dim foreboding" of these) is its currency. If this is Jewett's compensatory vision of a "community" that might gather around Joanna, it seems less necessarily assimilating and coercive, less normative and normalizing, than *inoperative*, in Jean-Luc Nancy's sense: built around the same elemental paradox, made up of precisely the incommunicable singularity that marks and is shared by every mortal person.[37] It may be, in other words, that not all longings for sociality are only, or finally, concessions to an at-least-implicitly homophobic symbolic order, intent on eradicating the disruptive unassimilability that is queerness. They are so only according to a leveling, abstracted sense of the undifferentiatedness of any and all forms collectable under the rubric of the Symbolic. Those forms are many and, as Jewett in her fine-grained attentiveness to the "elaborate conventionalities" of village life seems very much to insist, these are distinctions worth making. And it may be, too, that there are forms of queerness that themselves fall afield of the model of a disruptive and elemental unassimability, but are for that neither without value nor somehow *not queer*.

Still, whether or not Jewett shares too readily with Mrs. Todd an overeagerness to believe in the consoling power of worlds made by queer affinity—whether or not she sacrifices queer antisociality on the altar of queer sociability—her more pressing concern in *Firs* is plainly with the *fragility* of those worlds. She understands that fragility to be, again, a matter of temporal vulnerability. History is coming for them. In this respect, the gestures toward Joanna may be compensatory far less in their defense of a sociality Jewett badly wishes to ratify than in their poignant insistence on the enduring power, and enduring legibility, of Joanna's pain, her valor, her uncommonness. The vision of succeeding generations making pilgrimages to Shell-heap Island sits strangely and a bit uneasily—perhaps compensatorily—alongside the narrative's recurrent anxiety about the effects of something like modernity as it sweeps its way into the distant corners of coastal Maine. For Jewett, what that modernity seems most to threaten with disruption is precisely the quality of variable, errant, loose sociability that makes Dunnet Landing so attaching. Captain Littlepage strikes the note first. "I view it," he says, "that a community narrows down and grows dreadful ignorant when it is shut up to its own affairs, and gets no knowledge of the outside world except from a cheap, unprincipled newspaper" (*Firs*, 17).

The result of this decline of seafaring is clear: "There's no large-minded way of thinking now," he says (*Firs*, 18). But the effects of that want of large-mindedness come clearest in Mrs. Todd's conversation with Mrs. Fosdick:

> "I used to return feelin' very slack an' behind the times, 'tis true," explained Mrs. Fosdick, "but 'twas excitin', an' we always done extra well, and felt rich when we did get ashore. I liked the variety. There, how times have changed; how few seafarin' families there are left! What a lot o' queer folks there used to be about here, anyway, when we was young, Almiry. Everybody's just like everybody else, now; nobody to laugh about, and nobody to cry about."
>
> It seemed to me that there were peculiarities of character in the region of Dunnet Landing yet, but I did not like to interrupt.
>
> "Yes," said Mrs. Todd after a moment of meditation, "there was certain a good many curiosities of human natur' in this neighborhood years ago. There was more energy then, and in some the energy took a singular turn. In these days the young folks is all copy-cats, 'fraid to death they won't be all just alike; as for the old folks, they pray for the advantage o' bein' a little different." (*Firs*, 51–52)

Queer folks and greater curiosity, strayaways and the sad kindred of the recluses: when Jewett thinks of progress, she thinks, in a wholly familiar way, of decline and loss. Her nostalgia, that is, may indeed bear the traces of an imperial melancholy, but it does not seem to me reducible to it. The register in which loss appears to her is, after all, striking. She mourns the degeneration of the world into the uniformity and homogeneity of "copy-cats." It is the loss of a social world capacious enough to include errancy, variety, the curious, and the queer.

Curious, though, that in Captain Littlepage's account one of the offered harbingers of that homogenized world is, precisely as it had been a decade before for James in *The Bostonians*, the "cheap, unprincipled newspaper"

(*Firs*, 17). It would have been there, of course, that the scandalous news of Oscar Wilde, his trial, his crimes, and his conviction would have made itself known to Jewett, as well as the to the imaginary inhabitants of Dunnet Landing, just the year before. The connection, through the newspaper, is as suggestive as it tenuous. It might at the very least recall to us James's wistful and faintly heartsick letter of 1918 to Annie Fields, who had of course lived with Jewett for better than two decades in an intimacy broken only by Jewett's death in 1909. Writing from the other side of the ascent of the modern sexual taxonomies in which something like "homosexuality" might more readily appear as a claimable identity (as well as an affliction, and a crime), James does not celebrate that advent as much as mourn the vanishing of a world whose codes of intimate meaning were configured otherwise.

One way to read *Firs*, and I would suggest to read Jewett's work more generally, is as an intricate, exacting account of the qualities and contours of precisely that "otherwise," those intimate codes whose erosion so pains James and whose disappearance Jewett's characters seem anxiously to foretell. For Jewett such an "otherwise" comes most vividly to life as the scene of sociability around which her narrative, from the first moment, builds its love-plots. As we have seen, Dunnet Landing is distinguished by the gathering of ardor into a range of extramatrimonial assemblages, lived out as impassioned investments in the nonhuman object-world, as queer affinities between uncompanioned women and strayaway men, and, not least, as the unloosening of possibilities for intimacy between women. If these passions go largely unnoticed and unnominated within the strictures of the marriage plot Jewett's book persistently dissembles, neither do they come particularly clear, or emerge without distortion, in the hard taxonomies of hetero and homo that would grow only more prominent after Wilde. According to Dunnet Landing's inhabitants, the world that is coming over the historical horizon is homogenized, narrower, more normal, less varied, less curious, less queer. Twenty years later, offering his own more rueful backward view, James can only agree.

Mateless, Mysterious

For the inhabitants of *The Country of the Pointed Firs*, the nineteenth-century coast of Maine had not yet become the early twentieth-century England from which James writes his letter. The future that is coming for them has not yet arrived. So the narrator takes her leave of that world not with dim foreboding but, in a chapter called "The Backward View," a final glimpse of Mrs. Todd:

> Presently, as I looked at the pastures beyond, I caught a last glimpse of Mrs. Todd herself, walking slowly in the footpath that led along, following the shore toward the Port. At such a distance one can feel the large, positive qualities that control a character. Close at hand, Mrs. Todd seemed able and warm-hearted and quite absorbed in her bustling industries, but her distant figure looked mateless and appealing, with something about it that was strangely self-possessed and mysterious. (*Firs*, 101)

Mateless and appealing, but also mysterious: What, we might wonder, is the mystery that envelops so frank and forthright a figure as Mrs. Todd? Is it the mystery of what allows her to be heartbroken and uncompanioned, like poor Joanna, but also "strangely self-possessed," as well as "warm-hearted," still open to a world where she both found and fostered hurt? Or is it, perhaps, the mystery of Mrs. Todd's relation to those facts—of the inarticulable singularity of her being toward and within her own affective history, and the world in which it transpired? Jewett seems to gesture here in all toward the encompassing mystery of how such wounding and such sustenance, such hurt and such strange wholeness, might share space in one bustling, industrious woman's body.

For Jewett, then, to be hurt is not to be afflicted with an unalterable destiny, and to be whole is not to be unwounded. She gestures instead toward what Jeff Nunokawa calls those "other, less totalizing ideas of what binds self to society," with an especially sharp eye for "the interstices of social bonds from which no disengagement is possible," where we find "all kinds of looser, smaller social situations from which it *is* possible."[38] Part of the problem with the too-thorough captivation of narrative by the preordained conflicts and structures of the marriage plot, she suggests, emerges in the drive to *resolve* the question of anyone's relation to her world—anyone's relation to the history that, in some importantly unpredetermined sense, makes her—away from just these fissured and mixed, these mysterious, states of being. Queer historiography, I think, stands to gain from the example of Jewett's method, which expresses itself here as the desire to track the movements of a mystery. Inasmuch as queer scholarship still struggles toward an approach to the world that makes justice and pleasure compatible, Jewett's work might serve as something more than a rich account of a ripe moment in the history of sexuality—a moment that finds the scene of a queer sociality moving toward normalization under the aegis of an emergent modern sexuality. Revealing as that story is, Jewett might help us to envision as well a critical practice that itself moves away from a sense of history as, most elementally, a scene of such determining hurt that any investment in justice must be expressed as a kind of tallying of history's wounds and wounded. And yet that corrective emphasis in Jewett is itself not coincident with an understanding of pleasure—of the specificities of queer delight—as wholly predicated on an ecstatic inadmissibility to the structures of any legible world, an unassimilable excess or *différance* that marks the limit, and structuring internal incoherence, of the social as such. These are not Jewett's stories: neither captivation nor *jouissance*. The fate of desire and desiring errancy in the lived world lies, for her, elsewhere. Her obliquities make her, it is true, hard to assimilate to either of the major queer interpretive paradigms (historical or psychoanalytic, political or radical). But that fact does not render her, by definition, insufficiently political, insufficiently radical, or insufficiently queer. What we are left with instead is a stranger world, where passion often looks more like stillness than drama, and where woundedness and contentment, irreconcilability and abundance, share space, all mysteriously, in the lived world.

4

What Does the Polygamist Want?

Frederick Douglass, Joseph Smith, and Marriage at the Edges of the Human

What does *the polygamist want?* In a world already ordered by patriarchy, coverture, and the traffic in women, in a world in which the need for a clear dispensation of property along succeeding lines of men makes compulsory monogamy the rule for middle-class women in a way that it conspicuously is not for men, in a world where the de facto concubinage of chattel slavery renders only the more fanciful the very idea of a confining white male monogamy—in *this* world, where the yoke of marital exclusiveness falls upon white men quite loosely, what can it mean to insist, with an increasingly self-endangering vehemence, on the necessity, the divinity, and the world-renovating force of plural marriage?

Such at least is one way of framing the mystery that is the career of Joseph Smith, founder of the Mormon faith, author of its chief doctrines and documents, homegrown prophet, child of nineteenth-century New England, polygamist, heretical theologian, and, finally, martyr. Among these other nominations Smith is also, I want to suggest, one of the most underconsidered figures in the vast and messy archive of nineteenth-century American writers. As Harold Bloom wrote in 1992, with characteristic immoderation: "In proportion to his importance and his complexity, he remains the least-studied personage, of an undiminished vitality, in our entire national saga."[1] Whatever Bloom's hyperbole, it is the case that in Smith we find a man whose imaginings of (for instance) embodiment and divinity, sex and its uneasy confinement in prescribed intimate forms, the interchange between gods and men, or between otherworldly and resolutely earthly pleasures, make him strange kin to the likes of Thoreau and Whitman—differently tuned midcentury visionaries of unrealized sexual possibility—as much as to contemporaneous religious figures like John

Humphrey Noyes (of the Oneida Perfectionists, who preached "complex marriage"), Alexander Campbell, and (slightly later) Mary Baker Eddy. In the chapter that follows, I want to unfold some of the implications of Smith's vision for the history of sexuality in nineteenth-century America. His provocations, in this context, cut in several directions. In the first instance, he pointedly reminds us how, in Molly McGarry's words, "histories of secularism structurally underwrite histories of sexuality *and function to elucidate some forms of sexual subjectivity while occluding others*" (emphasis added). Considering the kinds of imagining of sex that have become more, rather than less, difficult to see in the wake of the advent of a modern, putatively secular sexuality, McGarry investigates "how some varieties of religious experience may have been a marker for an incipient, not yet materialized, sexuality." In this framing—so crucial to my own focus on futures that would not come to be—the relentlessly sacralizing Smith articulates one of the forms of possibility for sexual being that has been "occluded" by the de facto secular vision of modern sexuality, and clarifies too some of the ways the American context might itself make a substantial difference in the trajectories of sexual history we learn in and through Foucault, in which, as McGarry observes, the "Catholic confessional sits in a genealogical relationship to the psychoanalyst's couch."[2] The line from the confessional to the sciences of modern sexuality runs rather more crookedly in America—through the revival tent, through varieties of spiritualism, through wider derangements of embodied devotional experience—in ways that Smith's career, embroiled as it is in sexual meaning and sexual scandal, renders especially vivid.

At the center of that scandal, of course, is polygamy. With respect to the place and meaning of polygamy in Smith's career, there are at least two strong explanatory frameworks, related but distinct. The first reminds us that Smith's Mormonism, whatever the range and force of its peculiarities, is at its root a religion of restoration, a repudiation of the fallen state of contemporary Christian practice and belief expressed in the familiar, fundamentalist terms of a *return*, a radical reinhabiting of origins made inaccessible in the present tense by the accretion of centuries of misapprehension and flawed doctrine. No one turns this point more emphatically or more insistently than Bloom. Giving terse summary to his thesis about Smith's "uncanny recovery of elements in ancient Jewish theurgy that had ceased to be available either to normative Judaism or to Christianity," he writes: "The religion-making genius of Joseph Smith, profoundly American, uniquely restored the Bible's sense of the theomorphic, a restoration that inevitably led the prophet into his most audacious restoration, patriarchal plural marriage."[3] Polygamy on this account comes into meaning as the final, indispensable, crowning element in Smith's project of theological restoration—a project that as we shall see involves not merely a return to originary texts or intentions but, rather more audaciously, a restoration of the sense of the protodivine, of the incipience of godhead, in man himself.

Man himself—but not *humankind*. A second, equally strong reading of polygamy takes up this project of restoration in a different register: as a response to a world that, however incontestably and comprehensively governed by patriarchy, yet appeared to the imaginations of many to be somehow, distressingly, alarmingly, not patriarchal *enough*—a world, that is, quite insufficiently patriarchal, and growing less and less sufficiently so all the time. In a passage taking up what Mary Ryan describes as "the economic shift from the self-sustaining agrarian home to a cash economy" that unfolded across the early nineteenth century, and enabled the Second Great Awakening, with its multiplying evangelical and missionary "associations," Elizabeth Freeman writes: "These early societies threatened to replace parental and marital bonds with affinities between same-sex peers and undermine the patriarchal family and church as means of social control."[4] Yet if, as Freeman suggests, "the most radical sects such as the Perfectionists and Mormons translated these . . . shifts into a vision of expansive lateral association"—codified in plural marriage—the Mormons could also be understood to ratify that wider social horizon for men *on the condition of its radical curtailment for women*. This point was certainly not lost on the many, many antipolygamist, anti-Mormon novelists of the nineteenth-century who, as Nancy Bentley demonstrates, persistently figure the fate of the Mormon wife in the terms of servitude, abject confinement, and *enslavement*: Mormon polygamy, in all, as the white woman's enslavement.[5]

Both of these readings—emphasizing a fundamentalist return to Old Testament origins and a panicky, hyperpatriarchal reaction to loosenings in the social fabric of comprehensive male control—seem to me rich, suggestive, and true; I want here less to contest than to add to them. For Smith's recasting of what Bloom calls "the Hebrew Bible's vision of theomorphic men and women" suggests a trajectory toward polygamy—away from dyadic intimacy—with perhaps different resonances and analogues. Taking up the writings of Smith's final years, chiefly as they are collected in *Doctrine and Covenants* and in fragments of writing considered by critics and biographers as diversely disposed to Smith as Fawn Brodie, Richard Lyman Bushman, D. Michael Quinn, Todd Compton, and Terryl Givens, I want to pursue a related but distinct line of inquiry into the prophetic career of Joseph Smith.[6] My widest claim is that we stand to gain a great deal by taking him up as a theologian and fabulist who is also, beneath these roles, an extraordinary kind of *historian of the body*, where "history" is understood to be unconfined by secularist presumption.[7] I want to suggest that polygamy, that defining fabulation of Smith's, comes to seem the proper way to, as he says, *"learn how to make yourself Gods"* (emphasis added) because it begins to express—with what remains at the time of Smith's death a good deal of unresolved complication—how you might live out the unfallenness, the already-present but as-yet-insufficiently apprehended divinity, of your body.[8] To name the capacities of this radiant body "sexuality" is to speak no less accurately, and no more, than to call Walt Whitman "gay."

Of course, one can imagine ways of living out to the edges of such a body's capacities that do not entail either a dismantling of monogamous marriage or an insistence on patriarchal polygamy. To turn consecrated dyadic monogamy into the enemy of the body's unconstraint is to speak from a particular perspective—a fact brought home clearly enough by Frederick Douglass's conception of all that official marriage might do for American prophets of a different type and inclination: former slaves. I begin, then, with Douglass's rather different imagining of marriage (*not* with his experience with marriage, which is a different matter), though I do so not merely for the sake of his contrast to Smith. Polygamy and slavery are of course densely entangled across the nineteenth century, and not just as paired constitutional crises, or as the "twin relics of barbarism" they would famously be named in the first national Republican convention in 1856.[9] As I hope to show in what follows, they are joined, too, in a fashion considerably more uncanny and unsettling, by the ways both so relentlessly conjoin questions of the body—the body as a marker of, we might say, both the inner and the outer edge of an imagined *humanness*—with the question of what marriage does and is.

Love and Enfranchisement

We know, by now, the story of the story Frederick Douglass tells. As around few other of the texts of the enslaved and formerly enslaved, there has been established around the 1845 *Narrative of the Life of Frederick Douglass, An American Slave* an exegetical and historical framework of considerable accreted force, nuance, and sophistication. Students of the work struggle far less than they might have twenty years ago to see in this generically heterodox, unlikely, and tremendously politico-historically vexed document the clarity of a *narrative*: a movement from South to North; captivity to freedom; legal and historical nonentity to self-possessed subject, contracted laborer, and citizen. In the wake of Henry Louis Gates's early, now-canonical unpacking of the *Narrative*, it has become a critical commonplace to read the book as a story of the seizure, and self-creation, of a species of *autonomy*, routed crucially through the acquisition of literacy Gates so forcefully emphasizes—"In literacy lay true freedom for the black slave," he would famously write—but joined as well to burgeoning capacities for contract (first as a laboring slave, then as a free man, then as a *husband*) and to a style of self-possession coded masculine not least in its depiction, as in the slave's famous fight with the brutal Mr. Covey, of a kind of regeneration through violence. "You have seen how a man was made a slave," he writes in preface to the great fight with Covey; "you shall now see how a slave was made a man."[10]

In all, the story of the *Narrative* as the tale of autonomous individuality, seized from the teeth of forces seeking only to refuse it, is by now a familiar one, enough so that the text's very focus on autonomy and individuality has come to be, if not an object of critique, at the very least the means by which it is taxonomized as a distinctively male slave narrative, different in character and content from a similarly canonical narrative like that of Harriet Jacobs, in which the struggle to retain the integrity of the individual body against the unrelenting sexual assaults of a master expands into a differently calibrated struggle to retain the integrity of a *family*.[11] And yet, as resonant and revealing as these accounts are, I am not sure we do an ample enough kind of justice to the movements of Douglass's text if we consider it finally a casebook study in the slave's attainment of autonomy. In a way that I want to trace out briefly, the narrative also describes a trajectory whose chief polarities are not enslavement and autonomy but what we might name, with terms borrowed from Hortense Spillers, *kinlessness* and *attachment*. Considering Douglass's account of his infant separation from his mother, Spillers rises to this arresting query: "Could we say, then, that the *feeling of* kinship is *not* inevitable? That it describes a relationship that appears natural, but that must be cultivated under actual material conditions?"[12] Slavery withholds those conditions, Spillers suggests, in its effort to destroy kinship. In my reading of Douglass, it is the cultivation, the *conjuring* and subsequent nurturing of precisely these affiliative possibilities that takes center stage, not the achievement of defiant individuality. Curiously, as we shall see, what stands as the crowning destination for both narrative strands, those of autonomous self-possession and achieved kinship, is marriage.

"My mother and I were separated when I was but an infant—before I knew her as my mother," Douglass writes. "It is a common custom, in the part of Maryland from which I ran away, to part children from their mothers at a very early age. . . . For what this separation is done, I do not know, unless it be to hinder the development of the child's affection toward its mother, and to blunt and destroy the natural affection of the mother for the child. This is the inevitable result" (*NLFD*, 48). As Spillers notes, precisely this "blunting" comes to define, too, Douglass's relation to his siblings, of whom he says, "The ties that ordinarily bind children to their homes were all suspended in my case. . . . I had two sisters and one brother, that lived in the same house with me; but the early separation of us from our mother had well nigh blotted the fact of our relationship from our memories" (*NLFD*, 73). This is what Spillers has in mind when she speaks of the "enforced state of breach" that is the slave's experience of family, "where 'kinship' loses meaning, *since it can be invaded at any given and arbitrary moment by the property relations.*"[13]

But these are not Douglass's only avowals, at the *Narrative*'s outset, of what Spillers calls the "patterns of dispersal" (219) into which the material conditions of enslavement were designed to precipitate the enslaved. Consider the horrific scene with which the first chapter in the narrative famously concludes, that of the stripping and lashing of Douglass's Aunt Hester, a spectacle he describes as "the blood-stained gate, the entrance to the hell of slavery" through which the narrator is made to pass. Just before that sentence, though, Douglass offers a stranger framing of the scene. "It was the first of a long series of such outrages," he writes, "of which I was doomed to be a witness and a participant" (*NLFD*, 51). What explains the retrospective sense of *participation* in the outrage *here*? His "participation" in the later outrages done directly to him—his participation as object and victim—of course makes sense. But what are we to do with the fleeting intimation of something like guilt, of a kind of retrospective complicity in the scene to be narrated, we might hear echoing in the word "participant"? Consider again the young Douglass's response to the scene of torture, and consider it in particular in the context of the rest of the first chapter's account of slavery's enforced disarticulation of familial attachment:

> Her arms were stretched up at their full length, so that she stood upon the ends of her toes. He then said to her, "Now, you d———d b———h, I'll learn you how to disobey my orders!" and after rolling up his sleeves, he commenced to lay on the heavy cowskin, and soon the warm, red blood (amid heartrending shrieks from her, and horrid oaths from him) came dripping to the floor. I was so terrified and horror-stricken at the sight, that I hid myself in a closet, and dared not venture out til long after the blood transaction was over. I expected it would be my turn next. It was all new to me. (*NLFD*, 52)

"I hid myself in a closet," Douglass writes. "*I expected it would be my turn next.*" Is the implication here, in this chillingly unadorned sentence, that the young Douglass's so vivid horror is rooted not in an other-directed sympathy but a self-protective *fear*? That the grown Douglass suffers the memory of this violence as a "participant" inasmuch as he recognizes in the scene the degree to which slavery had *already* done to him much of its "soul-killing" work (*NLFD*, 58), expressed in the moment as an incapacity to identify with the suffering of another, *as* another's, except insofar as that suffering threatens to be visited upon the self? In a chapter all about slavery's radical disordering of familial affection, for slaves and masters both—recall his remarks about the slave offspring of masters, and how they "are, in the first place, a constant offense to their mistress" (*NLFD*, 49)—the scene of Aunt Hester's torture marks the young narrator's introduction to the sexual violence of slavery, even as it realizes, in the most spectacular and indelible way, Spillers's intimation that "the *feeling of* kinship is *not* inevitable," that it is the goal of enslavement both to deny in theory *and ravage in practice* the slave's very capacity for attachment.

Without discounting readings of the *Narrative* as an account of the seizure of autonomy and individuality by the enslaved man, I would suggest nevertheless that one can also describe the whole rest of the book, from the moment of Aunt Hester's assault onward, as the story of the painstaking assembly of precisely the affective, the *affiliative*, capacities denied and blunted at the outset. We watch, in other words, as the narrated Douglass emerges from the affective atomization with which he is so conspicuously marked at the narrative's opening to an ever-englarging affiliative openness to others. It is a capacity that begins with a kind mistress, extends eventually to other slaves, even to the white boys of Baltimore, and comes then to be the anchoring point of the concluding movements of the text. We are used to reading Douglass's lyrical contemplation of the sails of ships on the Chesapeake as among the text's chief climactic moments, and of course it is. But an equally dramatic turning point comes just a few pages later, as Douglass describes his "Sabbath school":

> I held my Sabbath school at the house of a free colored man, whose name I deem it imprudent to mention. . . . I had at one time over forty scholars, and those of the right sort, ardently desiring to learn. They were of all ages, though mostly men and women. I look back to those Sundays with an amount of pleasure not to be expressed. They were great days to my soul. The work of instructing my dear fellow-slaves was the sweetest engagement with which I was ever blessed. We loved each other, and to leave them at the close of the Sabbath was a severe cross indeed. (*NLFD*, 12)

And then, in case the gravity of the phrase *We loved each other* has passed us by, Douglass remarks again, of "the society of my fellow-slaves": "We were linked and interlinked with each other. I loved them with a love stronger than any thing I have experienced since. . . . We never moved separately. We were one" (*NLFD*, 121–22).

"*We were one,*" he says, marking a kinship forged beyond the parameters of familial life—and, as he began by underscoring, without the family as an established template—but no less ardent for that. Even as Douglass's resolve to escape slavery deepens and solidifies, he continues to remark on an escalating fear of *separation*, of an unjoining of the attachments he has forged. "I was ready for anything," he writes, "rather than separation" (*NLFD*, 129–30). Finally, as Douglass's last plan for escape ripens, he gathers up these previous notes of hesitation and offers this startling account, in which the force of his impassioned attachment threatens to overmatch the force of his desire for freedom and autonomy:

> It is impossible for me to describe my feelings as the time of my contemplated start drew near. I had a number of warm-hearted friends in Baltimore,—friends that I loved almost as much as I did my life,—and the thought of being separated from them forever was painful beyond expression. It is my opinion that thousands would escape from slavery, who now remain, but for the strong cords of affection that bind them to their friends. The thought of leaving my friends was decidedly the most painful thought

with which I had to contend. The love of them was my tender point, and shook my decision more than all things else. (*NLFD*, 142)

The trajectory from the young Douglass's state of pained familial and affective dispersal—his state of enforced kinlessness—to this scene of a love as ardent and binding as it is expansive could not be underscored more forcefully.

Yet Douglass is not done with the theme. For as the narrative rises to its conclusion, as Douglass moves from the "great insecurity and loneliness" of New York City to New Bedford, we find this passage, and this gesture of extratextual inclusion:

> At this time, Anna, my intended wife, came on.... In a few days after her arrival, Mr. Ruggles called in the Rev. J. W. C. Pennington, who, in the presence of Mr. Ruggles, Mrs. Michaels, and two or three others, performed the marriage ceremony, *and gave us a certificate*, of which the following is an exact copy—
>
>> "This may certify, that I joined together in holy matrimony Frederick Johnson and Anna Murray, as man and wife, in the presence of Mr. David Ruggles and Mrs. Michaels.
>> "James W. C. Pennington.
>> "New York, Sept 15, 1838" (*NLFD*, 145, emphasis added)

The inclusion in the body of the text of this certification, this mark of recognition, can plausibly be read as a crowning moment in Douglass's movement toward contract: toward the recognized authority and clarified self-possession that would allow him to undertake and be recognized in contractual relations. Yet the inclusion of the marriage certificate marks too, I think, a different kind of culmination. As Amy Dru Stanley astutely reminds us, "At law, marriage alone represented a hybrid of contract and status."[14] What is certified here also, and what operates in the terms of the text *as* status, is *the acknowledged binding force of Douglass's capacity for attachment*. The very affective aptitude that is underlined again and again in the run-up to escape is here acknowledged in the form of *official recognition*. The arc from enforced dispersal to civically certified affiliative attachment completes itself, precisely as scholars of nineteenth-century African-American marriage suggest to us it might, in matrimony.[15]

There is of course a long backstory to the understanding of the slave's specifically affective capacities as the mark of his or her aptitude for the rigors of larger spheres of belonging and affiliation: to the nation as citizen, or for that matter to humankind itself as cocreated child of Nature and of Nature's God. If Thomas Jefferson's *Notes on the State of Virginia* says of the blacks that he is determined to banish from the republic, "Their griefs are transient," and Harriet Beecher Stowe's scenes of sentimental apotheosis mark the possible equivalence of black and white on the grounds of their mutual susceptibility to wounding and loss, then Douglass enters this contested terrain with the assertion, "It is my opinion that thousands would escape from slavery, who now remain, but for the strong cords of affection that bind them to their friends"; or perhaps with the more simple declaration, "We loved each other." To be married, to be certified in one's intimate attachments, is for Douglass not only to carve a fragile place for the legitimacy of the slave's sex—to push back against white supremacy's simultaneous imputations of ungovernable animality in the slave, as well as impotent passivity, and an unlimited *availability* to sexual assault. It is also, as Douglass's narrative scripts it, to rebuke the kinlessness slavery mandates, and to have ratified a capacity for attachment that anchors claims to far, far wider forms of enfranchisement.[16] Marriage is the portal through which Douglass, at least in this early text, looks to enter an affiliative as well as contractual world that is not one of enslavement.

You Have Got to Learn How to Make Yourselves Gods

Perhaps William Lloyd Garrison had something of this wider claim for enfranchisement in mind when, in his preface to the 1845 *Narrative*, he remarked on "the godlike nature" of slavery's victims. But for a decade and a half before Garrison wrote these words, another radical had been busy recognizing the godlike nature of mortal men, and coming to expansively different conclusions about the worldly consequences of that godlikeness and its recognition. *"You have got to learn how to make yourselves Gods,"* Joseph Smith would say to his followers in a breathtakingly heretical oration from April of 1844 (later to be known as the King Follett Discourse) (*EJS*, 235, emphasis added). It was not through monogamous marriage that Smith imagined the path to this vast enlargement of the human to run.

"Joseph Smith did not wish merely to set his saints apart," Harold Bloom writes in *The American Religion*. "He wished them to become gods, and he decided polygamy was necessary for that apotheosis."[17] But what makes for this *necessity*? By what logic does the rupturing of monogamous marriage come to read as a necessary condition for the enactment of a cosmology as idiosyncratic as Smith's, a cosmology that includes the notion that God was man who enlarged himself to become God, and that humans might themselves follow a like trajectory toward godhead? First and above all, we need to remember that for Smith, this world—the mortal world of human striving and exaltation—is not some mistranslation of a divine after-word, is not an allegory of some inaccessible heavenly elsewhere. Terryl L. Givens frames the "common theme" of Smith's elementally heretical disposition aptly: it consists at its most basic in "the disintegration of that distance that separates the sacred and the profane, that defines religious experience as unfathomable mystery, that constitutes religious feeling as the presence of the ineffable, that renders such terms as holiness, worshipfulness, and reverence as constituting the very essence of religion."[18] Or, to put this differently, *the world is not fallen*. When we recognize as much, we begin to see how something as seemingly outlandish as polygamy emerges for Smith from premises that should be, at least to readers of the midcentury canon, not particularly esoteric.

Bloom is right to note Smith's "genius for restoration," his impassioned, time-collapsing identification with the figures of the Old Testament, among whom polygamy was not exceptional.[19] (The first sentences of Smith's polygamy revelation frame the matter as, precisely, one of Biblical precedent, an explication of how God "justified my servants Abraham, Isaac, and Jacob, as also Moses, David, and Solomon, my servants, as touching the principle and doctrine of their having many wives and concubines."[20]) And yet so much of the point for Smith is that his relation to Abraham, Isaac, and Jacob is *not* merely imitative, is emphatically not derivative. Where Emerson in 1836 famously reclaimed the privilege of a direct relation to nature, Smith polemicized thus: "Some say the kingdom of God was not set up on earth until the day of Pentecost. . . . But I say in the name of the Lord that the kingdom of God was set upon the earth from the days of Adam to the present time whenever there has been a righteous man on earth unto whom God revealed his word" (*EJS*, 168). Or again, striking a note that should startle no reader of "Self-Reliance": "Have I not an equal privilege with the ancient saints?" If the ancients are models for Smith, it is less because of the authority they offer through precedent than because he understands them to have lived in the world exactly the way he does in the present tense—that is, *in a state of revelation*, in possession of a capacity for the direct, in-the-flesh experience of divinity.

We can begin to see some of the stakes of Smith's crucial, career-wide insistence on the already-present sacredness of the extant world in his many critical remarks on speech, writing, and what we might call prophetic epistemology. Mark Twain famously described *The Book of Mormon* as "chloroform in print," chiefly in reference to its interminable genealogies, executed in a kind of poor imitation King James English, and the line still has undeniable sting. But *The Book of Mormon* was only the beginning, not the end, of Smith's career as a writer. We find, too, in Smith's writing, moments of strangeness, of combinatory vernacular oddity, that are not simply risible. "The people of the Lord," Smith would write in 1833, "those who have complied with the requisitions of the new covenant, have already commenced gathering together in Zion, which is in the state of Missouri" (*EJS*, 36). Little could better express Smith's insistent running-together of the divine and the quotidian, the otherworldly and the ordinary, than the punctuation of a sentence about "the requisitions of the new covenant" with the unexalted plainspokenness, and the complex indigeneity, of the word "Missouri."[21]

But plainspokenness, like indigeneity, proves to be a matter of some theological consequence to Smith. The very word "Missouri"—a French adaptation of an Illinois word, and the name of a Siouan tribe—reminds us that at its origins Mormonism is as much an attempted *indigenization* of Christianity as it is a project of restoration, in ways that (as we will see) richly complicate how the Mormons came to avow the kinds of intimate sociality, the disorderings of the dyadic nuclear family, that Smith had prophesied near the end of his life.[22] But before he arrives there he has much to say about ordinary speech and the perils of translation. In an exegesis from 1835 on Matthew, Smith contends that Jesus spoke in parables expressly and specifically to those afflicted by "their unbelief" (*EJS*, 70). To *these*, Smith says, Jesus could only speak in parables "because they did not or would not understand; and seeing they did not perceive: for this people's heart is waxed gross; their ears are dull of hearing, and their eyes they have closed, lest at any time, they should see with their eyes, and hear with their ears, and understand with their hearts" (*EJS*, 71). But this allows Smith to turn a different point:

Men are in the habit, when the truth is exhibited by the servants of God, of saying, all is mystery, they are spoken in parables, and, therefore, are not to be understood, it is true they have eyes to see, and see not; but none are so blind as those who will not see: And although the Savior spoke this parable

to such characters, yet unto his disciples he expounded it plainly; and we
have reason to be truly humble before the God of our fathers, that he hath
left these things on record for us, so plain that, notwithstanding the exer-
tions and combined influence of the priests of Baal, they have not power to
blind our eyes and darken our understanding, if we will but open our eyes
and read with candor, for a moment. (*EJS*, 71–72)

"Yet unto his disciples he expounded it plainly": here is one of the origins, and
one of the expressions, of what Givens describes as "the ease and brazen-
ness with which Smith appropriated heavenly matters to his simple, direct
discourse."[23] It is a point to which Smith will often return (perhaps nowhere
more disarmingly than when he says, "I love that man better who swears
a stream as long as my arm and [is attentive to] administering to the poor
and dividing his substance, than the long smoothed faced hypocrites" [*EJS*,
180]). What his reading of Matthew makes clear is that Smith insists on
plainspokenness because of his conviction that, for the believer, *the world
is not an allegory*. Only to apostates—to those under the "combined influence of the priests of Baal"—does knowledge of the world require obliquity,
indirection, figure. Only for those inured in unbelief is the sacredness of
the world in need of some effortful *translation* back into the legible terms
of the human. "There is no room left for dubiety upon the mind," he writes
as he concludes his reading of Matthew, "notwithstanding the cry of the
priests, parables, parables! figures, figures! mystery, mystery! all is mystery!"
(*EJS*, 73). The matter with humankind lies not in any innate and incurable
dislocation from the divinity of the extant world, not in some elemental
incapacity for contact with God. (Smith's Protestantism is, once again like
Emerson's, an all-points rebuke to Calvinism.) The problem resides rather
in the false belief, solidified over two millennia of misapprehension in the
name of Christian doctrine, that there *is* any inborn difficulty to be encountered in the perception of the sacredness of the living world. Christian tradition, in other words, is for Smith not the record of assembled knowledge but
of growing estrangement, of mistranslation, misapprehension, and finally
apostasy.[24]

The ramifications that follow from this are expansive, and Smith's
career might be understood as the pursuing, in an astoundingly compressed frame of time, of just a few of them. (*The Book of Mormon* is first
published in 1830; Smith is killed in Carthage, Illinois, in June of 1844.)
The largest and perhaps most frontally heretical is his revelation that God
is a being with a history, a kind of biography: that God was a man who

became a God. This is the heart of the sermon he delivered in Nauvoo in April of 1844, not three months before his death, in which he asked, "What kind of being is God?" (*EJS*, 233). Anticipating his conclusion, Smith says, "If men do not comprehend the character of God, they do not comprehend their own character" (*EJS*, 233). What follows is Smith's genealogical account of the career of God:

> What kind of being was God in the beginning, before the world was? . . . First, God Himself who sits enthroned in yonder heavens is a Man like unto one of yourselves—that is the great secret! If the veil were rent today and the great God that holds this world in its sphere and the planets in their orbit and who upholds all things by His power—if you were to see Him today, you would see Him in all the person, image, fashion, and very form of a man, like yourselves. For Adam was a man formed in His likeness and created in the very fashion and image of God. Adam received instruction, walked, talked, conversed with Him as one man talks and communicates with another. (*EJS*, 234–35)

The great secret is not just that there is a story of, as Smith says, "how God came to be God" (*EJS*, 235), but that once we know that story we come at last to understand "that we may converse with Him the same as one man with another," since He, too, "once dwelled on an earth the same as Jesus Christ himself did in the flesh and like us" (*EJS*, 235). If what makes such a vision possible is at base a kind of monism, an understanding of the shared and indivisible *matter* of the human and the divine—"All spirit is matter" Smith writes in *Doctrine and Covenants* (*D&C*, 266)—the larger point of such monism, for Smith, lies in how it point by point refuses any intimation of a human falling-away from the divine, *any diminution of the scope and scale of the human*. Whitman exalts the body no less than the soul, Thoreau reverences the wild no less than the good, and Smith insists that all "doctors of divinity say that God created [the soul] in the beginning; but it is not so. *The very idea lessens the character of man*" (*EJS*, 239, emphasis added)—insists, that is, that the human and the divine mark differences of degree, masking an elemental sameness of kind. Any framework that misstates this shared essence is for Smith inevitably, and unpardonably, demeaning. Hence his most central exhortation, his reminder his followers that *they themselves are embryonic gods*, and are with their earthly lives assembling moments in a temporal curve that bends inexorably toward divinity and timelessness: "You have got to learn how to make yourselves Gods in order to save yourselves and be kings and priests to God, the same as all Gods have done—by going from a small capacity to a great capacity, from a small degree to another . . . til you are able to sit in everlasting burnings and everlasting power and glory as those who have gone before, sit enthroned" (*EJS*, 235–36). There is no "redemption" here, no translation of the human into the radical otherness of the heavenly. Enlargement, improvement, the going from a small capacity to a great capacity: these, for Smith, are the trajectories of the human toward the divine.

Crucially, Smith continually returns us to the misperceived but already-extant divinity of the human, not only as soul or spirit but *in all its enfleshed materiality*. Again, as we are told, "There is no such thing as immaterial matter. All spirit is matter, but it is more fine or pure, and can only be discerned by purer eyes" (*D&C*, 266). Smith rebukes the notion of God as uncreated creator, and he does so because to believe otherwise is to split matter unjustifiably away from spirit, to split the human away from God, and finally to "lessen[] the character of man." But what is that character? Or rather, what are the features of human character that most beguile Smith's theological imagination? They are not, it transpires, qualities of goodness, charity, or devotion. Consider the astounding way Smith appends his revelation concerning the human origins of God, with a pair of sentences so curious, so surprising, they might well comprise the most beguiling moment in the whole of the discourse: "This is good doctrine," he says by way of summary to the thesis that God has a biography; and then, wonderfully, "*It tastes good*" (*EJS*, 240, emphasis added). What can we make of a redescription of Smith's most expansively heretical exegetical pronouncements that turns so conspicuously not on truth but on *pleasure*? What of the turn to a specifically sensual delightedness for the human subject who, as Smith says, is "bound to receive [these revelations] as sweet" (*EJS*, 240)?

The underscoring of this-worldly pleasure is in fact not isolated to this moment in Smith. The starchiness of the twentieth-century caricature of upright Mormon rectitude, of an almost parodic wholesomeness (often wedded in the popular imagination to an outsized capacity for retributive violence), obscures the earlier, rather different perception of Mormons as "the dancing Puritans."[25] Fawn Brodie's account of Smith returns insistently to Smith's attentiveness to, and captivation by, worldly delight: "Joseph was no hair-shirt prophet. He believed in the good life, with moderate self-indulgence in food and drink, occasional sport, and good entertainment. . . . 'Man is that he might have joy,' had been one of his first significant pronouncements in the Book of Mormon, and from that belief he had never deviated."[26] Thus, "To every man in love with life—with the tantalizing richness of learning, the sweaty satisfaction of hard work, the luxury of sensual pleasure—Joseph's heaven had profound meaning." She goes on to note that "it is no accident that his theology in the end discarded all traces of Calvinism and became an ingenuous blend of supernaturalism and materialism, which promised in heaven a continuation of all earthly pleasures—work, wealth, sex, power."[27] And Smith can in fact not too often mention the strange joyfulness of embodied life. ("Our organism," Brigham Young would write, "makes us capable of exquisite enjoyment."[28]) As he writes in 1842—in what was a spectacularly ill-advised letter to the nineteen-year old Nancy Rigdon, whom he was laboring to cajole into marrying him—"Our heavenly father is more liberal in his views, and boundless in his mercies and blessings, than we are ready to believe or receive" (*EJS*, 159). Like the divinity of the human and the human origins of God, just this inbuilt human capacity for delight is what the accreted misapprehensions of the Christian tradition have conspired to mystify. "Happiness is the object and design of our existence," Smith writes, and it is God's plan that "in the end they shall have joy" (*EJS*, 158, 159).[29]

We do well to follow Brodie in recognizing Smith as that rarest of things: a theologian in love with life. (Once more, these terms recall quite precisely those in which Whitman's followers would take him up.[30]) For Smith, the saints do not merely live in an unfallen world. Life transpires as well *in an unfallen body*, a body that like the rest of the material world does not require artful translation into the bracing otherness of sacral terms but is already the site of divinity's unfolding, is already in fact composed of the stuff, the matter, of godhead. So when Smith says to the saints "*You have got to learn how to make yourselves Gods*," part of what he means is that they must learn to live in, and out to the edges of, the divinity of their bodies. And though the path to that realization is, as we shall see, an arduous one—the fact of God's liberality, he writes to Nancy Rigdon, is not easy "to believe or receive"—Smith comes later in his life to a clear sense of how can be accomplished: "Then shall they be gods, because they have no end; therefore shall they be everlasting to everlasting, because they continue; then shall they be above all, because all things are subject to them. Then shall they be gods, because they have all power, and the angels are subject unto them" (*EJS*, 194; also *D&C*, 132:19–20, 268–69).

"*Then shall they be gods*": so writes Smith in July of 1843, in his revelation concerning "The Principle and Doctrine of Having Many Wives and Concubines." Plural marriage, we might say, is the becoming-normative of the heavenly language of the body, its rendering in the vernacular of daily life. It is for Smith the mode by which one might best live out the almost inconceivable fact that one is living in the body of a God not yet enlarged, a body whose intensities of delight—as Brigham Young says: "Our senses, if properly educated, are channels of endless felicity to us"[31]— forever vouchsafe to it the fact of its divinity. It is a body that partakes of the enlargement, the fullness, above all the *numerousness* Smith so associates with godhead. Polygamy, then, is the intimate form proper to life in an unfallen body, and not simply because the ancient prophets, who walked and conversed with God in the flesh, themselves enjoyed such a privilege. If you are today the likeness of Abraham and Jacob, it is not least because like them you too live in the flesh. Or, to put it differently: How do you know you are not fallen away from divinity but advancing ever closer to godhead? Because you live in a body, with all its self-startling pleasures and faculties.

In Nothing Did They Sin

Perhaps not surprisingly, living in the body is also, as Smith frames and reframes it, a way of being in the world that is difficult to endure—and not only for the women forced to walk "in sacred loneliness," as Todd Compton titled his detailed history of the plural wives of Joseph Smith. (As Compton makes clear, and as we shall see, their afflictions are extraordinary.) We hear something of this in what is perhaps Smith's most famous utterance—"No man knows my history"—when he says, "I don't blame you for not believing my history. *If I had not experienced what I have, I could not have believed it myself*," implying, if not a distinction between the human and the divine, then a distinction between the human experience of its own incipient divinity and a capacity to *know* it, or believe in it, "to believe or receive," as he writes to Nancy Rigdon (*EJS*, 245). As Jared Hickman puts it, "In Mormonism's profoundly monistic cosmos . . . it need not be presumed that direct dialogue with God relieves one of the burden of interpretation any more so than direct dialogue with one's fellow human being."[32] So while it is indeed the pleasures of the body—their intensities and derangements—that vouchsafe to Smith, in the first place, the daring intimation that living persons are not fallen clay but gods in embryo, those intimations are as disquieting as they are exhilarating. The love of life, in other words, is no uncomplicated thing, and the revealed world, in the very grain of its intensity of delight, is as much a kind of provocation to Smith as a comfort or security.

In early 1844, Smith would dwell on just this point with something like exasperation:

> But there has been a great difficulty in getting anything into the heads of this generation. It has been like splitting hemlock knots with a corndoger for a wedge & a pumpkin for a beetle; even the Saints are slow to understand. I have tried for a number of years to get the minds of the saints prepared to receive the things of God, but we frequently see some of them after suffering all they have for the work of God will fly to peaces like glass as soon as any thing Comes that is Contrary to their traditions. They cannot stand the fire at all. How many will be able to abide a Celestial law & go through & receive their exaltation I am unable to say but many are called & few are Chosen. (*EJS*, 212)

To recognize the things of God requires, here, preparation but also resilience, stamina, fortitude. When Smith wonders, "How many will be able to abide a Celestial law," he points not chiefly to a kind of declension, I think, but to the ways living out a life at last revealed to be that of a God in embryo might itself be trying, disquieting, a thing one struggles to endure.

This begins to explain the strange, strangely repetitive emphasis in the polygamy revelation on *crime*—or rather on things that seem criminally contrary to nature only in terms that are not those of God. Abraham is of course the Biblical model most pertinent to Smith: "This promise is yours, also," the revelation says of polygamy, "because ye are of Abraham" (*EJS*, 195). But consider Smith's framing of the Abraham story:

> God commanded Abraham, and Sarah gave Hagar to Abraham, to wife. And why did she do it? Because this was the law, and from Hagar sprang many people. This, there, was fulfilling, among other things, the promises. Was Abraham therefore under condemnation? Verily, I say unto you, *Nay*; for I the Lord commanded it. Abraham was commanded to offer his son Isaac; nevertheless, it was written, thou shalt not kill. Abraham, however, did not refuse, and it was accounted unto him for righteousness. (*EJS*, 195)

We underread this passage, I think, if we understand it to be essentially a kind of coercive scripture mongering, a way to bully Smith's wife Emma into countenancing what was after all a violation of her marriage. (The revelation culminates in a command to "Emma Smith" in particular "to abide and cleave unto my servant Joseph, and to none else" [*EJS*, 197].) It is that, without question, but it is also an expression of what I would call the lived incoherence of polygamy for its practitioners, of the ways it cannot *not* feel like a crime even to those propounding it. "David also received many wives and concubines, as also Solomon, and Moses my servant . . . and in nothing did they sin," Smith writes, and it is not at all clear that the only person he is trying to convince of the sinlessness of plural marriage is Emma (*EJS*, 196).

Perhaps nowhere else is the folding-together of exaltation and an encroaching sense of shame more vivid than in Smith's letter of 1842 to Newel and Elizabeth Ann Whitney, and to their daughter Sarah Ann Whitney, to whom, God has revealed, Joseph is to be sealed. "If you both agree to covenant and do this," the revelation reads, "then I give you S. N. Whitney my daughter to Joseph Smith to be his wife" (*EJS*, 165). But here is Smith speaking to the Whitneys not in the voice of God but *in propria persona*: "I am now at Carlos Graingers, Just back of Brother Hyrams farm, it is only one mile from town, the nights are very pleasant indeed, all three of you can come . . . it is next to the cornfield, I have a room intirely by myself, the whole matter can be attended to with most perfect safty" (*EJS*, 166). And then, in perfect completion of an image not at all that of the fearless prophet and leader of men, he goes on:

> the only thing to be careful of; is to find out when Emma comes then you cannot be safe, but when she is not here, there is the most perfect safty: only be careful to escape observation, as much as possible, I know it is a heroick undertaking; but so much the greater friendship, and the more Joy, when I see you I will tell you all my plans, I cannot write them on paper, burn this letter as soon as you read it; keep all locked up in your breasts, my life depends upon it. (*EJS*, 166)

Here is the quintessential image of the cringing Joseph Smith, skulking in the dark of night like the most dismally commonplace of philanderers. Why does he dress up this skullduggery as some "heroick undertaking"? One possibility, of course, is that Smith fears the apostate world will misrecognize him, and see not an emergent God in the dress of a man but an all-too-ordinary man dressing up his foibles and frailties in sanctimony and godliness. But I think we might sense instead in Smith's fearful secrecy—as in his larger unwillingness to publicize the revelations about polygamy to any but a small cadre of saints, which would do so much to foment the radically hierarchal insularity, the secrecy and silence, that characterize institutional Mormonism even now—something graver. What we hear is perhaps something of Smith's own misgiving, his own glancing suspicion that the cosmology he believes himself called to embody and to prophesy is itself fraudulent, a thing made not by the will of a liberal God but by his own least sanctified and least governable impulses. In Smith's polygamous world, that is, "sex" marks the experience of a possibility for nearly unimaginable plenitude, folded around a pervasive, disquieting, no less vast intimation of shame.

These are only the first of the incoherencies surrounding plural marriage. There are others no less pressing. For instance: If it is true in Smith's terms that the human species is elementally godlike, awaiting not transformative redemption as much as progressive enlargement, then can *women* be understood to inhabit the bodies of gods? Is women's embodiment as much an experience of inflooding divinity as men's? It is true, of course, that all the Old Testament polygamists are men, and the institutions of Christianity itself unrelievedly patriarchal, but Smith, as we have seen, is hardly shy about upending Christian tradition. The polygamy revelation, though, is where Smith seems most to say NO, in thunder. "They belong to him," he writes, "and if one, or either of the ten virgins, after she is espoused, shall be with another man, she has committed adultery, and shall be destroyed" (*EJS*, 198). Here Smith makes maximally clear the brutal inequality, the forms of sweeping curtailment, upon which the breadth of his vision of embodied possibility may be said to rest. What's notable in these terms is less Smith's unconventionality than his radicalization of *conventional* gender arrangements, his insistence not merely on patriarchy but a kind of cosmologically ordained superpatriarchy: the patriarchal sublime.

Even here, though, are unlikely incoherencies, further testament to the provisionality of Smith's theology, its unsystematized incompletion and its openness to still unforeclosed possibilities, as it unfolded on the ground in the last years of his short life. In a sermon Smith is recorded to have delivered in 1842—appearing before the Female Relief Society, which as Brodie writes, "Joseph had organized in mid-March 1842 with Emma as president"[33]—he makes a few remarks that, though equivocal at best, still suggest some wider latitude for understanding the like capacities, and perhaps like divinities, of men and women. The occasion for his remarks is gossip: "some little things was circulating in the Society, that some persons were not going right in laying hands on the sick, &C" (*EJS*, 160). This talk he wishes to put to rest:

> Prest. Smith continued the subject by adverting to the commission given to the ancient apostles "Go ye into all the world" &C. No matter who believeth; these signs such as healing the sick, casting out devils &C. Should follow all that believe whether male or female. He ask's the Society if they could not see by this sweeping stroke that werein they are ordained, it is the privilege of those set apart to administer in that authority which is conferr's on them—and if the sisters should have faith to heal the sick, let all hold their tongues, and let every thing roll on. (*EJS*, 161)

Or again: "there could be no more sin in any female laying hands on the sick than in wetting the face with water. It is no sin for any body to do it that has faith" (*EJS*, 161). Of course, the duties for which women are given sanctification here—tending to the sick—are wholly conventional. And though Smith concludes his remarks with the still-more-normative injunction that "this Society teach how to act towards husbands, to treat them with mildness and affection," still there are glimpses of larger possibility. "Females, if they are pure and innocent can come into the presence of God," Smith avers (*EJS*, 162). More than this, women, he insists, share with men a capacity for expansion and, that hallmark of the trajectory toward godhead, *enlargement*: "Not war, not jangle, not contradiction, but meekness, love purity, these are the things that should magnify us" (*EJS*, 163). That these all are traditionally female virtues, rooted more in passivity than, say, embodied joy, surely mitigates the potential capaciousness of Smith's reference to "us," though it does not, I think, cancel it or invalidate the fleeting intimation that men and women aspire *together* toward a magnification into divinity. After all, as Smith says earlier in his address, in a moment that for those auditors hungering for such notes may have seemed more richly promising, "Who knows the mind of God? *Does he not reveal things differently from what we expect?*" (*EJS*, 161, emphasis added). The revelation of plural marriage as a kind of hypertrophied patriarchy was not, we might say, at all different from what one might have expected. That the practices and doctrines surrounding polygamy might have developed otherwise had Smith lived beyond 1844, or had the church not passed into the control of Brigham Young, is perhaps unlikely. But that is not because the seeds of a contrary theological development, however meager and however scattered, were not there. They were.[34]

That contrary rendering might likely return to the point I have suggested lies at the center of Smith's thought about polygamy: his regard for the living body as the scene of an exquisite joy, of delights so manifold they at once explode the traditions by which that body has been legible to itself and recall to the self nothing less than the divinity of the elements of which it is compounded. It is this kind of body—so reminiscent of Whitman and, particularly in its intimations of an enlarged future, Thoreau—that I think McGarry has in mind when she recalls to us how secularizing accounts of the history of sexuality *misplace* certain varieties of religious experience, since it is a body on which we are given only a very limited kind of purchase by the taxonomies of attachment and extension that would arrive at century's end, and travel under such nominations as "heterosexuality." It is no great surprise, then, that for the radiant body of Mormon theology one can imagine, even from the breadcrumb trail of Smith's own writings, modes of realization and enactment that are *not* plural patriarchal marriage, even if Smith's emphasis on number, on magnification through numerousness, seems to lock him into a logic of bioreproductive fecundity. One of them, given its most articulate historical treatment by D. Michael Quinn, finds Smith striking a note that should startle us with its familiarity: "Let me be resurrected with the Saints, whether to heaven or hell or any other good place," Smith says in 1843, where his heretical strain rises to an almost Satanic willingness to oppose the joys he knows to any that might or might not be sanctioned. "What do we care if the society is good?" To which he adds: "Friendship is the grand fundamental principle of Mormonism, to revolution[ize and] civilize the world, [to] pour forth love" (*EJS*, 200). Sounding remarkably like the "Calamus" Whitman, Smith makes monogamous marriage seem an impossibly narrow form with which to ratify the sorts of joyous fellowship, of impassioned intimacies extending well beyond the dyadic couple, that the industrializing century had brought more and more into relief, and that Smith here understands to be "fundamental" to the revolutionary restorative project that is Mormonism. Or as *Doctrine and Covenants* 130 puts it, after noting that the Savior "is a man like ourselves": "And that same sociality which exists among us here will exist among us there, only it will be coupled with eternal glory, which glory we do not now enjoy" (*D&C*, 130:1–2, 264). Heaven is, in this rendering, less the site of hetero-reproductivity run celestially amok than the scene of an expansive lateral sociability far less easily coded back into heterosexualizing frameworks.

What discloses itself here might be understood as the lost futures of the early Mormon social and sexual imaginary: the possibilities that would not come to be. There are of course many ways to narrate precisely how, from the seeds of Smith's possibly capacious (indeed, possibly Satanic) counterimaginings of intimate possibility, the forms that developed around the Mormons as they ventured West under the leadership of Brigham Young would come to be as unyieldingly, hyperbolically patriarchal as they did.[35] But one line of reasoning returns us to the matter we have approached only glancingly thus far: Smith's fashioning of Mormonism as an *indigenization* of Christianity. For as Bethany Schneider, Mark Rifkin, Andrea Smith, Deborah Miranda, and other scholars of native studies remind us, Smith's restoration of polygamy as a vector of what Bloom calls his "near identification with the ancient Hebrews" grows complex indeed when we remember that, throughout *The Book of Mormon*, Smith understands the direct descendants of those ancient Hebrews *to live on still*: they are in America and, quite significantly, are themselves the architects of modes of intimacy and sodality that fall hard aslant the normative.[36] "It has been said by many of the learned, and wise men, or historians," Smith writes in 1835, "that the Indians, or aborigines of this continent, are of the scattered tribes of Israel" (*EJS*, 66). What's so densely complicating about Smith's writing of Mormonism as an indigenization of Christianity here is that it was precisely Native arrangements of gender, property, and intimate life— precisely the way "the kinship structures of . . . tribal relation stood directly against the heteronormative structures of private property ownership and inheritance"—that rendered native peoples the object of a new and immensely punitive kind of racialization (a racialization, as Mark Rifkin argues, *through* imputations of sexual errancy).[37] For the Mormons, this racialization through a reading of intimate forms could only have expansive, unsettling consequences.

We are allowed here, I think, some purchase on the strange fate of plural marriage after Smith's death. By virtue not only of their origin myths but, more troublingly, *of their own derangements of dyadic intimate forms*, Mormons found themselves propelled into a layered, unstable, and spectacularly fraught identification with North American Native peoples. In the light of the state's efforts toward the forcible erasure or violent

reorientation of vast structures of gender and sex among native peoples—
"gendercide," in Deborah Miranda's formulation[38]—we can hardly wonder at the Mormon drive to turn their *own* alternative kinship structures
into a kind of hyperpatriarchy. For to allow the ampler and less uniform
possibilities of Smith's unsystematized visions of plural marriage to flourish would be to invite the indigenizing drive of Mormonism to corrode
into something more directly, and for the early Mormons more intoler-
ably, *racializing*. (The invocation of a historically misplaced *barbarity*, in
the famous phrase referring to slavery and polygamy as the midcentury's
"twin relics of barbarism," comes into especially rich meaning in just this
context.) In this vein, the turning of plural marriage into hypertrophied
patriarchy comes into meaning as a gambit of invidious distinction, fueled
by some dangerous proximities: a bid to shore up not only the straightness but the *whiteness* of the Mormons who, as they ventured deeper and
deeper into the West, risk appearing before the American imagination as
possessed of too little of both. Only one irony here is that the effort to cut
a hard, violent difference between native and Mormon intimate forms, or
between nonstandard intimacies that are degenerate and those that are
somehow *hypernormative*, would fail spectacularly. (The Mormon church
was forced to renounce polygamy officially in 1890.) Whatever its con-
solidating push toward patriarchal verticality after Smith, the radically
lateralizing intimate imagination of early Mormonism—the making of
a heaven of sociality itself, say, where humankind learns to expand itself
toward godhead—could not so easily be routed back into the channels of
the normative.

And with this gesture to the heavenliness of sociability we are returned,
at a new angle, to Frederick Douglass, for whom marriage—monogamous, state-certified marriage—operates precisely as a kind of recognition, the consecration of a humanness made most legible in the embodied
self's capacity not merely for labor but for connectedness, entanglement,
mutuality, extension. We come back here because, in the strangest kind
of crossing, marriage is for Smith, too, a measure of the human. For the
escaped slave, as we have seen, marriage is the portal through which to
enter into a wider enfranchisement: as legal citizen, contractual subject,
and participant in the affective fellowship of what is sometimes called
the human family. For Smith, it is the portal through which to enter into
a different but related enlargement, a magnification of the human out
toward the divinity that is its destiny: an enfranchisement of the human,
we might say, *as* divine. In Smith's rendering, marriage is not a perpetual

woe, a patient endurance, and even less a suffering of the chastisement of mortal flesh in the expectation of an eventual release into a divine hereafter. It is more an unlearning, a steady erasure of two millennia of apostasy and calcified falsehood, which live not only in mistranslated scripture but *in the flesh*. If, as Givens suggests, Mormonism is at its root a "demystification of Christianity itself," then polygamy—Smith's unwriting of monogamous marriage—is perhaps best understood as an effort toward the demystification of *embodied life*.[39] It is the fashioning of an intimate form that recognizes in the extravagances of sensation of which the body is capable, its deranging pleasures, the need for a like derangement of what is in many respects, as later Mormons would discover, the very bedrock of the nation's consensual real: the sanctity of monogamous marriage. So it was that in 1890 the Mormon Church officially renounced polygamy, paving the way for the ratification of Utah's statehood in 1896—and also transforming Mormonism into, essentially, another strand of American Protestantism. Thus did plural marriage, with its many-pleasured body driving toward a future of vast enlargements, begin its unquiet career as the relic of a repudiated past.

Coda

Unceremoniousness

In the world of "toasts," "roasts," and "boasts," in the universe of unreality and exaggeration, the black female is, if anything, a creature of sex, but sexuality touches her nowhere.
— Hortense J. Spillers, "Interstices: A Small Drama of Words"

The history of sexuality that Michel Foucault famously begins to outline in his introductory first volume is, of course, conspicuously European. The movement from Catholic pastoral to expert rational discourse, for instance, looks markedly different in an American context that *begins* with Protestant reform, and is convulsed across the nineteenth century by revivalisms of various pitches and intensities, of which Joseph Smith's Mormonism is only one especially vivid example.[1] But the Americanist reader of *The History of Sexuality* might be startled, too, by Foucault's turn to what he calls "racism": to the strand of racism, rooted in a sense of the "degeneration" of the lower orders, that emerges in the nineteenth century. That sexually anchored racism, which for Foucault offers a foretaste of fascist eugenics, lives a considerably more manifest, more Manichean, and of course differently chronological life in the American context, shaped as it is not only by racist epistemologies of science but by the specific practices of antebellum slavery—practices that made the order of alliance (based on stasis, the transfer of property, the proper name) both problematic and necessarily ineradicable, whatever its penetration by the different technologies of sexuality, in ways distinct from European history.[2] The whole of the vast horror of miscegenation lives in the space of this paradox, where the prevalence of rape as tool of both terror and property expansion runs headlong into the imperative to maintain the purity of white lineage.

Slavery, in other words, makes the history of sexuality in America a thing not so easily convertible to the master chronology of *Volume 1*. And, as Frederick Douglass already suggested to us so vividly, marriage—marriage law and marriage custom—is one of the chief switching points for the coming into meaning of sex in a racialized world. In the simplest terms, this is almost self-evident: marriage and slavery are both at their root structures of property distribution and entailment. And yet for Douglass, as we have seen, the conjoining of sex to *meaning* was also much of the point. Marriage extended to him the promise not only of a kind of affective ratification but offered as well—as marriage does—a framework within which all that is disreputable or threatening about black sexuality might be made amenable to hygienic narratives of social stability and social reproduction. At its most basic, marriage codes sex into a kind of legibility, translating whatever is worryingly ungovernable in it into normative, stabilizing terms. For the subject of "race," buffeted by presumptions of impotence and insatiability, those contrary legibilities would be welcome indeed.

All of which makes only the more remarkable Harriet Jacobs's famous declaration at the end of *Incidents in the Life of a Slave Girl*: "Reader, my story ends with freedom; not in the usual way, with marriage."[3] By way of brief conclusion to this section on the woe that is in marriage, I want to take up Jacobs's meditation on sex and matrimony for the female slave, at the center of which is neither the question of "alliance" nor of "sexuality" as such, but rather of "recognition" in its broadest, most epistemologically vexing senses. Though of perhaps lesser gravity than her struggle against the predations of Dr. Flint, or to secure her own freedom and that of her two children, Jacobs's Linda contends throughout the text of *Incidents* with what we might think of as a problem of *translation*—with the difficulty of finding a framework that might allow her to bring into legible coherence what have been her own lived experiences as a female slave. As critics like Valerie Smith and P. Gabrielle Foreman have argued, *Incidents* records one woman's struggle with the formal articulability of the story that, as she keeps reminding us, she has *lived*.[4] If that thematics of inarticulacy recalls the psychoanalytic framework of trauma, it has, also, other and perhaps more curious resonances. What's striking in particular, I want to suggest, is how closely Jacobs's struggle with legibility, especially in and around sex and marriage, aligns her work in the book with a novel that seems on the face of it to harbor quite different ambitions. Her work can, I think, be set in illuminating dialogue with another of the midcentury's great literary adventures into the uncharted, into some extremity of experience that leaves its survivors disfigured and frantic, in pained possession of a story that does not know how to tell itself.

Consider this passage, and its characteristic density of rhetoric:

> So that there are instances among them of men, who, named with Scripture names—a singularly common fashion on the island—and in childhood naturally imbibing the stately dramatic thee and thou of the Quaker idiom; still, from the audacious, daring, and boundless adventure of their subsequent lives, strangely blend with these unoutgrown peculiarities, a thousand bold dashes of character, not unworthy a Scandinavian sea-king, or a poetical Pagan Roman. And when these things unite in a man of greatly superior natural force, with a globular brain and a ponderous heart; who has also by the stillness and seclusion of many long night-watches in the remotest waters, and beneath constellations never seen here at the north, been led to think untraditionally and independently; receiving all nature's sweet or savage impressions fresh from her own virgin, voluntary, and confiding breast, and thereby chiefly, but with some help from accidental advantages, to learn a bold and nervous lofty language—that man makes one in a whole nation's census—a mighty pageant creature, formed for noble tragedies.[5]

Moby-Dick is a book about what happens to selves—as well as to affect, relation, being—once they are unhooked from the securities and clarities of the landed world and cast out into a kind of elemental extremity, there to receive "all nature's sweet or savage impressions fresh from her own virgin, voluntary, and confiding breast." According to the passage, among the things reshaped by such exposure is language itself: we see this in Ahab's "bold and nervous lofty language," but also in Ishmael's, whose own singular idiom (its neologistic hyperproduction of Miltonic prefixes and suffixes, say: "unworthy," "untraditionally," and, especially, "*unoutgrown*") speaks to the fact of his own exposure, and of his own labors as the last living witness, he only alone escaped to tell the *Pequod*'s tale.

Much of the comedy of the first part of the novel comes, in fact, from the sharp collision between the narrative disposition we are taught to recognize as Ishmael's—that strange, cheerful, but vastly *dismissive* mode of openness to any and all of the world's proffered forms—and the character Ishmael is at the outset, before his immersion in the chaos of the elements has led him "to think untraditionally and independently." New Bedford and, especially, Nantucket, those early settings for the novel, are locales in which the locked-in-lathe-and-plaster certainties of landed life begin to erode, or at least to undergo transformation, as they are encroached upon by the sea and its rewirings of order and conventionality. ("In New Bedford, fathers, they say, give whales for dowers to their daughters, and portion off their nieces with a few porpoises a-piece" [*MD*, 32].) Ishmael's experiences there are a kind of laboratory in which we see him taking the first steps on a trajectory from prickly, pious, defensive schoolmaster ("and you, sir, *you* I mean, landlord, *you*, sir" [*MD*, 18]) to world-devouring ironist, possessed of what he will call a "free and easy sort of genial, desperado philosophy" (*MD*, 226). And the first harbinger of that transformation involves, as it proves, race and sex and marriage.

Here is how Ishmael himself describes the first station of his rebirth:

> As I sat there in that now lonely room; the fire burning low, in that mild stage when, after its first intensity has warmed the air, it then only glows to be looked at; the evening shades and phantoms gathering round the casements, and peering in upon us silent, solitary twain; the storm booming without in solemn swells; I began to be sensible of strange feelings. I felt a melting in me. No more my splintered heart and maddened hand were turned against the wolfish world. This soothing savage had redeemed it. There he sat, his very indifference speaking a nature in which there lurked no civilized hypocrisies and bland deceits. Wild he was; a very sight of sights to see; yet I began to feel myself mysteriously drawn towards him. And those same things that would have repelled most others, they were the very magnets that thus drew me. I'll try a pagan friend, thought I, since Christian kindness has proved but hollow courtesy. (*MD*, 50–51)

Ishmael's melting here at the edge of the sea, his elasticization ("yet see how elastic our stiff prejudices grow when love once comes to bend them" [*MD*, 54]), is in part a matter of foreswearing his own particular prejudices, as critics like Samuel Otter and Geoffrey Sanborn have argued so convincingly—his suspicions of "this 'dark complexioned' harpooner," or his objections to "the unbecomingness of [Queequeg's] hugging a fellow male in that matrimonial sort of style" (*MD*, 15, 27).[6] Another way to frame these early transformations, though, is to read them as Ishmael's first intimations of what *an uncoding of his body* might entail, an unloosening of corporeal selfhood from the codes by which it knows itself. To say that this uncoding is sexual *and* racial is, in a sense, a poor way of speaking, since sex and race figure here, in his matrimonial embrace with the dark-complexioned cannibal, as elements of the same melting, simultaneous mappings of a body that, once properly touched, overspills its parameters.[7] The transgression of bodily propriety here issues less in any alternate configuration—interracial homosexuality, say[8]—than in dispositions, mutualities and resonances, that for Ishmael are available in language only as approximations: "You had almost thought I had been his wife" (*MD*, 25). An unmooring of the body, a melting into new possibilities for extension and connection: this is what sex looks like at the outer edges of the land.

Yet the mutuality between Ishmael and Queequeg *is* figured, at least here on land, as marriage. "When our smoke was over, he pressed his forehead against mine, clasped me round the waist, and said that henceforth we were married; meaning, in his country's phrase, that we were bosom friends; he would gladly die for me, if need should be" (*MD*, 51). In some ways, such nominations make narrative sense. The matrimonial, we might assume, becomes in this instance but another object of Ishmael's all-devouring impiety, what Bersani calls his "cannibalistic encyclopedism," in which he consumes as many epistemologies, as many landlocked modes of knowing the world, as he can, only to inhabit them with so much genially demolishing absurdism and irony as to leave each and all of them hollowed out, dispossessed of whatever authority or ontological gravity might have accrued to them.[9] Just so, with the coupling of Ishmael and Queequeg he offers an expansion of the notion of "marriage" beyond its most immediate markers of legibility, and out to the point of epistemological bursting. In this reading, marriage comes to be analogous to naturalist taxonomy, jurisprudence, Shakespearean bibliography, and all the other forms of knowledge and order the novel replicates in the register of giddy parody. But if the splendid unceremoniousness of Ishmael and Queequeg's marriage is but another expression of what Cesare Casarino calls Ishmael's "condition of abandon," just one more derangement of one of the landed world's more prominent order-giving forms, it is also something else again.[10] Marriage, here, is for Ishmael the approximate name for the new form of intimate connectedness of which the embodied self is capable when it *begins* to be deterritorialized. It is, we might say, the novel's designation for the form of intimacy proper to the liminal space of the shore, where inherited conceptual structures remain unoutgrown, and still possess a modicum of referential authority, however extravagantly attenuated.

Things look very different at sea. Indeed, intimate attachment there is distinct enough from the sex on shore that marriage—at least heterosexual marriage—comes to stand for the novel as something like the *opposite* of the forms of bodily interrelation proper to landlessness. Famously, those entanglements appear here:

> Squeeze! squeeze! squeeze! all the morning long; I squeezed that sperm till I myself almost melted into it; I squeezed that sperm till a strange sort of insanity came over me; and I found myself unwittingly squeezing my co-laborers' hands in it, mistaking their hands for the gentle globules. Such an abounding, affectionate, friendly, loving feeling did this avocation beget; that at last I was continually squeezing their hands, and looking up into their eyes sentimentally; as much as to say,—Oh! my dear fellow beings, why should we longer cherish any social acerbities, or know the slightest ill-humor or envy! Come; let us squeeze hands all round; nay, let us all squeeze ourselves into each other; let us squeeze ourselves universally into the very milk and sperm of kindness.
>
> Would that I could keep squeezing that sperm for ever! For now, since by many prolonged, repeated experiences, I have perceived that in all cases man must eventually lower, or at least shift, his conceit of attainable felicity; not placing it anywhere in the intellect or the fancy; but in the wife, the heart, the bed, the table, the saddle, the fire-side; the country; now that I have perceived all this, I am ready to squeeze case eternally. In thoughts of the visions of the night, I saw long rows of angels in paradise, each with his hands in a jar of spermaceti. (*MD*, 416)

Though it features no less prominently than the earlier scene a "melting," this vision of a now-lost "conceit of attainable felicity" is no marriage, and Ishmael is no man's wife. Indeed, in the reflected light of this later scene, the uncoding of the body in Ishmael's seaside encounter with Queequeg is made to seem markedly *preliminary*. As Casarino puts it, in the Deleuzian terms that I think are wholly appropriate to these moments in the novel, "If in Ishmael and Queequeg's Badaliya we witnessed a loss of self—in the sense that no subject was allowed to crystallize there and that the only viable modality of being in it was the being-in-common and the sharing of hospitality—here we are faced with a loss of body *tout court*, or, at the very least, with a fluid redrawing of bodily boundaries."[11] That initial expansion into newly habitable attachments moves in the sperm squeezing scene into a much more comprehensive sort of loosening, a dissolving of the self, *almost* completely, not only into the otherness of other people but into a porousness that melts it nearly indistinguishably into the raw stuff of the physical world. Mistaking hands for globules, his own fingers feeling more and more "like eels," Ishmael does more than speak to the deranging joys of male shipmate intimacy. He invites us to think back on the like kinds of porousness between men and men and, especially, between men and *other flesh*—men and whales' heads, men and whales' skin, men and whales' blubber, men and whales' immeasurable bodily recesses—that more and more obtain as the *Pequod* sails deeper into the "everlasting terra incognita" of the sea (*MD*, 273). There is Tashtego, who "with a horrible oily gurgling" slips into the whale's head, and loans it for a moment some of his own animation: "Looking over the side, they saw the before lifeless head throbbing and heaving just below the surface of the sea, as if that moment seized with some momentous idea; whereas it was only the poor Indian unconsciously revealing by those struggles the perilous depths to which he had sunk" (*MD*, 342). And there is of course the mincer who skins the whale's penis and "lengthwise slips himself bodily into it" (*MD*, 420). A turning of self into assemblage, an unwriting of the body and of territorializations of the self as *white or cannibal*, as well as *man or whale*, *fish or fowl*: this is what sex at sea looks like in the novel, and "marriage" it most certainly is not.[12]

And yet *Moby-Dick* is not, or is not solely, a joyous story of deterritorialization, however joyously Melville may present us, as Casarino claims, "with a nonteleological sexuality and a posteschatological sexual world," producing "same-sex desire as a constellation of bodies in pleasure," perhaps rather too precisely as Foucault would have him do.[13] To be free of the self-conjugating strictures of the landlocked world may indeed be to encounter the possibility of inhabiting a body less forcefully coded by race and sex, or the imperatives of alliance or sexuality both, and so to discover a body capable of new and thrilling alignments. But remember that Ishmael says he *wishes* he could abide in such zones of delight, wherein he and his shipmates can forget their terrible oath. As the novel is at pains to teach us, though, what looks at some moments like deterritorialization, a freedom from worldly captivation, looks at others like something significantly less habitable: like, precisely, exposure, in its rather more harrowing senses. Before we even begin to see what such exposure might actually involve, we know that it is, in a curious way, hard to *tell*. There at the outset is the solitary and sober, "somewhat aloof," and conspicuously unquoted Bulkington, who soon wordlessly vanishes from the novel. But there are also other retuning sailors: "After we were all seated at the table," Ishmael says, "and I was preparing to hear some good stories about whaling; to my no small surprise nearly every man maintained a profound silence. And not only that, but they looked embarrassed. . . . A curious sight; these bashful bears, these timid warrior whalemen!" (*MD*, 30) Ishmael hungers at the breakfast table for "some good stories" but what comes in their place, from the mouths of men who have encountered what yet awaits him, is "profound silence."

But the destructiveness and incommunicability of being unmoored has a much more potent emblem in the book. From "The Castaway":

> But it so happened, that those boats, without seeing Pip, suddenly spying whales close to them on one side, turned, and gave chase; and Stubb's boat was now so far away, and he and all his crew so intent upon his fish, that Pip's ringed horizon began to expand around him miserably. By the merest chance the ship itself at last rescued him; but from that hour the little negro went about the deck an idiot; such, at least, they said he was. The sea had jeeringly kept his finite body up, but drowned the infinite of his soul. Not drowned entirely, though. Rather carried down alive to wondrous depths, where strange shapes of the unwarped primal world glided to and fro before his passive eyes; and the miser-merman, Wisdom, revealed his hoarded heaps; and among the joyous, heartless, ever-juvenile eternities, Pip saw the multitudinous, God-omnipresent, coral insects, that out of the firmament of waters heaved the colossal orbs. He saw God's foot upon the treadle of the loom, and spoke it; and therefore his shipmates called him mad. (*MD*, 414)

Not surprisingly, the paragraph is prefaced by a question about communicability: "The intense concentration of self in the middle of such a heartless immensity," Ishmael exclaims, "my God! *who can tell it?*" (*MD*, 414, emphasis added). Ishmael informs us in the next moment that he suffers a "like abandonment" himself at the novel's conclusion, which encourages us to understand the oft-noted wild idiosyncrasy of his narrative form as something like an *idiolect*, a language blasted by its exposure to "the unwarped primal world" into near incomprehensibility. Contact, as offered here, seems to contort language—language figuring not only as that which distorts or misapprehends but that which *protects*. That it is Pip who, of all the sailors, exemplifies such incommunicable exposure, Pip the poor Alabama boy who is also native to Tolland County, Connecticut—Pip, perhaps, the figure of the fugitive slave[14]—is more than telling. The matter is not only that "Pip loved life, and all life's peaceable securities," and earlier had nominated the heedless sailors as "men that have no bowels to feel fear" (412, 178)—or that he *longs* for the protection of secure forms, and finds in sexual errancy the fittest emblem of their jettisoning. Beyond these ironies are more dire implications.

Like all Westerns, *Moby-Dick* is a story about the difficulty of returning from the wilds of some unwarped primal world with enough language intact, enough battered sense, to be able to make legible to the uninitiated what is found there. In the novel's terms there is, of course, great urgency to that project, since the uninitiated *need to know*: the fate of the ship of the nation, we might say with a text like "Benito Cereno" in mind, depends intimately upon the story's ability to be told and to be read. Failures of telling issue in cataclysm: this is what novelist Frederick Busch has in mind when he says that for Melville "fiction is a matter of life and death."[5] Hence *Moby-Dick's* fascination with prophets: Elijah, of course, but also Fedallah, Gabriel, Ahab, and the Fates themselves. Pip can be read alongside these figures, but also aslant them. For in Pip, poor Alabama-boy Pip, the novel finds its chief emblem of *blighted* prophecy, of an experience untold and perhaps untellable. The significances here are clear: the rendering of Pip as the novel's foremost blighted prophet—Pip whom Stubb threatens to sell back in Alabama—argues as clearly as anything else in the novel that the danger and the terror for the nation that is launched with such heedlessness out onto the open seas of history is that it carries within it—not exterior to it—a story that cannot find a language in which to tell itself. Pip's incommunicability suggests a hole at the center of the nation, an extremity of experience that struggles to translate itself into something approximating legibility.

Incidents in the Life of a Slave Girl is that story. Or, to put it differently, it is an account of enslavement that at every moment foregrounds the problem of translation, of making communicable an experience that eludes even its subjects. A small but revealing moment comes early in the text, as the grandmother of Jacobs's narrative stand-in, Linda, witnesses the sale of her youngest son: "Could you have seen that mother clinging to her child, when they fastened the irons upon his wrists; could you have heard her heart-rending groans, and seen her bloodshot eyes wander wildly from face to face, vainly pleading for mercy; could you have witnessed that scene as I saw it, you would exclaim, *Slavery is damnable!* Benjamin, her youngest, her pet, was forever gone! She could not realize it" (*ILSG*, 23). One moral it seems *can* be made clear, according to Jacobs: slavery is wrong, is "damnable," and requires only witness. In some measure Jacobs's narrative, like others of the genre, means to provide precisely such witness through the mediating and distributive mechanisms of print and publication. But another, more deeply insoluble problem comes to the fore here as well, one that will mark the rest of the book's unfolding. "*She could not realize it,*" Jacobs writes, and intimates an incomprehensibility, a stark resistance to knowledge, at the root of the experience of enslavement. (This causes a tremor to run through the phrase "as I saw it," since part of what Jacobs may be seeing is the inadmissibility of slavery to acts of witnessing proper, even by those who experience it.) If this is the very definition of trauma—trauma as an occurrence that, because it cannot be assimilated in its totality *as* experience in the first place, must be returned to—Jacobs rings detailed and significant changes on the story of what *renders* the experience of enslavement so troubling to knowledge, what sets it so apart from the grids of comprehension in which one might try to figure it.

Several passages from a single chapter in the book, "A Perilous Passage in the Slave Girl's Life," bring the matter into exceptional clarity. Here Jacobs labors to give narrative form to a confession that, as she repeats, pains her terribly. Having, almost miraculously, held off her master's advances, and having parted with her first impassioned love—a free black man—she writes of becoming pregnant by "a white unmarried gentleman" (*ILSG*, 60). Here are the first stages of her approach:

> And now, reader, I come to a period in my unhappy life, which I would gladly forget if I could. The remembrance fills me with sorrow and shame. It pains me to tell you of it; but I have promised to tell you the truth, and I will do it honestly, let it cost me what it may. I will not try to screen myself behind the plea of compulsion from a master; for it was not so. Neither can I plead ignorance or thoughtlessness. For years, my master had done his utmost to pollute my mind with foul images, and to destroy the pure principles inculcated by my grandmother, and the good mistress of my childhood. The influences of slavery had had the same effect on me that they had on other young girls; they had made me prematurely knowing, concerning the evil ways of the world. I knew what I did, and I did it with deliberate calculation. (*ILSG*, 53–54)

The passage wrestles with a language of intention—alternatively of agency and culpability—that it finds neither satisfying nor dispensable. To offer a "plea" of compulsion or innocence is to misperceive her deliberateness, the self-possession with which she has acted. But what must figure too in her "calculation" are the malign "influences" of enslavement, and their range of "effect[s]." Conspicuously, there seems for Jacobs to be no secure ground in which to stake such claims of, in essence, agency and constraint in simultaneity.

The encounter with this groundlessness comes clearest in the astonishing density of a passage a few paragraphs later, whose stinging poignancy lies as much in its shifting microclimates of tone as in its famous ascent into declarative defiance.

> So much attention from a superior person was, of course, flattering; for human nature is the same in all. I also felt grateful for his sympathy, and encouraged by his kind words. It seemed to me a great thing to have such a friend. By degrees, a more tender feeling crept into my heart. He was an educated and eloquent gentleman; too eloquent, alas, for the poor slave girl who trusted in him. Of course I saw whither all this was tending. I knew the impassable gulf between us; but to be an object of interest to a man who is not married, and who is not her master, is agreeable to the pride and feelings of a slave, if her miserable situation has left her any pride or sentiment. It seems less degrading to give one's self, than to submit to compulsion. There is something akin to freedom in having a lover who has no control over you, except that which he gains by kindness and attachment. A master may treat you as rudely as he pleases, and you dare not speak; moreover, the wrong does not seem so great with an unmarried man, as with one who has a wife to be made unhappy. There may be sophistry in all this; but the condition of a slave confuses all principles of morality, and, in fact, renders the practice of them impossible. (*ILSG*, 54–55)

"He was an eloquent and educated gentleman," Jacobs writes, and then, striking the note of the ingénue, of the naïf in a novel of seduction, she avers, "*too eloquent, alas, for the poor slave girl who trusted in him.*" And yet nothing could be more rebuking to the tone of wounded innocence, and the conventions that attach to it, than the sentence that follows hard upon it, with its cynic's world-weary knowingness: "*Of course I saw whither all this was tending.*" Even to the propriety-shattering insight to which she soon turns—"There is something akin to freedom in having a lover"—Jacobs appends qualification, worrying that "there may be sophistry in all this."

What sounds here, I think, is not only Jacobs's pained ambivalence in relation to a standard of feminine propriety she can neither believe in, so badly does it misappraise the situation of the female slave, nor wholly renounce, not least because of how deeply she experiences that code of behavior in relation to the grandmother whom she loves and needs. (Dana Luciano explicates just this excruciated ambivalence as part of a dialectic of what she calls "*blameworthiness*," at the heart of which is "the sexualized female body as the unspeakable origin of maternal affection."[16]) Nor are its multidirectional evasions solely evidence of what Foreman calls Jacobs's strategy of "the undertell."[17] The swift movements between registers, the uneasy adoption of one language after another after another, the casting about among modes of self-explication that feel misapprehending, all speak pointedly instead to the anguish of a specific kind of *dispossession*. When Jacobs says, "the condition of a slave confuses all principles of morality," she underscores not so much her young self's naiveté as a frightening vacancy in the place where some adequate conceptual grounding of her experience might have presented itself, but did not. It is in these terms that I think we can most amply understand Lauren Berlant's claim that "Jacobs experiences as a fact of life the political meaninglessness of her own sensations," where that meaninglessness signifies in the register of an ungroundedness, a fearful dispossession, in the realm of intimate experience.[18]

And Jacobs herself has an account of this ungroundedness, of what sustains it and why it is so:

> But, O, ye happy women, whose purity has been sheltered from childhood, who have been free to choose the objects of your affection, whose homes are protected by law, do not judge the poor desolate slave girl too severely! *If slavery had been abolished, I, also, could have married the man of my choice; I could have had a home shielded by the laws; and I should have been spared the painful task of confessing what I am now about to relate*; but all my prospects had been blighted by slavery. (*ILSG*, 54, emphasis added)

Or again, when thinking of her first lover, whom she decides she must send away: "Even if he could have obtained permission to marry me while I was a slave, the marriage would give him no power to protect me from my master" (*ILSG*, 42). Or, more concisely than any of these: "*Why does the slave ever love?*" (*ILSG*, 37, emphasis added). Jacobs's experience is one of an intimate life cut away from the forms of protection, which are also the forms of *intelligibility*, that might allow her to "realize" it, or at least to make it narratable, even if not in what she calls "the usual way." Law, marriage, *love itself*: none of these ways of coding the body's extensions, or the sphere of its most intimate attachments, quite obtains for Jacobs. (When asked by Dr. Flint if she loves the man, Linda responds, "I am thankful that I do not despise him" [*ILSG*, 59].) This is part of what it means for her "to be entirely unprotected by law or custom" (*ILSG*, 55), this standing at the center of a vacancy filled chiefly by the affects that most register her dispossession: confusion, shame, occasional exhilaration, grief, pain. Startlingly like the immersive confrontation with the unwarped primal world that explodes Pip's lexicon, Jacobs's enslavement figures as a kind of exposure, an extremity of experience that devours the languages brought to the scene of its explication.

"O reader, can you imagine my joy?" Jacobs writes of her reunion with her son, and famously rejoins: "No, you cannot, unless you have been a slave-mother" (*ILSG*, 173). The moment of course offers as concise a critique as could be wished for of what Glenn Hendler describes as the sentimental "fantasy of experiential equivalence," wherein feeling with and for another becomes an erasure of the differences between the self and the object of sympathetic attachment.[19] But it is also, I would argue, a restatement of the problem at the heart of *Moby-Dick*, which concerns the simultaneous urgency and arduousness of making somehow comprehensible a shattering extremity of experience, an experience located in the spaces language won't go. A bit like *Moby-Dick*, at least in the figure of Pip, Jacobs locates that extremity in no far-off ocean but in the heart of antebellum American life—specifically, in the uncodable entanglements of ardor, calculation, compulsion, shame, and fear that is slavery's intimate life.

When Hortense Spillers asks us to wonder if the black woman can be said to possess a "sexuality"—when she observes that "the black female is, if anything, a creature of sex, but *sexuality* touches her nowhere"[20]—she has in mind, I think, a version of Jacobs's story, or her story's struggle. "The structure of unreality that the black woman must confront," she writes, in terms that again bring to mind *Moby-Dick*'s structuring figures,

> originates in the historical moment when language ceases to speak, the historical moment at which hierarchies of power (even the ones to which *some* black women belong) simply run out of terms because the empowered meets in the black female the veritable nemesis of degree and difference. . . . I am not addressing the black female in her historical

apprenticeship as an inferior social subject, but, rather, *the paradox of non-being* (emphasis added).[21]

Assimilable neither to emerging technologies of sexual science nor to an alliance model of generation, though shaped by the pressures of both, the sexuality of the female slave emerges in Jacobs as an insoluble incoherence, less deterritorialization than dispossession. As *Incidents* continually reminds its readers, the slave woman's dispossession, and the violence that enforces and accompanies it, magnetizes as well each and every one of the normative forms that live in contact with it. "That cage of obscene birds," is how Jacobs, borrowing from the Book of Revelation, refers to the slaveholding household, figuring there the derangement of *all* intimate forms entangled by what Spillers names the "chaos" mantling the sex of the black female slave (*ILSG*, 52). Slavery is, in this way,

> a curse to the whites as well as to the blacks. It makes the white fathers cruel and sensual; the sons violent and licentious; it contaminates the daughters, and makes the wives wretched. And as for the colored race, it needs an abler pen than mine to describe the extremity of their sufferings. (*ILSG*, 52)

It's true that Jacobs finds in the encounter with that space of chaotic, eroticized bearing toward the world, or in moments of its unfolding, "something akin to freedom." But such incoherence also brings to her, with what seems to be far greater insistence, an exceptional quantity of anguish. For *that* extremity, *Incidents* insists, no ordinary pen suffices, no ceremony avails, and marriage is no cure.

PART THREE

Speech and Silence

Reckonings of the Queer Future

5

The Tenderness of Beasts

Hawthorne at Blithedale

Favorable or Otherwise

What would it mean if, just this once, we were to read Hawthorne straight? With respect to *The Blithedale Romance*, nothing, it seems, has been less easily accomplished. In his famous preface to that novel of 1852—famous largely for its meditation on the perils and possibilities, for the "the American romancer," of "Fiction" in its relation to "everyday Probability"[1]—Hawthorne begs us to recall that the novel that follows, whatever its origins in "the Socialist Community" established at Brook Farm, emphatically does not "put forward the slightest pretensions to illustrate a theory, or elicit a conclusion, favorable or otherwise, in respect to Socialism" (*BR*, 1). This is perhaps the least believed-in sentence Hawthorne would ever write.

Over many decades, and for a range of plausible reasons, Americanist literary criticism has found the notion of Hawthorne's demurral from conclusiveness especially hard to credit, taking it, for the most part, as still another expression of the book's sustained and elegant duplicity. We might well wonder, though, what shape this "brightest" and "liveliest" of Hawthorne novels (as Henry James had it) might finally acquire if we were to read it apart from the set of morals we are often assured it elaborates: that philanthropy and utopian politics more generally are undertakings dangerously entangled with both fatuous self-deceit and megalomaniacal narcissism, and tend in this way toward various kinds of "moral obliquity," as our narrator Miles Coverdale puts it; that Brook Farm was accordingly a terrible failure; that, more abstractly, languages of mass politics and intimate politics function each as misarticulations of the sphere of the other, consigning both to terminal dissatisfaction; and that powerful women, whatever the strength and tenacity of their convictions, can be brought low by the errant swervings of their heart's passion.[2] Read in this way, *Blithedale* seems a not untypical exercise in what we might call

Hawthornean conservativism: an ambivalent, in many ways not wholly unsympathetic, account of the dangers, to the self but not only to the self, that come trundling in with the overstepping of the narrow parameters of tradition and convention and ordered social propriety.

No one would suggest there is nothing to such a reading, because of course there is. Any even cursory approach to the very plot of the novel, or to the fate of its main characters, would seem to confirm it: Zenobia is destroyed, Hollingsworth lives on a broken and diminished man, and Miles passes through the world meekly and melancholically, laboring to find, among his accumulated failures, a long-spent ambition to be proud of having once possessed. *Blithedale* reads in all these respects (and in ways that set it in intriguing conversation with the work of Hawthorne's Concord neighbor Thoreau) as a novel about disappointment, in its most spectacularly public and obliquely inward dimensions. Or so it would appear. But once we begin to take seriously even the glancing possibility that Hawthorne, in his admonition to his reader, might be doing something other than, for instance, *lying*, then precisely this sense of the book, as a rueful and satiric brief against heedless reformist zeal, changes its bearings dramatically. What sort of story does it become if we take that disavowal of specific political intent—which is also of course a reading of the novel—to express *not* the elemental duplicity Hawthorne shares with his famously unreliable narrator; not his carving out of a space free from strictly "political" discourse from which he might offer a different caliber of nevertheless explicitly political commentary;[3] not duplicity, masked intent, indirection, guarded but genuine contempt, or anything at all other than a frank avowal of broad agnosticism with respect to socialism and reform more generally, and a corollary desire to trace out the complexities of other sorts of questions and other sorts of dilemmas? What if the novel is *precisely* as described in the preface, holding in abeyance what are called "positions" with respect to the many vectors of contemporaneous politics that pass through it—the better, perhaps, to understand how such positions, dressed up in the guise of "theories" or "conclusions," might themselves be duplicities, masks of a sort, vehicles for other species of fear or longing?

If in what follows I do not accede wholly to the view that the novel expresses, with singular force, something like Hawthorne's visionary conservativism, it is less because I think such a reading untenable than because it is, in a way I want to specify, partial, pulling our attention as it does away from much of what I take to be most intriguing, unsettling, and finally suggestive about the novel. Following out different lines of interest, this chapter does not much address itself to the complexity of the book's views, favorable or otherwise, with respect to agrarian reform, communal living, nineteenth-century philanthropy, or transcendentalist-cum-utopian politics more generally. (We will not be dwelling much on Brook Farm itself, its history, or Hawthorne's time there in the early 1840s, nor for that matter on the question of "Romance" and its perils and possibilities, as adumbrated by a narrator so self-conscious about the practice of narrative.[4]) The readings that follow are anchored instead in a sense of the book as fascinated, above all else, by twinned conceptual dilemmas: by the problem of sexuality—and for this book, as we shall see, sexuality is in its promptings, urgencies, and bewilderments nothing if not a problem—in a moment of heightened social flux; and, relatedly, with the problem of freedom, of a specifically political and for the novel distinctively American sort of freedom, in its relation to what might be termed, in a word, terror. Freedom, terror, sex: these are the keywords in the readings that follow.[5]

Over the previous chapters I have been arguing that the mid-nineteenth century was a particularly vexed era in the history of sexuality, one that is distinguished by a fundamental uncertainty, very much at play in a novel from 1852, about just what is meant, and can be meant, by the word "sexuality." This is a moment, as we have seen, before the taxonomies that would come to seem simply commonsensical (the dividing of people into hetero-, homo-, and bisexual identities, say) had achieved their wide and solidified currency, but in which the movements toward that new mode of categorization were beginning to be felt. One of the great and edifying pleasures of *The Blithedale Romance*, I want now to suggest, is the exquisite clarity with which it renders the special tensions that so mark that moment, and renders, too, the *consequences* of those tensions, and the way they might branch fractally into other vectors of social life. "The text of *Blithedale* may be studiously chaste," Michael Colacurcio observes, "but its urgent subtext—*like the social pretext of this most daringly suggestive novel*—is unblushingly sexual," and it is just that coming-together of sexual subtext with political pretext that I wish to explicate (emphasis added).[6] With some pointedness, the novel reminds us that, whatever the languages of self-nomination available or not at midcentury, 1852 was plainly not a moment in which those later, as-yet-unsolidified forms of sexual stratification, of ordering in the sphere of sexuality, had no gravitational pull whatsoever. For Miles Coverdale at least, the linking of gender performance and gender difference to pathologies of sex is a process well underway, if not yet fully elaborated and coordinated. (It is precisely in the open spaces of that incomplete coordination that Coverdale, all unreliability and self-occlusion, is pleased to maneuver.) *Blithedale* gives us the story of a man who might plausibly be read according to a number of available midcentury types—the sexually ambiguous "bachelor" not least among them—but whose deepest anxieties suggest instead the unsettling *encroachment* of modes of sexual typology and specification still decades away from their rise to prominence. The novel in this way invites a reading less in terms of dreamed-toward futures that would not come to be (as we had seen in, say, Thoreau), or for that matter in conventionally Foucauldian terms of what hardens into contemporaneous "discourse," than as something considerably more untimely: the sketch of an anxious moment in which fragments of an unripened future made their first premonitory impressions.[7]

Following out these terms, I want to pick up on notes struck by critics like Benjamin Scott Grossberg, Barbara and Allen Lefcowitz, Lauren Berlant, and especially Robert K. Martin and Jordan Stein, and argue that *The Blithedale Romance*, despite its appearance some forty years before the infamy of Wilde, is one of the great American novels about homophobia.[8] (Not, crucially, a homophobic novel, but a novel *about* homophobia.) It is, that is, a novel both about the fear of the possibility of desire and sexual exchange between people of the same sex, and about a more cripplingly intimate fear of the possibility of such desire *in oneself.* And what gives the latter fear its shape in the novel, as it turns out, is, precisely, *politics*—or, in Hawthorne's own terms, theories, conclusions, typically of a politically condemnatory nature. Robert Levine astutely observes that even Coverdale's suspect political idealism ought not to be sweepingly dismissed but "taken seriously, for it speaks to Hawthorne's own attraction to the possibilities of reform."[9] Lauren Berlant, speaking of attraction to possibility, writes that, "As with Zenobia, Coverdale is attracted to Hollingsworth, and repulsed by his attraction."[10] Both of them, I think, are correct, which suggests much about how the crosswiring of intimate and social desire works in the novel. I take *Blithedale* finally to be the story of a man in panicked headlong flight from the kinds of specifically sexual freedom to which he is, to his own dismay, also powerfully attracted. His politics, which are so often taken for Hawthorne's own, are the form that flight takes.

Hawthorne's Givens

Why the persistence of readings of *Blithedale* as, finally and decisively, anti-utopian? Surely Hawthorne's own public political commitments inflect the matter, particularly as they were expressed in his now-infamous campaign biography of Franklin Pierce, his classmate and dear friend from his days at Bowdoin College. There, his ameliorationist stance toward slavery, and his hot disdain for the recklessness of abolition, expresses itself with little enough ambiguity, as Hawthorne lionizes the future president (who would reward Hawthorne with a hugely lucrative consulship, and who would later be ranked among the nation's more disastrously inept commanders-in-chief).[11]

More persuasive than any of this merely biographical evidence, though, are surely the veerings of the novel itself, which does not want for flights of satirical fancy with respect to reformers, and reform. There is the irony, listing toward something more like sarcasm, that again and again seeps through the pages. ("No sagacious man," Miles observes, "will long retain his sagacity, if he live exclusively among reformers and progressive people, without periodically returning into the settled system of things, to correct himself by a new observation from that old stand point" [*BR*, 140–41].) But there is also, more resonantly, the impassioned articulacy of sharper passages, moments less sarcastic than wrenching. Of the climactic moment in which Coverdale at last refuses Hollingsworth's plan to federate with him in a scheme to convert Blithedale into an institution for the reformation of criminals (a plan in which Coverdale finds "nothing but what was odious. . . . A great black ugliness of sin" [*BR*, 133]), he writes,

> Had I but touched his extended hand, Hollingsworth's magnetism would perhaps have penetrated me with his own conception of all these matters. But I stood aloof. I fortified myself with doubts whether his strength of purpose had not been too gigantic for his integrity, impelling him to trample on considerations that should have been paramount to every other (BR, 134).

Here we have one neatly telegraphed account of the oft-cited moral of the book: a reading of it as a story of the dangers, corrosive and evidently contagious, that attend the forcing of sympathy, a disregard for the weight of tradition, and the single-minded pursuit of some lofty ideal or other, whatever its assumed benignity of purpose. Under the force of such gusts of eloquence, fortified like Coverdale with such moral and political doubts, readers can hardly be blamed for taking up the book according to what Robert Levine describes as the "general consensus that *Blithedale* has to be read in conservative terms as an attack on the sentimental culture of reform." (*BR*, 224)[12]

The first point one might make with respect to such a consensus—and Levine makes it—is that the impassioned voice in the passage above belongs not to Nathaniel Hawthorne but to Miles Coverdale, of whom it seems fair to say (as Nabokov says of Humbert) that there are many points on which he and Hawthorne do not agree. Accordingly, not a few of those critics who reproduce, more or less entirely, this and similar perorations of Coverdale's as the moral of the novel itself, do so with an occasional sense of disquieting irony. But even when they do pause over the uncanny identification of the so unreliable Coverdale with the implied moral center of the novel itself—or, more plainly, with Hawthorne *in propria persona*—they persist in the claim that these indeed are Hawthorne's views (his conclusions, we might say), condensed and refracted in the enlivening form of a novel, and granted there a special kind of richness, complexity, and ethical density, not least *through* their placement in the mouth of a character so flawed. (Hawthorne, we might say, on this account gets to have his critique, to critique it, and to have it still.) In *Hawthorne's Shyness*, for example, Clark Davis follows critics like Charles Swann and Richard Brodhead in noting the especially pressing oddity of the fact that so spectacularly compromised a narrator, in a phrase he repeats, "sounds very much like Hawthorne."[13] "Given Hawthorne's skepticism," he argues, we can best appreciate Coverdale's narration as a meditation on ethics, point-of-view, and the practice of a species of political engagement pursued "not in spite of but *by means* of disengagement."[14]

But this is to beg the essential question: why, in the first place, take Hawthorne's skepticism as, in Clark's words, "given"? For my own part, I am not certain what Nathaniel Hawthorne—Bowdoin graduate, resident of Salem and Concord, and citizen of the American nineteenth century—believed about reform, though I might venture some informed surmises. Whatever Hawthorne himself did or did not believe, though, *The Blithedale Romance* is only very naively read as a transcription, or complex encoding, of those beliefs. To take up the novel as either political testimony or subtle code, to assume from the start the given-ness of Hawthorne's skepticism, is to discount the possibility that Hawthorne finds in his Miles Coverdale a vehicle with which he might *interrogate*, perhaps even to the point of disintegration, his own vexed inclinings and impulses (inclinings toward, for instance, conservativism). It may be, in other words, that the novel is only limitingly, and limitedly, approached as a kind of externalization, in fictional form, of what are Hawthorne's expressed "politics," his views, favorable and otherwise. Perhaps, to borrow a bit from Foucault, Hawthorne grants himself, in the fairy-land of fiction, a freedom even from his own morality when he writes. And perhaps he takes that freedom as an occasion to worry, in the most searching and articulate terms of which he is capable, over the very impulses he finds himself cherishing in his waking, public, political life.[15] All of these possibilities suggest a greater need to prize apart Coverdale and some hypothesized "Hawthorne" than is accomplished even with terms like "unreliable narrator" or "self-referentiality" or "irony." The relation between these figures, author and authored-author, pulses with a greater density, a richness of possibility and possible errancy, than such frameworks quite allow.

It is not, after all, merely the fact that the moralizing language employed with respect to reform comes from Coverdale that ought to give us pause. For the language itself—particularly the invocation of "a great black ugliness of sin"—echoes, in extravagantly complicating ways, other moments and other declamations in the novel. And, of course, whatever else is at stake in the climactic crisis between Miles and Hollingsworth, the passage is also, quite vividly, a break-up scene. How this is so, how it has come to this, requires some explication.

Love in the Ruins

What kind of man is this Miles Coverdale? He is, as we know, a poet— Zenobia begins by suggesting he is an accomplished one, though we may come eventually to suspect that this, on her part, is more finely-calibrated flirtation and flattery than honest assessment. As befits a man of such socially dubious occupation, Miles, at the outset, inhabits a demimonde that lies just on the outer edges of social propriety. Here is the novel's first sentence: "The evening before my departure for Blithedale, I was returning to my bachelor-apartments, after attending the wonderful exhibition of the Veiled Lady, when an elderly man of rather shabby appearance met me in an obscure part of the street" (*BR*, 5). Where do we find ourselves? We learn here that Coverdale is (not wholly unlike Hawthorne's Concord neighbor, Henry David Thoreau) a bachelor, and whatever resonance of sexual irregularity gathers in that word is only amplified by the other supplied details: his late-night presence in an "obscure part of the street," his involvement there with a person of "shabby appearance," and not least his attendance at "the wonderful exhibition of the Veiled Lady," an entertainment that is certainly not akin, in its measure of respectability, to a strip-show, but that is nevertheless hardly the most decorous way a respectable young man might spend his evening, or the most unbesmirchably chaste.[16] The whole atmosphere that surrounds Coverdale as we are introduced to him speaks to a kind of bohemian laxity—a life, again, placed on the blurred outer edges of respectability, with the possibility of some not necessarily *not* sexual sort of impropriety hovering, unconfirmed and unconfirmable, around and about it all.

This begins to explain why he takes up the opportunity to reside at the as-yet-unnamed Blithedale, despite his many and oft-repeated bouts of weariness, self-doubt, and cynicism. (He knows himself to be not really cut out for the labors he's set himself and, in case we have missed the point, he takes dreadfully ill *before* the first day's work commences.) For Blithedale, as we quickly come to learn, is a place where Coverdale might enjoy an intoxicating sort of freedom: a freedom, as it turns out, from the very codes of propriety and respectability toward which, back in his city life, he had stood in such intriguingly unsettled relation.

Perhaps the first thing we are given to note about Blithedale—beyond even the awkward class-mixing or naïve righteousness that come under such broadly satiric scrutiny—is the extraordinary quality of sexual frankness that prevails there, heralded not least by Zenobia, her singular beauty, and her equally singular forwardness. Fast upon his arrival, she begins flirting with Miles. (No fool, she goes right to his tenderest spot: she flatters his poet's vanity.) Coverdale's imagination, which we soon understand is an engine prone to overheating, needs little more prodding than Zenobia supplies to give itself over to this new climate of openness bordering on indelicacy. After Zenobia concludes a barbed and suggestive exchange with the assertion that, "As for the garb of Eden . . . I shall not assume it til after May-day!," Coverdale gives us an account of the range of her effects upon him. Look at this wonderful exchange, as Miles and Zenobia pursue their flirtation:

> Assuredly, Zenobia could not have intended it—the fault must have been entirely in my imagination—but these last words, together with something in her manner, irresistibly brought up a picture of that fine, perfectly

developed figure, in Eve's earliest garment. I almost fancied myself actually beholding it. Her free, careless, generous mode of expression often had this effect of creating images which, though pure, are hardly felt to be quite decorous when born of a thought that passes between man and woman. (16–17)

We will return in a moment to what Coverdale describes as the "fault" in his imagination. For now we can note merely that Coverdale himself recognizes the fact that to imagine, with whatever degree of vividness and detail, Zenobia standing before him quite completely nude is an exercise "hardly felt to be decorous"—is, in fact, a bit indecent. Neither, though, is the pleasure of that freedom of imagination lost on Miles. So intense is that pleasure, and so immediate and complete is his retreat from the actual labor of the farm, that we might at this point begin to suspect that it is the prospect of just this ambiguous sexual freedom, a freedom unto indelicacy, that had made the whole notion of Blithedale alluring to labor-averse Coverdale in the first place. He finds there, or thinks he finds there, a freedom to speak, look, imagine, and perhaps actually to live according to pleasingly remapped parameters of intimate life.

Zenobia is the first flashpoint for this attraction to Coverdale, and it is worth considering closely just what it is he finds so attractive in and about her. There is, of course, the resonant fact of her body. But Coverdale says intriguing things not only about the form and shape of that body, but about how it is worn, and its relation to the carriage of the other sorts of bodies, particularly female bodies, he has observed. "It did one good to see a fine intellect," he says of Zenobia, "so fitly cased." Her body, that is, expresses—to Coverdale, at least—something extraordinary about her mind, her person, her very being in the world. He specifies this as he goes on:

She was, indeed, an admirable figure of a woman, just on the hither verge of her richest maturity, with a combination of features it is safe to call remarkably beautiful, even if some fastidious persons might pronounce them a little deficient in softness and delicacy. But we find enough of those attributes, everywhere. Preferable—by way of variety, at least—was Zenobia's bloom, health, and vigor, which she possessed in such overflow that a man might well have fallen in love with her for their sake only. In her quiet moods, she seemed rather indolent; but when really in earnest, particularly if there were a spice of bitter feeling, she grew all alive, to her finger-tips. (15–16)

In the place of the attributes Coverdale associates with everyday femininity—softness, delicacy—he sees in Zenobia not just a refusal of conventionality but a fine and captivating sort of excess, the issue of which is a vitality, a full-blooded, positively luxuriant expansiveness of sensual being that Miles admires precisely because it outstrips, it "overflows," the chastening refinements and deadening constraints on feminine embodiment that he sees, as he says, "everywhere." (He routes that admiration through a typically circuitous kind of indirection, saying of her sensual vitality that some hypothetical "man," neither necessarily Miles nor not-Miles, "might" fall in love with her—and so would not necessarily do so—just for its sake alone.) If Coverdale is attracted to Zenobia—and "attraction" seems a toothless word for his feeling—that attraction has at its root Zenobia's capacity to exceed, to overspill, the strictures of merely conventional femininity. "We seldom meet women, now-a-days, and in this country," Coverdale says, "who impress us as being women at all; their sex fades away and goes for nothing, in ordinary intercourse. Not so with Zenobia" (*BR*, 17). The problem with standard-issue domestic, sentimental, white womanhood, in this reading, is not the compromised timidity of its politics or the forced falsity of its sentiments but, beyond all that, its thoroughgoing effacement of the *sex* in femininity—a sex that is, as Miles envisions it through Zenobia, no longer anemic and dematerialized but luxuriant, sensual, vital.[17]

Of course, much of the pleasure of Zenobia, and of the way she inhabits a womanliness that exceeds the confinements of "the feminine system," is for Coverdale the availability *to* him—to his speech, his sight, and above all to his imagination—that seems to follow from her unconventionality. (In a characteristic gesture of projection, Miles insists that it is Zenobia's demeanor, and not any lasciviousness of his own, that "has the effect of creating images" that are other than pure.[18]) As a range of critics and historians have observed, one of the chief consequences of the codes of middle-class gender propriety in the antebellum North—codes that increasingly isolated feminine virtue in the private sphere, where, through the saving power of "influence," it could work its tutelary magic upon men made corrupt by the market-driven avarice of public, commercial life—was the ever-increasing separation of men from women, and particularly unmarried men from unmarried women. The ideology of separate spheres played out not only in cleaving of public from private but also, less spectacularly but no less consequentially, in the more intimate realm of gendered and sexual *exchange*. It is G. J. Barker-Benfield's recurrent point in *The Horrors of the Half-Known Life* that young men had vastly more to do with each other than with young women, and vice-versa, such that respectable unmarried men and women were virtual strangers, if not to each other personally, then certainly to the worlds the other inhabited.[19] Neither the varied mystifications of sex that might follow from this circumstance, nor the intensities of same-sex attachment and devotion that would follow as well, are difficult to imagine.

We see the effects of this ideology of separateness—or rather, of its breaching—unfold in wonderfully vivid detail in the person of Miles Coverdale himself. Zenobia is so unabashedly frank in her manners and speech, her body displays such a richness of sensual vitality, that Coverdale cannot stop himself from imagining—and imagining, and imagining, and still again imagining—that she was somehow in possession of "a destiny already accomplished," that with her "the great event of a woman's existence had been consummated," and that she was "a woman to whom wedlock had thrown wide the gates of mystery" (46–47). "Zenobia," Miles tells himself in a kind of paroxysm of irresistible fancy, "is a wife!" It is a moment that recalls to us Coverdale's invocation, when he is first gazing upon Zenobia and picturing her naked, of the "fault" in his imagination. For here, Miles responds to what he calls "the freedom of her deportment" (*BR*, 47) with an answering freedom of imagination that begins with conjuring her disrobed and escalates swiftly from there, so much so that the incompleteness of his access to her, to her person, and the particularities of its history, begins to irk him. He says, amazingly, "A bachelor always feels himself defrauded, when he knows, or suspects, that any woman of his acquaintance has given herself away" (*BR*, 48). The feeling of having somehow been "defrauded" speaks as eloquently as any of Miles's other words or deeds to the degree to which Zenobia's freedom of manner has come to invest him with a remarkably expansive sense of his own entitlement *to* her. Zenobia herself notices the mutedly predatory aspects of Miles's attention: "I have been exposed to a great deal of eye-shot in the few years of my mixing in the world," she says to Coverdale, "but never, I think, to precisely such glances as you are in the habit of favoring me with" (*BR*, 47).

So Miles Coverdale, by this point, answers with wonderful readiness to any of a number of historical analogues in relation to which one might read him. In his infatuation with the kinds of access Zenobia's freedom from conventionality affords him, he exemplifies the tangled mystifications, of desire, sexual exchange, and women more generally, that a gendered ideology of separate spheres might provoke, particularly in a man who likes to think of himself as virtuously sexually progressive but who very much wishes as well to retain the considerable privileges his gender affords him. (It is an earlier instance of Coverdale's vacillation between a certain pleasure in aspects of gendered unconventionality and an ambivalent longing for the rewards, as well as the self-protections, of conventionality.) In the comforts of his unmarried and under-committed life, he seems to ring changes, too, on the figure of the bachelor, familiar in American literature since Irving and Cooper, at least, and brought into heightened legibility at midcentury by the publication of the wildly popular *Reveries of a Bachelor; or, A Book of the Heart* by IK Marvel (Donald Grant Mitchell).[20] There are also the more explicitly sexual contemporary scandals hanging in the air around Blithedale: the specter of a free-love radicalism (with ties to Fourier), of Mormon-like polygamy, of open marriage under the guise of communitarian reform. And we could note as well, returning to the matter of the "fault" in Coverdale's bachelor imagination, that Hawthorne invites for him a still-more-specifying sexual typology. For in his so thorough possession by flights of erotically tinged fancy—in that so vivid excess of imagination—Coverdale reads a bit like a monitory figure lifted from the pages of that early sensationalist/sexological genre, the anti-onanist tract. Coverdale, that is, in his reveries and almost involuntary passages of indecent imagining, seems very much to be suffering from the malady that would (as Eve Sedgwick, Vernon Rosario, and Thomas Laqueur have underscored) give shape to one of the earliest iterations of modern, specifically sexual, identity—that of the masturbator. He is, as the genre pioneered by Sylvester Graham with his 1848 *Lecture to Young Men* predicts, plagued by an imagination that will not be restrained, that leads him toward narcotically addictive visions of indecency and excess, and away from the forms of productive labor, economic and familial both, to which a man of his age should by now have turned himself.[21]

These historical analogues all are there to be read, certainly, and the novel can and will answer tellingly to all of them. But the trajectory of the novel also draws us, I think, in different directions, away from the basic fact of these available analogues, these typologies of sexual being with which Miles Coverdale's character, and the hothouse atmosphere of Blithedale, seem to accord, and out toward other dilemmas and possibilities. Especially in its dramatic turn toward Coverdale's own sudden and in many ways puzzling misgivings about the people with respect to whom he, early on, professes such ardor, the novel opens out toward questions parsed less easily in terms of contemporaneity than of, perhaps, the *premonitory*, of shards of a future not arrived but glimpsed in passages of anxious anticipation. Just as Coverdale's faulty imagination suggests the outlines of that premonitory figure of modern sexuality, the masturbator, so does the novel invite us to consider the dawning of the very possibility of sexual specification—of something like modern sexual identity, that would draw in and consolidate so many aspects of being and experience that had once been separable—and the shaping anxieties that possibility might provoke. *Blithedale*, then, is perhaps less an account of one man *as* a sexual category than of a man experiencing, with a radically disruptive ambivalence, the inchoate emergence of what we would later call "modern" sexual identity as such.

Dreadful Peculiarity

This emergence comes clearer when we recall that Zenobia is not the only figure to whom Miles becomes so deeply, if complicatedly, attached. There is also, as we have begun to see, Hollingsworth himself, who nurses the sickly Miles with "more than brotherly attendance" (*BR*, 41). That Miles finds Hollingsworth attractive, magnetic—indeed, that he loves him—is clear. Of that extraordinary sick-room care he writes,

> Hollingsworth's more than brotherly attendance gave me inexpressible comfort. Most men—and certainly I could not always claim to be one of the exceptions—have a natural indifference, if not an absolutely hostile feeling, towards those whom disease, or weakness, or calamity of any kind causes to falter and faint amid the rude jostle of our selfish existence. The education of Christianity, it is true, the sympathy of a like experience and the example of women, may soften and, possibly, subvert this ugly characteristic of our sex; but it is originally there, and has likewise its analogy in the practice of our brute brethren, who hunt the sick or disabled member of the herd from among them, as an enemy. It is for this reason that the stricken deer goes apart, and the sick lion grimly withdraws himself into his den. Except in love, or the attachments of kindred, or other very long and habitual affection, we really have no tenderness. But there was something of the woman moulded into the great, stalwart frame of Hollingsworth; nor was he ashamed of it, as men often

are of what is best in them, nor seemed ever to know that there was such a soft place in his heart. (*BR*, 41–42)

Two things are said here, though somewhat obliquely. The first is that, as far as Coverdale is concerned, Hollingsworth loves him. He is not kin to Miles, nor have they known each other long: his tenderness, the passage quietly avers, is the function of love. But Miles also intimates that whatever passion he feels for Hollingsworth kindles not in spite of but *for* the way he puts to rout to conventions of gendered behavior—for the way that something womanly is grafted onto him—and, importantly, for the way that womanliness is unaccompanied, in him, by *shame*. Hollingsworth appears to Miles as undisfigured by any corrosive sense of inadequacy, impropriety, or self-contempt; he feels what Miles considers to be an extraordinary freedom from shame with respect to his own capacities for tenderness—with respect, we might say, to the gendered errancies of his person, which in this instance express themselves in an ability to love outside the terms usually proscribed by masculinity. So it is that, in the throes of his illness, Coverdale comes to desire Hollingsworth, and him alone, for his "death-bed companion" (*BR*, 42).

We can note, at this point, the neat symmetry that seems to have been unfolded around Coverdale: as he was drawn to Zenobia and the way her rich carnality puts to rout the petty confines of proper femininity, so is he drawn precisely to and by that in Hollingsworth that runs sharply counter to the conventionalities of *his* gender. Evidently, Miles is a man deeply attracted to people—women or men—who refuse to conform to the expectations of their gender, and who accordingly live their lives in one measure or another at a distance from the "systems" of masculinity and femininity that circumscribe the respectable world of middle-class New England life. What Coverdale finds at Blithedale is an amazing freedom not only from the tawdry cares of the commercial world but from the rigid confines of gender that accompany that world. And this is a freedom, as we have seen so vividly with Zenobia, that swiftly translates into a beguiling sort of *erotic* possibility, the force of which, at the outset, all but sweeps Miles Coverdale off his feet. Coverdale himself (in retrospect, and through the distancing prism of other people's lives) recognizes as much, in a phrase that gathers up each and every lubricious resonance to be heard at midcentury in the term "association." He observes that "the footing, on which we all associated at Blithedale, was widely different from that of conventional society. While inclining us to the soft affections of the Golden Age, it seemed to authorize any individual, of either sex, to fall in love with any other, regardless of what would elsewhere be judged suitable and prudent. Accordingly, the tender passion was very rife among us" (*BR*, 72).[22] The tender passion is rife at Blithedale, and no wonder, since it is a place where freedom from specific gender constraints seems to pave the way for a whole set of as-yet-unexplored erotic possibilities. Dreaming the naked Zenobia before him, imagining himself handed into death by the loving and tender Hollingsworth, Miles himself appears to be, at first, no stranger to that passion's promptings.

It is here, though, that the novel begins to get, in what we might think of as the Nietzschean sense of the word, *interesting.*[23] For *The Blithedale Romance*, whatever else it may be, is not the story of a man who, unhappy with the dull confines of his life in the city, finds a freer community in which to take part, and there discovers unsuspected capacities—for love, for sex, for fulfillment more generally—which, in this new environment, he pursues toward their fruition. It might be more aptly described as the story of a man who, upon his removal into this new and freer environment, discovers in himself yearnings and inclinations and possibilities that fill him far less with hopeful expectation than with tremors of shame, of panic, and increasingly with something a lot like terror. What the rest of the novel narrates, in other words, is not Coverdale's embrace but his headlong flight from, his multifaceted and self-conflicted refusal of, the kinds of possibility, and specifically the kinds of love, Blithedale coaxes from him. The subtle contortions of that refusal—the misrecognitions, the obfuscations, the jarring substitutions—are worth looking at in some detail since they give to the rest of the novel its trajectory and form. But those alibis of Coverdale's, with all their chastening vehemence, give shape to something else as well: they comprise, finally, his *politics*, politics that, as we have seen, are regularly described as belonging no less to the novel, and to Hawthorne, than to Coverdale himself.

We can now consider more exactingly what is in many respects the first climax of the novel, the scene of Miles's break, or break-up, with Hollingsworth—and consider, too, the array of claims that surround it. "As I look back upon the scene," Coverdale writes,

> through the coldness and dimness of so many years, there is still a sensation as if Hollingsworth had caught hold of my heart, and were pulling it towards him with an almost irresistible force. It is a mystery to me how I withstood it. But, in truth, I saw in his scheme of philanthropy nothing

but what was odious. A loathsomeness that was to be forever in my daily work! A great black ugliness of sin, which he proposed to collect out of a thousand human hearts, and that we should spend our lives in an experiment of transmuting it into virtue! Had I but touched his extended hand, Hollingsworth's magnetism would perhaps have penetrated me with his own conception of all these matters. But I stood aloof. I fortified myself with doubts whether his strength of purpose had not been too gigantic for his integrity, impelling him to trample on considerations that should have been paramount to every other. (133–34)

Mark first how Coverdale says he experiences his own attraction to the possibility of life with Hollingsworth as something absolutely exterior to himself: he is not himself drawn to such a notion, this language insists; rather, it was "as if Hollingsworth had caught hold of my heart, and were pulling it toward him with an almost irresistible force." And notice, too, the swift escalation of condemnatory language he uses to describe not the possibility of a life-defining intimacy with Hollingsworth but the philanthropic enterprise he proposes: "A loathsomeness. . . . A great black ugliness of sin." It is absolutely Hawthornean language, familiar to us from early-career stories like "Alice Doane's Appeal" right through novels like *The Scarlet Letter*. But is *philanthropy* what's on Miles's mind here? Is the reformation of criminals what calls from him such high-flown vehemence? We have, after all, heard something of this language before, not only in "Young Goodman Brown," and not in reference to Hollingsworth's philanthropy.

Here is the language with which Hollingsworth himself, earlier in the novel and after much insinuating goading from Coverdale, had described Charles Fourier, the social theorist who has had the temerity to place sexual liberation—particularly the abolition of property in women via marriage and monogamy[24]—at the center of his social scheme:

"Let me hear no more of it!" cried he, in utter disgust. "I will never forgive this fellow! He has committed the Unpardonable Sin! For what more monstrous iniquity could the Devil himself contrive, than to choose the selfish principle—the principle of all human wrong, the very blackness of man's heart, the portion of ourselves which we shudder at, and which it is the whole aim of spiritual discipline to eradicate—to choose it as the master-workman of his system? To seize upon and foster whatever vile, petty, sordid, filthy, bestial, and abominable corruptions have cankered into our nature, to be the efficient instruments of his infernal regeneration!" (*BR*, 53)

Hollingsworth throws his Calvinist revulsion before ineradicable human depravity into high gear here, turning sex into a monstrosity the horror of which cannot, it seems, be exhausted by any hyperbole. "The Unpardonable Sin . . . the very blackness of man's heart": this is rich rhetoric indeed. But it does not disappear in the novel. For when Coverdale, the better to fortify himself against Hollingsworth's sinister "magnetism," describes that man's philanthropic project to himself, he applies to it exactly this language of moral opprobrium, a language first employed in relation to a blackness of human sin that is anchored, quite particularly, in the depravities of sex. And this magnetizes Coverdale's earlier, striking intimation that "there was a stern and dreadful peculiarity in this man, such as could not prove otherwise than pernicious to the happiness of those who should be drawn into too intimate a connection with him. He was not altogether human" (*BR*, 70). If we suspect that Miles's attacks on Hollingsworth—his stories about him—draw some of their urgency from fears of Miles's own, then what the coordination of these sentences underscores is that Miles's keenest fear is of an attachment to Hollingsworth, a deeper intimacy that will in its intensity and peculiarity somehow be tinctured by the threatening possibility of sex. More than this, the specter of sex, of some desiring element in Hollingsworth's so passionate attachment to him, has provoked in Miles a broad condemnation of Hollingsworth's very personhood, has anchored an account of some dire and disfiguring "peculiarity" in him that unbalances the whole of his moral character and estranges him, in Miles's view, from any familiar human-ness. It is a peculiarity that Miles evidently fears might infect, and perhaps work its own disfiguring magic within, his own identity, should his resistance to it waver in the least.

Is this to suggest that Hollingsworth, or for that matter Coverdale, is homosexual? In one fairly limited sense, the answer has to be no: we ought not to describe these characters as "homosexual" or as "gay men" because built into those terms are ways of conceptualizing desire and its relation to identity, to personhood, that (as we have seen) in the mid-nineteenth century simply had not come into currency, and would not for nearly fifty years. But the fact that there is no easily applicable contemporaneous terminology for what looks to us, today, like homosexuality plainly does not mean that there was not intimacy, ardor, attraction, desire, or indeed sex between people of the same gender, even if it does make same-sex intimacy in the era before our commonplace taxonomies intriguingly difficult to read, inasmuch as we must labor to see through and around the prism of our own conceptual categories and into an experience that was, necessarily, ordered and conceived differently. (Hollingsworth, for instance, expresses a patent horror of sex—he calls it, in his least gothic appellation, the "selfish principle"—but we are left to wonder if that horror is reserved for the *procreative* sex Fourier has in mind, for sex between men and women specifically, and so not for whatever forms of impassioned intimacy he might imagine can take place between men like himself and Coverdale.) But Coverdale's fits of panic allow us to see with splendid clarity how, in the first place, the unloosening of gender constraints—that unloosening so nurtured and encouraged at Blithedale—might itself carry in its wake new and bracing and, for Coverdale at least, deeply unsettling possibilities for desire, for intimacy, and for sexual exchange. In an era before the hardening of nonnormative sexual practices into stigmatized identities, Hawthorne gives us a novel about not only the undiscovered possibilities for sexual exchange that may lay just beyond the horizon of the current upheaval in gender, but about the varieties of fear—of intimate, duplicitous self-fear—those possibilities might provoke.

What seems finally more crucial than the designation of Coverdale or Hollingsworth as this or that "type" of character—bachelor, sex-radical, homo or hetero—is the fury of defensiveness Hollingsworth's proposal, and indeed his whole magnetic person, comes to evoke in Coverdale. He rejects the philanthropic endeavor that Hollingsworth proposes to make the basis of their life together, but rejects it as though it were an unwanted sexual advance—the attraction of which, as we have seen, Miles labors quite strenuously to locate outside of any impulse in himself. (That attraction is, Miles says, solely a function of the penetrating magnetism of that other man, the one with some inhuman peculiarity in him.) For Coverdale, it seems, there is something deeply beguiling about gender nonconformity; we have seen it in his relations with Zenobia no less than in his relations with Hollingsworth. But it seems clear as well that gender nonconformity broaches possibilities—for attraction, for love, for sex—that are to Miles so intimately disquieting, so disordering to his sense of who he is and must be, that he refuses even to grant them conscious audition, of whatever sort, preferring instead—in absolutely typical Hawthornean fashion—to project outward, onto proximate others, all the possibilities for errancy he cannot bear to acknowledge in himself. As Robert K. Martin has it, "Coverdale's thoughts express, of course, an anxiety on his part that originates not so much in Hollingsworth's violation of gender categories as his own."[25] And this self-terror—Miles, we might say, *is* a man who is acutely ashamed of what Hollingsworth, for one, believes might be best in him—speaks as well to an encroaching but clearly disquieting anxiety about the comprehensive ways errant possibilities for attraction or love or sex might unravel personhood itself, might, in the language of critics that would come much later, spoil the whole of an identity that Miles, whatever his momentary investments in gender and sexual unconventionality, is unwilling to surrender. His subsequent longings for conventional gender roles—his ambivalent envy of the domineering Westervelt and Hollingsworth, his urges to shame Zenobia for her high-handedness with him—are part of his self-defensive retreat from the unnerving sexual possibilities that errancies in gender seem to him to raise. An unloosening of restraints in gender broaches the possibility of specifically erotic unconventionality at Blithedale. But that possibility broaches in turn the prospect of a marking of moral character, of personhood more broadly, *according* to erotic predilection, that Miles cannot abide. His is an intimation of something like sexual identity—specifying, saturating the character, expressing itself as a peculiarity of self at once distinguishing and ineradicable—and he wants nothing of it. It is a novel in which a form of sexual typology that would arrive fully only decades later casts its shadow, as it were, backwards: a novel of intimation, untimeliness, and, above all else, fear.

These recognitions—historical recognitions, we could say, or recognitions of the staggered temporality of the novel's sexual historicism—carry with them, I think, some expansive critical consequences, not least where the novel's much-remarked politics are concerned. For when Miles recoils in horror before the idea of Hollingsworth's philanthropy, we do well to read that horror, that utter condemnation, with special care. As he himself all but says, Miles's horror in these moments draws much of its force from his need to scare himself away from what he otherwise might desire (a life with Hollingsworth, say, and all that may, or may not, imply). He needs, very badly, to "fortify himself with doubts" about Hollingsworth, to establish some kind of resistance to an attraction he labors to locate not in his own desires but in Hollingsworth's magnetism. What horror is heaped upon Hollingsworth as amorally selfish, on philanthropy as a species of misbegotten egotism, and on the naiveté of utopianism more generally, is in this way excruciatingly difficult to separate from Miles's own smothered self-horror, from the homophobia that is so much the novel's point of fascination. Political critique, that is, works chiefly for Miles as a kind of prophylaxis, a shield against his impassioned, vibrant, unacceptable attractions. All of the seemingly clear and stark moral compass points of the novel come unstuck when we recall Miles's passionate investment in the reading of the people surrounding him at a certain self-protective angle, an investment chiefly energized, as I have tried to suggest, by the effort to mask the unsettling yearnings he has found not in other people but in himself. Of course, the famous stammering last line of the novel ("I—I myself—was—in love—with—Priscilla") does much to confirm just this reading, as it is there that Miles assures us that, no, he was never passionately attached to any of the magnetic, beautiful, gender nonconforming figures he has paraded across the stage, but was always, in truth, in secret, in love with the very most tame, the very most conventional, the very most submissive and utterly normative character in the whole of the narrative. To the degree that we understand Miles to be in the protracted throes of a kind of sexual panic, to just that degree must our sense of the novel as performing some sort of sweeping condemnation of Hollingsworth, of Zenobia, or of utopian yearning itself be significantly mitigated. For this to be the essentially conservative novel it is often taken to be, it would, finally, have to think far more uncritically than it does of the way its narrator *uses* nominally political condemnation to police his own desires, and to have less sharply in focus Coverdale's horror in the face of all that he might become.[26]

None of this is to say that Hollingsworth is not iniquitous in his plotting, nor that Zenobia is not ruthless when she endeavors to return Priscilla to her weird captivity with Westervelt and in so doing loses her inheritance, which Moodie/Fauntleroy then bestows upon Priscilla (causing Hollingsworth to take *her* up, causing Zenobia in turn to drown herself). But our reading of Miles as in the grip of an anxiety at once sexualized and strangely anticipatory—anticipating the precipitation of something like a spoiled identity through his affiliation with a man like Hollingsworth—does complicate accounts of the novel as an expression of Hawthorne's vexed but finally stolid conservatism, his cautionary distrust of cause-driven social engineering, the discarding of traditions however entrapping, and the pursuit of ampler freedoms. Those notes are there in the novel, to be sure, but the more prominent dilemmas the work engages involve instead the complicated self-deceptions that sustain Miles Coverdale and allow him to keep forever at bay the desire, in himself, to live otherwise. Sex, as we have seen, is at the root both of the other life Coverdale begins to imagine for himself and of his passionate efforts at self-deceit.

Freedom and Terror

To say sexual possibility and sexual anxiety stand at the defining center of *The Blithedale Romance* is not to reduce the novel to sex, or to collapse what might be called its political imagination into the realm of frustrated erotics. I take the point to be, rather, that sex operates for Hawthorne as a key vector for thinking through other sorts of problems, national and political problems among them. As intimate life finds itself less in the sway of hardened identities than of new, half-formed emergences, Hawthorne offers sex as a suddenly exquisite register of the most pressing questions of national life and what he might have called national character. In this instance, and like many authors before him—like many in his immediate surround—Hawthorne seems to me finally interested, in *The Blithedale Romance*, in capturing something of the intricacy of the experience of freedom. Of course "freedom," in one conceptual shape or other, had long been an anchoring note in American self-conception by the time Hawthorne wrote, and was an already indispensable element in the stories the nation liked to tell itself about itself. This was indeed the substance of so much of the cultural energy and optimism radiating out of a Transcendentalist hub like Concord. Born in a moment of decisive break from an Old World ancestry, Americans could enjoy the pleasure of imagining themselves the inheritors of a whole range of freedoms: the freedom to venture (which would often translate, more mundanely, as a freedom to acquire), the Gatsby-like freedom to change, to reinvent oneself, to be born anew, or for that matter the freedom to rebuild the world, to make, as some of the Puritan forefathers had it, a new Jerusalem here in this land located at a safe remove from the corruptions and decay of old Europe. As his Puritan tales of violent and guilty origins make evident, Hawthorne had a keen and skeptical ear for this sort of national imagining.[27] So it is perhaps not surprising that when he comes to anatomize the *experience* of that freedom, he imagines it in terms rather more bracing and uncomforting than otherwise. In and through the person of Miles Coverdale, Hawthorne envisions the experience of freedom at midcentury to be quite densely interwoven not only with dilemmas of sex and sexual possibility, but more generally with sharp senses of isolation, dread, estrangement, instability, and finally a kind of *terror*. (In Miles's case, this is an escalating self-terror.) To be cut loose from the familiar moorings of self-definition, to be set down in an environment charged more with possibility than with constraint, to be confronted by the chaos of an unstructured world with no protective membrane of customary practices and beliefs and rituals to shield the self from the world's violence and tumult: these are not, for Miles at least, altogether pleasant experiences. We could call this an expression of Hawthornean conservatism but this seems to me to misappraise the matter. In all, the unmooring of the self that freedom promises is an experience every bit as terrorizing as it is exhilarating—we might think here of Emerson, who in Nature famously finds himself "glad to the brink of fear"—and Hawthorne's is an especially responsive book about the density and ramifying complexity of one man's recoil from just that terror.

And Miles is not alone. We can think of many an analogue: there is Hawthorne's impetuous former friend Herman Melville, whose rollicking novel of whale-hunting begins in an atmosphere of expansive unconstraint—signing himself up as a sailor, for Ishmael, is an escape from the land-locked pieties and plaster-bound strictures of daily life and into the illimitable possibility of the sea—only to darken, as Melville begins to worry, deeply and passionately, over what such freedom might entail. Recall, in this respect, the unmoored crew's utter vulnerability to the tyrannical magnetism of Ahab; or, better still, think again of cast-away Pip, the black cabin boy who, when dropped into the ocean behind a chasing whale-boat and abandoned in the midst of the sea, experiences that widening unconstraint as unbearable and, finally, self-obliterating, and so falters into madness. Whatever its exhilarations, to be unmoored, Melville's novel suggests, is painfully proximate to being orphaned, or to being cast away into frantic and death-stricken incommunicability.[28] Or think finally of *The Adventures of Huckleberry Finn*, a novel whose astounding rhetorical agility and sustained humor can distract us from the fact that its hero, unbroken and irrepressible though he may be, also spends a great deal of the book literally struck dumb with fear, oppressed by a loneliness so intense and so paralyzing that he is only able to live out and make use of his freedom when he is accompanied by a man not his father, not kin to him, and pointedly, painfully, *not* free: the slave Jim, without whose presence Huck's freedom is unbearable to him.[29]

All of which is only to say again that the conjoining of terror and freedom, which seems so modern a concern, has a long and storied history in American literary imagining. Hawthorne rings changes on this tradition by offering the story of a man who is, finally, terrified by what it is he might want—by the kinds of love his strong attractions seem to imply—and who ties himself into knots in the effort to evade or outpace that terror. Here, several generations before the advent of the categories of sexual deviance that are the very grammar and syntax of today's sexual common sense, is a novel about, again, *homophobia*: an intimate sexualized self-fear. And this so intimate fear is, no less intriguingly, a terror linked back to freedom, specifically a freedom from gendered conventions that broaches alarming new possibilities for intimacy. Like not a few other American texts of the nineteenth century, *The Blithedale Romance* suggests, with some force, that freedom is neither the opposite of terror nor its cure, but the substance from which it is born.

6

Made for Love

Olive Chancellor, Henry James,
and The Bostonians

In the early course of her intimacy with Kate Croy—an "intimacy as deep as it had been sudden"—Milly Theale, death-stricken heroine of Henry James's 1902 novel *The Wings of the Dove*, wonders over the labyrinthine silences that so strangely animate her new fast friendship.[1] "What had happened," James writes, his free indirect discourse routed in this instance through Milly's consciousness,

> was that afterward, on separation, she wondered if the matter hadn't mainly been that she herself was so 'other,' so taken up with the unspoken; the strangest thing of all being, still subsequently, that when she asked herself how Kate could have failed to feel it she became conscious of being here on the edge of a great darkness. She should never know how Kate truly felt about anything such a one as Milly Theale should give her to feel. Kate would never—and not from ill will nor from duplicity, but from a sort of failure of common terms—reduce it to such a one's comprehension or put it within her convenience. (*WD*, 177)

Milly's curiosity poses a series of questions that are themselves writ large across the whole of *Wings*, a book famously about "the unspoken" and what it can effect, suspend, or sustain.[2] Through Milly James seems to wonder: What happens between people when they want for "common terms"? What happens to something—a relation, a wish, an aspect of being—when it is unnameable, or is somehow rendered so? What does the corralling of something expansive, protean, and elusive—a relation, a wish, an aspect of being—in the narrow parameters of a name, of "common terms," do to it? Is that namelessness a kind of brutality? ("Kate wasn't brutally brutal—which Milly had hitherto benightedly supposed the only way; she wasn't even aggressively so, but rather indifferently, defensively and, as it might be said, by the habit of anticipation" [*WD*, 171].) Or is it pleasure? ("Yet on the spot [Milly] . . . knew herself handled and again, as she had been the night before, dealt with—absolutely even dealt with for her greater pleasure" [*WD*, 243].) Is it important to maintain, even momentarily, the distinction between these anguishes and delights?

James's consideration of the limits of the speakable are also, that is to say, explorations of the efficacies of wordlessness and namelessness, and they mark his late fiction especially dramatically—fiction composed after the catastrophic failure of his play *Guy Domville* in 1895, which is also, of course, the year of Wilde's gripping, terrible trials.[3] Whatever else they may have done, those trials could only have brought home the more forcefully to James a painful intractability in questions of sex and sexual naming, an intractability he would spend much of the next decade turning into a singular, even exemplary style of modernist fiction.[4] For Wilde's suit and countersuit mark the moment in which homosexuality, particularly in men, comes at once to be persecuted in the most spectacularly punitive ways but also to establish itself, in "common terms," *as* an identity (and, so, as a mode of recognition as well, a locus for a shielding sort of community of organized resistance to the tenor of those common terms).[5] We have seen in previous chapters the array of losses entailed in that hardening-into-place of modern sexual identity, losses of errant, oblique, expansive ways of imagining sexual being. James's career spans the breadth of the period of transformation we have been considering. We have remarked already, in his 1914 letter to Annie Fields, James's wistful nostalgia for the looser codes, and perhaps more occult legibilities, of a moment before Wilde—and this squares well with the familiar sense of the late fiction as preoccupied with silence, and with the singular power of things left protractedly unspoken. But James's disposition was not always thus. Perhaps surprisingly, a younger James found room to wonder over not the freedom but the pains, even unto anguish, of *namelessness*.

Such pain is on richest display in *The Bostonians*, a novel published in 1886, set in the 1870s, and, for my purposes, perhaps most aptly contextualized by Annamarie Jagose. Jagose astutely reminds us that "the novel's narrative ambivalence is structured less across character than across a sexual field whose defining coordinates have not yet hardened off," with the result that, by 1885, "on the cusp of its possible sexualization . . . the Boston marriage see-sawed between respectability and perversion." So it is, Jagose argues, that the novel finds James "taking up the disconnected discourses of a not fully superceded female homosociality on the one hand and a not fully intelligible female homosexuality on the other, and running the former as interference for the latter."[6] The matter is not that this novel from the in-between time before the Wilde cataclysm finds James any less suspicious of explicitness than he would be in the later fiction, with its famously unresolving attenuations (attenuations inflected perhaps by the vividness of Wilde's excoriation). But *The Bostonians* does find James far more preoccupied than he would become with the question of how one might suffer under the condition not of naming but of unnameability, of a silence experienced less as freeing than as asphyxiating. The vehicle for James's consideration of such suffering, I want to suggest, is Olive Chancellor.

This is in certain ways a counterintuitive claim, though it is far less so now than it would have been only a few decades ago. The emergence of a queer James in criticism has made it appreciably easier to limn the lines of identification, however fraught, between James and the "morbid" Olive. (Of that emergence Tessa Hadley writes pithily, at the outset of her *Henry James and the Imagination of Pleasure*: "There has been a quiet revolution: new readings in the last ten years or so have overturned our perceptions of the erotic in Henry James's fictions."[7]) But for decades, as Alfred Habegger notes, readings of the novel tended to underscore the ferocity of its satire of, in effect, all that Olive might be imagined to stand for: feminism, progress, benevolent causes, and, for that matter, the legitimacy and integrity of her Boston marriage with Verena Tarrant. Not at all unreasonably, the novel has been taken to represent James at his most arch, crypto-conservative, and cheerfully, even hysterically misogynist. From its exuberantly belittling account of reformers, the atmosphere of their sociability, and the tenor of their ambitions, we can see the justice of some of these appraisals.[8]

Without quite disputing the reading of the novel as committedly, perhaps even hysterically, misogynist, I want to take up the strand of James criticism (pioneered especially by Judith Fetterley, Joseph Litvak, Valerie Rohy, and Annamarie Jagose) that might allow us to see more clearly the novel's strange and often torturous generosity to Olive Chancellor, the ardent feminist, would-be reformer, and above all the impassioned partner of Verena, the young woman with whom she enjoys an intimacy in which there are "elements which made it probably as complete as any (between women) that had ever existed."[9] Olive's love for Verena, that is to say, is the novel's figure for the unprecedented. This unprecedentedness is what makes Olive, in a novel preoccupied with the bearing of history in an increasingly crass and commercial present, so much a problem, and her story so much a tragedy.

In a piece not itself about James, Eve Sedgwick gives us one template for understanding how this might work. She wonders, in *Tendencies*, about how far desire might "swerve"—"how radically will it misrecognize itself," she asks—in the absence of an articulate set of terms in which it might come into meaning.[10] For Olive, I want to suggest, reformist feminism is the closest approximation of a language in which her passion for Verena might find a kind of shelter. If the novel delightedly and mean-spiritedly and indeed misogynistically heaps opprobrium on that feminism, it nevertheless nurtures an open-heartedness and a generosity toward Olive that is rooted in precisely the sense of feminism as a sort of forced and debilitating *misapprehension*, an inadequate substitute in the place of which there are, for Olive, no immediately better options. The silence that veritably constitutes Olive has at its heart a yearning, outsized in its passion, for articulacy. The novel may satirize the language it finds for itself, and even Olive's swerving accession to it. But James treats with an astounding tenderness—even a kind of reverence—the yearning itself.

Along the way to limning the possibility that even a woman like Olive Chancellor is (as Basil says of Verena) "made for love" (*B*, 257), the novel invites us to consider, too, the complications involved in what we have been calling, thus far, earliness and expectancy. Expectancy travels under different names in the novel, and the most essential of them is, simply, *progress*. (One of the things James sets against progress, as we shall see, is "taste.") The novel's investment in competing rhetorics of "the emergent," that is, speaks not least to its attentiveness to what Jennifer Fleissner calls "the ongoing presence of an as yet unrealized future within the confines of the historical instance."[11] Writers are not prophets, but it is not difficult to imagine how the fate of Wilde might have sharpened the skepticism James proffers in *The Bostonians*, with an only slight leavening of ambivalence, about the happily forward march of progress, particularly where sex is concerned. And yet, if *The Bostonians* finds James unwilling to embrace hopeful expectancy as any kind of sufficiently rigorous disposition toward the world, *neither will he foreswear it*, nor dismiss how great a human necessity it might be for those afflicted by any number of kinds of silence. In the person of Olive Chancellor, the novel finds a way to respect—even, finally, to cherish—the vast hunger for relief that might stand behind expectancy, that yearning for some upheaval that might at last give words to an otherwise disfiguring namelessness.

Silent Sufferings

In a characteristically forceful reading, Leo Bersani, in *Intimacies*, describes James's story "The Beast in the Jungle" as a searching, if finally timid, meditation on the possibilities for radically defamiliarized sorts of attachment, intimacies rooted not in the "psychic density" of consolidated subjecthood but in the "pure virtuality," "the unrealized being" certain species of talk, freed from the possibility of sex, appear to liberate.[12] He reads John Marcher's famous unresponsiveness to the love May Bartram offers him in "Beast" as something other than it has commonly been known: neither a paralytic fear of love nor the mark of a foreclosed homosexual possibility. It is instead, to Bersani, an exploration of the contours of what he calls "impersonal intimacy," a notion he adapts from a Lacan-inflected understanding of the unconscious less as "the hiding place of the repressed" than "the reservoir of possibility, of all that might be but is not" (29, 24, 25). Talk, exemplified for Bersani as much by the psychoanalytic exchange as by Bartram's with Marcher, is what nurtures this "hypothetical subjectivity"—"a special kind of talk unconstrained by any consequences other than further talk"—and it aims "to free desiring fantasies from psychological constraints, thereby treating the unconscious not as the determinant depth of being but, instead, as de-realized being, as never more than potential being" (*I*, 28). Bartram allows Marcher access to this mode of subjectivity through the nonsexual talk she occasions and sustains, a subjectivity lived out, by Marcher, chiefly as what Bersani calls "*a constant sense of expectation*" (*I*, 29, emphasis added).

For Bersani, the delicate parsing of "conversation suspended in virtuality" (*I*, 28) is both the triumph of "Beast" and the scene of its gravest disappointment. Thinking of the melancholy ending of the tale (where Marcher weeps at the grave of Bartram, whom he recognizes himself as having failed to love), Bersani essentially scolds James for a failure of nerve and a concession to the normative. The story, we are told, "retreats from its images of indefinitely suspended being" (*I*, 29). (Or again: "James retreats from the remarkable singularity of his story . . . by specifying Marcher's 'it' as the reprehensible failure to add passion to talk" [*I*, 27].) And perhaps this is the tale's moral. Yet it might be possible to understand James's disappointing "retreat" from the prospect of virtual being and impersonal intimacy as something other than a failure of nerve. (There is, it must be said, little more conventional at the moment than accounts of James as a man whose nerve, sexually speaking, is forever failing him.) What if we understand that "retreat" less as cowardice than as, say, a species of calibrated, considered *ambivalence*? What if James turns away from states of being defined by suspension and an unbroken constancy of expectation not in deference to some conventionality, sexual or otherwise, but in consideration of the kinds of confinement, debilitation, and even anguish that might accompany them? Ambivalence, that is, is not necessarily the same thing as failure.

Olive Chancellor, in *The Bostonians*, knows what it is to live a life of expectancy. Her commitment to causes, after all, can be generalized as a commitment to *progress*: to the bringing about of a future that ameliorates, upends, or redresses what are, to her, the inequities of the present. "It was the usual things of life," we are told early on, "that filled her with silent rage; which was natural enough, inasmuch as, to her vision, almost everything that was usual was iniquitous" (*B*, 11). To be in sympathy with the new ideas, as she fears her exotic Southern cousin Basil will not prove to be, is not only to be firm in the belief in "the iniquity of most arrangements" (*B*, 23) but to live in the expectation of a better day's arrival. Yet Olive does not experience this reformist expectancy with anything like tranquility, or for that matter with any of the release of virtual being. Expectation, for Olive, is a state far more grinding, and ceaselessly tumultuous, than expansive. (Her nature, we are informed at our very first introduction to her, "was like a skiff in a stormy sea" [*B*, 10].) For her, to live in expectancy is, most often, to be captivated by an uncomfortable, even frantic sort of yearning. If Thoreau's yearning takes the form of a complex disappointment, Olive's lives out, chiefly, as suffering.

This is so, at least in part, because the condition from which that yearnful expectation emerges is Olive's *silence*—recall from above her "silent rage"—a feature no less than elemental to her character and her being in the world. Speaking of "her shyness," the novel specifies it as "the conscious, anxious silence to which she was so much of the time condemned" (*B*, 119). (Indeed, in his initial sketch of the novel sent to his publisher, James defines Olive and Verena's relationship in precisely the terms of the latter's speech-making fluency and the former's pained silence.[13]) Readers of the later James, in particular, are by now used to rather different, largely valedictory accounts of silence, figured often—and often by James *in propria persona*—as a kind of haven for a satisfying expansiveness of meaning, undistorted by mere denotation and its narrow confinements. Perhaps the most famous passages to this effect come in James's preface to *The Turn of the Screw*, where he argues for the superiority of aesthetic effect achieved by an ambiguity, resolutely unresolving, that is sustained through protracted *refusals* of naming, an unceasing turning-away from "weak specifications." "Portentous evil," James writes there, "how was I to save that, as an intention on the part of my demon-spirits, from the drop, the comparative vulgarity, inevitably attending, throughout the whole range of possible brief illustration, the offered example, the imputed vice, the cited act, the limited deplorable presentable instance?"[14] Meaning freed from denotation, possibility unmoored from action or determination: as Bersani rightly intuits, these are at the very core of late-Jamesian fiction, with its deferrals, its suspensions, its infinite attenuations, and its exquisite delicacy with respect to any particular cited act or "imputed vice."

It is remarkable to consider how little this is Olive's silence. Basil is correct when in his first blush of meeting Olive he notes that "exhilaration, if it ever visited her, was dumb," though James leaves it to his reader to grasp in that phrase a larger and more awful implication than Basil yet surmises (*B*, 17). For all the intensities of being by which Olive wishes to define herself (rage, captivation, delight), there are, it seems, no words— only an echoing silence, and the strange variety of shame that goes with it, visited upon her in "fits of tragic shyness, during which she was unable to meet even her own eyes in the mirror" (*B*, 10). Nothing more completely anchors Olive's devotion to feminism than this afflicting, corrosive silence, a point to which the novel, at the outset, returns with something like relentlessness. "I want to enter into the lives of women who are lonely," Olive proclaims to Mrs. Farrinder, "who are piteous. I want to be near to them—to help them. I want to do something—oh, I should like so to speak!" (*B*, 30). Or, as we are told shortly after this exchange: "The unhappiness of women! The voice of their silent suffering was always in her ears" (*B*, 30). In fact, when Olive herself puzzles over the nice matter of how, precisely, pert young Verena "had got her 'intense realization' of the suffering of women," she comes to an inevitable conclusion: "Olive was sure that Verena's prophetic impulse had not been stirred by the chatter of women (Miss Chancellor knew that sound as well as any one); it had proceeded rather out of their silence" (*B*, 67). For Olive, wordlessness is the condition that underpins the "tragic shyness" in which she feels so often and so helplessly entrapped. And it is on the basis of precisely that feeling—of a shamed, exposed, imprisoning sort of wordlessness—that Olive builds not only her love for Verena (who with her easy fluency *can* speak) but her own passionate identification with the hard and lowly lot of women. Despite the provisions of her wealth, it is the feeling that defines for her the experience of womanhood.

It is hard not to read precisely this turn—Olive's identification with the suffering of women via her own acute sense of being silenced—as, in effect, the ground-zero of the novel's withering satire. Particularly in the novel's first book, though not solely there, we are invited to regard Olive's embrace of feminism with perhaps less blustering affront than her sister, Mrs. Luna, but with about as much bemusement. Again and again the narrative hastens to remind us of the patent mismatch between, for instance, Olive's material circumstances (recall the splendid interior of the home into which she first welcomes Basil, which strikes him, naïf that he is, as veritably opulent[15]) and the states of oppression with which she longs to identify and cast her lot. We could think of the sharp comedy of Olive's exchange with the imperious reformer Mrs. Farrinder ("Mrs. Farrinder, at almost any time, had the air of being introduced by a few remarks" [*B*, 25]) in which Olive is essentially, and gracelessly, primed by the famous woman for her cash. Or think of Olive's fumbling efforts "to know intimately some *very* poor girl":

> This might seem one of the most accessible of pleasures; but, in point of fact, she had not found it so. There were two or three pale shop-maidens whose acquaintance she had sought; but they had seemed afraid of her, and the attempt had come to nothing. She took them more tragically than they took themselves; they couldn't make out what she wanted them to do, and they always ended by being odiously mixed up with Charlie. Charlie was a young man in a white overcoat and a paper collar; it was for him, in the last analysis, that they cared much the most. They cared far more about Charlie than about the ballot. (*B*, 29)

The awkwardness and misunderstanding here, as between people sharing no language between them, underscores what we might take to be the novel's broadest strain of satire, a mocking—not always gentle—of the pretensions of a person as rich in comfort as Olive laying claim to so forceful an identification with the downtrodden.[16] In this respect, *The Bostonians* can seem to be about the folly, evidently quite common in Boston, of mistaking private unhappiness for legitimate public grievance.

And yet it is not clear that this and the novel's other, more and less hysterical assaults on reform in general and feminism in particular amount to *the same thing* as a maligning of, or thoroughgoing distaste for, Olive Chancellor. In a complicated way, it might be, with respect to Olive, another vector of its strange and unsettled love. In the first place, the mismatch between her sensibilities and the environments of reform is a fact hardly lost on Olive herself. "With her immense sympathy for reform," we are told, "she found herself so often wishing that reformers were a little different. . . . All sorts of inferior people lived [in Beacon Street], and so brilliant a woman as Mrs. Farrinder, who lived at Roxbury, ought not to mix things up. It was, of course, very wretched to be irritated by such mistakes; but this was not the first time Miss Chancellor had observed that the possession of nerves was not by itself a reason for embracing the new truths" (*B*, 28). If this is a cause of fresh pain for Olive—she experiences her pangs and scruples as "wretched"—still what we might call her acuity with respect to status and taste is as ineradicable a part of her character as her prodigious capacity for suffering: "Even among reformers, she discriminated; she thought all wise people wanted great changes, but the votaries of change were not necessarily wise" (*B*, 66). Indeed one of the most potent through-lines of the narrative's unforesworn affection of Olive seems to reside precisely in her capacity, underscored here, for *discrimination* and its corollary: her finely-tuned sense of the vulgar. "Olive Chancellor," we are assured, in case the narrative had not yet been sufficiently clear on this point, "despised vulgarity, and had a scent for it which she followed up even in her own family" (*B*, 87). Not unlike the occluded but at moments nevertheless positively punitive narrative voice, Olive knows vulgarity when it presents itself, in whatever garb.[17]

The matter is not only that the novel finds common ground with Olive in an essentially elitist savoring of invidious distinction. At least part of the point here, too, resides in the redoubled suffering this trait—call it, for the moment, her "taste"—brings to Olive, a wretchedness rooted both in her exposure to a vulgarity that disheartens her and in her sense that the very impulse to notice such vulgarity is a mark of some grave insufficiency of devotion, or of genuineness, in respect to reform. The mismatch between her sensibilities and the movements with which she longs so passionately to identify herself is, in other words, the occasion for still another variety of pain for Olive. This seems to me to complicate a reading of the novel as being at Olive's expense (though it does so without much dismantling the novel's elemental anti-feminism). For it is the *clarity* of that pain in the narrative—an insistence on its special gravity—that, more than any disparagement of Basil, everywhere counter-balances the mocking depictions of Olive's pretenses to broad solidarity. The vividness of that pain returns us to what James would have us understand as Olive's special predicament, her ill-at-homeness even in the worlds in which she hopes to find succor and relief. Her suffering, James insists both mockingly *and* tenderly, is not the same as that of other women, and has no easy equivalence in the world of reformers. It is, perhaps, a silence not to be ameliorated even by the winning of the ballot.

At the center of that silence, of course, is what Jagose calls Olive's "unmarriageability"—her comprehensive estrangement from the styles, the rituals, and the manifold forms of belonging, comfort, privacy, entitlement, and more general *meaning* that travel under the sign of heterosexual marriage. Such is at least part of what is at stake in the novel's famous account of Olive: "There are women who are unmarried by accident, and others who are unmarried by option; but Olive Chancellor was unmarried by every implication of her being. She was a spinster as Shelley was a lyric poet, or as the month of August is sultry" (*B*, 16). Critics are of course right to point to this as a moment in which Olive's protolesbianism speaks up particularly forcefully. And yet this quasi-ontological account of Olive's unmarriageability is I think far less crucial to the novel than the *yearning*—impassioned, convulsive, very nearly disabling—that accompanies it. For Olive, to be unmarried by every implication of her being is most elementally, as the novel portrays it, to be in the grip of a constant, perplexing, buffeting sort of desire, for which there seems, at least until the advent of Verena, no available satisfaction, and precious little hope of one. (Hence Jagose's splendid description of Olive as "the saddest sexual community of one, her dispositions marking her out as a 'type' without the bolstering context of those others whom she might typify."[18]) We are told of Olive, as she considers the affect-effect of her first sight of Verena, "Her emotion was still acute . . . and what kept it, above all, from subsiding was her sense that she found here what she had been looking for so long—a friend of her own sex with whom she might have a union of soul" (*B*, 63). What most gives shape to Olive's restlessness, her uneasiness in the worlds in which she finds herself, is precisely this *wish*, this hunger for a woman with whom she might have, as James puts it with signature breadth, a union of soul. It is a desire that comes coupled in the novel with the other defining ardor of her life: "The most secret, the most sacred hope of her nature was that she might some day have such a chance, that she might be a martyr and die for something" (*B*, 12). And this pairing makes sense. Where there is a yearning so swallowed up by wordlessness, James implies, there is the concomitant wish to turn the unrelieved pain of it into something other than silence, something monumental and above all available for a kind of recognition, a kind of *history*: a martyrdom, then, a suffering exteriorized and made other than unsignifying.

Olive's unmarriageability, I mean to suggest, is a function less of what Basil is pleased to call her morbidity than of her *passion*. For all her reserve, all her brittle sobriety, Olive lives as the novel's emblem of the impassioned life. (Sorrow too, we might say, is one of the passions.) Consider the conclusion to which Basil himself is drawn at the novel's climax, as he prepares to spirit Verena away from her great public debut, and from Olive:

> The expression of her face was a thing to remain with him for ever; it was impossible to imagine a more vivid presentment of blighted hope and wounded pride. Dry, desperate, rigid, she yet wavered and seemed uncertain; her pale, glittering eyes straining forward, as if they were looking for death. Ransom had a vision, even at that crowded moment, that if she could have met it there and then, bristling with steel or lurid with fire, she would have rushed on it without a tremor, like the heroine that she was (*B*, 348)

"*Like the heroine that she was*": if Olive is a heroine—and in this moment the novel seems to insist, I think unironically, that she is—it is a heroism anchored in precisely a Joan-of-Arc-like passion, an outsized, all-consuming yearning made only the more lacerating for the confusions, silences, and misapprehensions that entangle its aim. At certain moments, though, that aim appears quite unmystified. Take this revelation, from the midst of Olive's agonized day of waiting for Verena to return from her afternoon's sojourn with Basil ("It was a day she was destined never to forget; she felt it to be the saddest, the most wounding of her life" [*B*, 316]): "Oh, Olive knew that she loved him—*knew what the passion was with which the girl had to struggle*" (*B*, 317, emphasis added). Olive *knows* what Verena struggles with in respect to Basil: what elsewhere goes under the sign of "a union of soul" is here, in her recognition of Verena's own struggle, called simply "love." What Basil says of Verena we might take as the novel's own account of Olive: despite being "profoundly unconscious of it," despite the way "another ideal, crude and thin and artificial, had interposed itself," still, beyond all this, she is "made for love" (*B*, 257).

If there is little unclear about the belittling unseriousness of the novel's regard for the projects of feminist reform it features—if the novel finds it virtually impossible to grant genuine gravity to the idea of an elemental injustice done to women *as* women—it nevertheless takes the contours and complications of Olive Chancellor's suffering very seriously indeed. Her suffering, and the impassioned yearning that fuels it, make her, in James's own terms, the novel's heroine. We could treat this fact as evidence of the work's failure to be, in any conceptually rich sense, political: as a matter, say, of its adherence to the delimiting, privatizing conventions of domestic fiction, in which private turmoil, however framed by social conditioning, trumps political or institutional analysis, imagination, and critique.[19] From the perspective of the novel's treatment of feminist reform, this may be fair enough. But there may be something more, and perhaps more complex, to James's regard for feminism as the misbegotten sign of, and vehicle for, Olive's suffering. What afflicts Olive, as we have begun to see, is a desire for what the novel itself names simply "love," a desire that can accrue to itself so little in the way of sufficiently ratifying languages that Olive experiences her longing as, most elementally, an immersion in silence. Her awkwardness, her dryness, her embarrassment, all the pains of her life in the social world: these are not, then, the after-effects of something like repression, of a refusal to give conscious audition to desires she fears to name. Olive suffers instead something closer to what Judith Butler helps us to recognize as the melancholia proper to an object not so much repressed as foreclosed—the blocked mourning, that is, for a loss that was itself never articulable, that could never take shape as a possibility that might, in turn, be subject to refusal or repression.[20] In this reading, "feminism" becomes the emblem of Olive's specifically queer melancholia. It marks the foreclosed possibility of the love for which she yearns so passionately; and it carries, too, all the distortion, all the misapprehension, and of course the pain, proper to melancholia.

Or perhaps we should put it a bit differently. Through the prism of misapprehensions of his own, we might say, James finds in Olive a way to anatomize the fate of a person made for love, but not heterosexuality, in the dwindling moment before new names for that queer love would achieve a definitive prominence. As we saw in the introduction, James did not regard that coming-into-articulacy with relief, or gratitude, or much of anything other than a melancholic longing for the time *before*, with its more oblique forms of signification and also, perhaps, with the greater freedom that obliquity afforded. (Recall once more W. D. Stead's letter to Edward Carpenter: "A few more cases like Oscar Wilde's," he wrote, "and we should find the freedom of comradeship now possible to men seriously impaired to the permanent detriment of the race."[21]) In *The Bostonians*, though, whatever sheltering wordlessness the older James would mourn appears as its own kind of affliction, the condition that drives Olive, with her unanswerable yearnings, to endeavor to embody herself in a cause that, whatever its self-distortions, at least promises her the possibility of a kind of articulacy, and so a kind of relief. Both options, as James depicts them, issue in pain. (As Olive pushes Verena toward her public unveiling, the better to render her unfit for Basil, Ransom surveys the scene and recognizes the turmoil it has all represented for Olive: "what he saw was Olive, struggling and yielding, making every sacrifice of taste for the sake of the largest hearing, and conforming herself to a great popular system" [*B*, 335].) To be made for love but not heterosexual romance in the 1870s, in James's account from the 1880s, is to be caught on the horns of a dilemma. For Olive, it is to be caught between a hunger for articulacy that might make the constant pain of muteness somehow less, on the one hand, and on the other languages that misrecognize that love in ways that are themselves painful and even disfiguring. So it is that Olive is all of the above: made for love, dry, brittle, heroic in passion, and possessed above all of a fearful power of suffering.

Sex, Taste, Time

What does it mean, though, to describe feminism as a misrecognition of Olive's desire, a swerving (in Sedgwick's terms) away from its proper if unavowable object? What precisely *disqualifies* feminism, or the discourses of reform more generally, as viable languages of relief for Olive, at least as James would have us understand them? And what for that matter disqualifies the ideal of romantic friendship, what Jagose refers to as "the discourse of a not fully superceded female homosociality"? If, as Jagose suggests, the novel takes place in the midst of a shift from female homosociality to "a not fully intelligible female homosexuality," then what are we to make of Olive's sustained refusals, her ill-at-homeness in either language?[22] In other words, there *are* modes of understanding, emerging languages and forms, that might be imagined to provide Olive some means of recognition. Why do they not? What fuels her refusal, and with it what James wishes us to understand as her misrecognition of herself in the languages of feminism and reform?[23]

These questions take us in new directions, as well as some old ones. To suggest that *The Bostonians* is a novel of sex and misrecognition might be, in the first place, to ring changes on an oft-told story of the novel: it might, that is, be a way of noting how James produces a strong, surpassingly subtle reading of the work of one of his most admired forebears. That James has Hawthorne's *The Blithedale Romance* somewhere in mind as he fashions *The Bostonians* is, I think, beyond dispute, although as far as James seems to read it *Blithedale* is instructive not only as a work about the ironies of sympathy and reform, or of women in public life. It is most telling for James's purposes, I think, as a kind of case study in the intimacy of desire and revulsion, and in the misapprehensions that intimacy generates. (Recall the Miles Coverdale we described in the previous chapter: powerfully attracted to gender unconventionality, and in a panicked projective flight from that desire.) *The Bostonians* inherits and inflects these visions of desire and misrecognition and shapes them around a sexual dispensation that has shifted in important ways since the 1850s. In his own moment, James takes up a novel about homophobia—Miles's paralyzing self-fear—and emerges with a work less about its heroine's homophobia than about the seeming remainderlessness of heterosexuality and its institutions, and about the intimate distortions and misperceptions that might follow from so airless a state of affairs.

So what is it that renders feminism so poor and misapprehending a vehicle for Olive? If it is so poor, why does she take it up, and with such vehemence? In some ways, the question is out of order. We need only to remember the unseriousness of the novel's regard for feminism as a political cause—an unseriousness punctuated at moments (to which we will soon turn) but steady enough across the breadth of the book that readings of it as finally and irremediably misogynist make, at the very least, a viable kind of sense. A more theoretically-minded reader might, in Sedgwickian terms, appraise Olive as a figure who anticipates the necessarily vexed, ever-unsettled relation of feminism to queer studies: modes of inquiry and critique that can neither function coherently without acknowledgment of one another, nor without distinction between them. Both approaches can be, I think, fruitful. But the novel's own terms of evaluation seem to me differently calibrated. For the viability of feminism for Olive is not quite a theoretical problem, of the sort that might be familiar to us from decades of queer scholarship that has sought to distinguish sex from gender without severing the ties between them. In *The Bostonians* it is more a problem of *time*. Or, in James's own terms, as well as Olive's, it might properly be described as a problem of "taste."

Nothing diagnoses the fluctuating state of "feminism" in the novel's scales of value more clearly than the treatment of one of its incidental characters, Miss Birdseye. And nothing makes clearer than that treatment the terms in which the novel's sense of value accrues. Miss Birdseye's initial appearance finds James at not only his most ungenerous but also, manifestly, his most unsubtle. The broadside assault on her character that appears in chapter four proceeds without even the familiar deflection, or ironic modulation, of indirect discourses. She is, we are told, "a confused, entangled, inconsequent, discursive old woman, whose charity began at home and ended nowhere, whose credulity kept pace with it, and who knew less about her fellow-creatures, if possible, after fifty years of humanitarian zeal, than on the day she had gone into the field to testify against the iniquity of most arrangements" (*B*, 23). This unforgiving estimation of Miss Birdseye comes not from the refracted, necessarily limited consciousness of one of the novel's other characters but, in a way that is startling, from the omniscient narrative voice itself. "She was in love," we are told acidly, "only with causes, and she languished only for emancipations" (*B*, 23), and her personal lovelessness—so opposed to the high passions about to engulf Olive, Basil, and Verena—reads here as a mark of her wholesale moral inconsequence, and of the absurdity of any movement that could revere her.

But then something strange happens. It is hard on this passage, with its nod to Miss Birdseye's "delicate, dirty, democratic little hand" (*B*, 23), that we are told that, in her life among reformers, Olive's "most poignant suffering came from the injury to her taste" (*B*, 25)—which might induce us to wonder: of what is Olive's taste made, exactly? We see a bit of it of course in the rich interior of the home to which she welcomes Basil at the novel's outset: "He had never felt himself in the presence of so much organised privacy or of so many objects that spoke of habits and tastes" (14). But another indication of how precisely "taste" signifies comes in what we might call the novel's softening toward Miss Birdseye, a modulation of regard that, given the initial treatment, is itself remarkable. That softening commences with a meditation of Olive's, in the period of her deep study with Verena.

> It struck Miss Chancellor that this frumpy little missionary was the last
> link in a tradition, and that when she should be called away the heroic age

of New England life—the age of plain living and high thinking, of pure ideals and earnest effort, of moral passion and noble experiment—would effectually be closed. It was the perennial freshness of Miss Birdseye's faith that had had such a contagion for these modern maidens, the unquenched flame of her transcendentalism, the simplicity of her vision, the way in which, in spite of mistakes, deceptions, the changing fashions of reform, which make the remedies of a previous generation look as ridiculous as their bonnets, the only thing that was still actual for her was the elevation of the species by the reading of Emerson and the frequentation of Tremont Temple. (*B*, 139)

If Miss Birdseye seems less absurd here it is because she suddenly appears in, and actually *as*, history, as "the last link in a tradition." What disperses the dirty democratic vulgarity with which she is initially charged is, in this account, nothing other than a sense of her historical embeddedness. Just that embeddedness is crucial to Olive, particularly in the urgency of her desire, as Fleissner has it, "to remove Verena from the vagaries of the present day altogether, to submerge both of them in the grand sweep of history."[24] In the absence of that time-ripened quality there are, it seems, only injuries to taste.

Miss Birdseye's apotheosis in the novel, it transpires, unfolds in just these terms. At the end of the novel, before her death but in the period of her decline, Basil discovers Miss Birdseye asleep, with a beautiful seaside New England view spread before her: "She appeared to him, as the minutes elapsed and he sat beside her, the incarnation of well-earned rest, of patient, submissive superannuation. At the end of her long day's work she might have been placed there to enjoy this dim prevision of the peaceful river, the gleaming shores, of the paradise her unselfish life had certainly qualified her to enter, and which, apparently, would so soon be opened to her" (280). From a grubby purveyor of mindless and inefficacious charity to, finally, one of heaven's anointed: the revolution in the novel's regard for Miss Birdseye is complete. A figure of and agent in history, she no longer affronts the "taste" the narrative repeatedly invokes, and accordingly finds a place of value, surprisingly high, in the novel's parsing of worth. Having served history, she is freed from it, mantled in nobility. Her final peroration, too, does its part to unsettle any easy sense of the novel as, uninflectedly or monolithically, antiprogressive. "You mustn't think there's no progress," she says, "because you don't see it all right off; that's what I wanted to say. It isn't till you have gone a long way that you can feel what's been done. That's what I see when I look back from here; I see that the community wasn't half waked up when I was young" (*B*, 310).

The strange career of Miss Birdseye shows us more than the instability of James's putative hostility toward feminism and reform. Her gentle admonition stands as a kind of counterpoint in the novel, here offered perhaps not wholly without ironic inflection but as gently, and as generously, as anywhere else. But Miss Birdseye's emergence as the novel's chief figure for historical unfolding, and for the accretive movements visible only over deep time, also gives point to the dilemma through which Olive suffers, and which is most on James's mind. Like the omniscient narrative consciousness that sometimes limits itself to her perspective, Olive experiences the world around her through the prism of an ineradicable, to her often painful, sense of "taste." For the novel's purposes, that taste consists in something more than an attentiveness to the codes, forms, and usages of social propriety. It signifies, too, a cultivated sort of bearing in and toward *time*. Taste, that is, names a specific sort of historical-mindedness, for James a sensitivity to the density of meaning and resonance that accrues over life spans, in the slow time of generations. In this way the niceties of taste emerge less as comic embroidery in the novel than as markers of one of its chief preoccupations: How, James worries, can a nation as unballasted by centuries-deep history make room for vital new emergences, without the unprecedented devolving into the cheapness of capitalist publicity culture, with its proliferating commodities and its ravenous hunger for mere novelty? What space can there be for the unprecedented, and for the vitality it might bring, in a world as dense with sensationalist vulgarity as the one ushered in by newsman Matthias Pardon or his covetous shadow Selah Tarrant?

Olive, of course, suffers her taste acutely, and on a number of fronts. It keeps before her, always, what she understands as the uniform brutality—the brutality of men, to women—of all of history; complicatingly, it sponsors in her an unwelcome discomfort with respect to the sociability, and parvenu atmosphere, of reform movements. And perhaps more than any of this, it leaves her with passions, involving the possibility of a union of soul with another woman, that fall so far afield of what might be ratified by precedent to be, as we have seen, virtually unavowable. Think of how Olive bristles when the nature of her passion for Verena comes in even remote proximity to direct naming—perhaps as the "not wholly intelligible," but then not wholly *illegible*, "female homosexuality" to which Jagose refers. There is this splendid exchange between Olive and the imposing Mrs. Burrage, mother of Verena's suitor:

"It's very true that you may ask me," added Mrs. Burrage, smiling, "how you can take a favourable view of a young man who wants to marry the very person in the world you want most to keep unmarried!"

This description of Verena was of course perfectly correct; but it was not agreeable to Olive to have the fact in question so clearly perceived, even by a person who expressed it with an air intimating that there was nothing in the world she couldn't understand. (*B*, 238)

To be understood in the presence of so cultivated and insinuatingly "worldly" a figure as Mrs. Burrage, and in the context of talk of the rituals of heterosexuality, is for Olive almost as wretched as to be smothered in silence.

We have seen over the course of several chapters now a number of expressions of what we have called the earliness of sexuality—of a sexuality not yet bound into the coordinated linkages it would come to be under the sign of modern sexuality, and not yet wholly captivated by the languages in which it more and more found itself spoken. In the figure of Olive Chancellor, earliness take shape neither as the condition that permits a freedom for errant imagining (such as we see in Thoreau and Whitman) nor even the shelter from vulgar nomination James would later suggest in his letter to Annie Fields. Earliness, for Olive, is instead a mode of affliction. What makes feminism painful to Olive is, we are told, the wounds it delivers to her "taste"—which is one way of gesturing toward its only marginal historical embeddedness, at least as James offers it. (The more deeply it can be woven into an historical narrative, granted an enriching past—as in the person of Miss Birdseye—the more viable it becomes in the novel.) But what makes feminism indispensable to Olive is the absence of any even comparably marginal precedent, any rich and accessible and legitimating *past*, for her desires. To be without precedent for Olive is at once a thing she longs for—in her politics, in her intimacy with Verena—and a thing that fills her with grave disquiet. She suffers, throughout, exactly this dichotomy.

In this respect the "contest" between Olive and Basil is scarcely that. Though possessed of wealth, security, status, and no shortage of fierce passion, Olive's desire—for a union of soul with another woman—is forever being set against not just Basil, with his handsome face and slender prospects, but the vastness of precedent, only barely distinguished from History itself, he carries about in his pocket, strictly by virtue of his capacity to offer Verena what Olive categorically cannot: marriage, as time-saturated institution and ritual, and with it singular access to a breadth of accumulated meaning and legitimacy with which there is, literally, nothing to compare. There is perhaps a kind of shelter for her desire, a room for respectability and disavowal both, in the increasingly antiquated languages of female friendship, as critics have observed. But as Olive keeps being bluntly reminded, there is not, in such friendship, anything like the absolute form of shelter and deference and privacy—without which, of course, desire itself can exist only as sickness, sin, or crime—that might be claimed by the time-enriched institution of marriage. Sharon Marcus may indeed be correct when she insists that, in England in the 1860s and '70s, "the female couple was accepted as a variation on legal marriage, not treated as a separate species," as well as in her claim that the resulting "female marriage" was "readily integrated into even the most restrictive ideas of social order." But even that acceptance, the function, as Marcus keenly observes, of a social *network* and pointedly not a *subculture*, suffers no less from the delibility, the comparative historical weightlessness, proper to an intimate formation that is, whatever its local recognitions, *detachable* from the temporally-accumulative institutions of culture and of law.[25] The worldly-wise Mrs. Burrage speaks this damning truth to Olive. "Don't attempt the impossible," she tells her. "You have got hold of a good thing; don't spoil it by trying to stretch it too far" (*B*, 243). This is Olive's pain in a word: she knows what it is to be impossible.

For all its satire, the novel, as I have suggested, makes Olive its "heroine," and at least part of what invests her with a tragic sort of heroism is how manifestly overmatched she is in the battle she has no choice but to fight, pitched as it is less against the person of Basil Ransom, whatever his charms, than against the weight of accumulated time itself, as neatly and, for her, brutally condensed by and in marriage. To be at once unmarried by every implication of your being *and* made for love, as the novel suggests is the case with Olive, is as James understands it to be wounded by history—we might think again of Jameson: "History is what hurts"—but, cruelly, not sufficiently *in* it, or of it.[26] It is to be extant but impossible. It is to be left to grapple as best you can with disfiguring silence, misrecognizing articulacy, and a species of unprecedentedness that, if you are tuned like Olive or, for that matter, like the organizing consciousness James orchestrates, leaves you ever-vulnerable to a sense of your own unviability. And so there is Olive as we first find her, "unable to meet even her own eyes in the mirror" (*B*, 10).

Accreted Time

How James imagines his own reflection is of course another matter, in respect to which *The Bostonians* provides at best a very limited kind of evidence. And yet it is immensely, almost irresistibly suggestive to think of Olive as one of the sorts of reflections into which James could gaze with searching attentiveness—a reflection put at a manageable distance by decades, by geography, and by gender. We might, for instance, think of the world of female friendship, and its decline into something more erotically suspect, as seeming to James an especially ripe theme. He might, that is, take up the decline of female friendship as a vehicle for exploring a similar, though less specifiable and less precise contraction: the loss of the open world of male intimacy whose other name, as Eve Sedgwick long ago reminded us, is *patriarchy*. That decline is something James intuits, and in *The Bostonians* protractedly worries over—again, at a distance, and through the threatening sexualization of a more familiar, more legible intimate form, the Boston marriage.[27]

But there is more than this. We know well enough that James was, temperamentally, no heedless Emersonian. Where Emerson everywhere valorized the emergent over the established, the unforeseen over the settled notion—and so built up a framework for the valorization of American intellectual and artistic achievement—James fretted, memorably and at length, over the impoverishment of American cultural inheritance. His 1879 biography of Hawthorne, with its famous catalogue of all that America must do without ("no country gentlemen, no palaces, no castles, nor manors, nor old country houses, nor parsonages, nor thatched cottages nor ivied ruins"), reminds us that the effect of the comparative historylessness of America "upon an English or a French imagination, would probably as a general thing be appalling."[28] Removing himself to Europe, and immersing himself there in the denser sociability to which his novels constantly refer, James lives out a preference for what we might call accreted time: for a world saturated in whatever of time gathers, accumulates, becomes monumental. In this, he marks a distance from the figures we have seen already—Whitman, Thoreau—that is as much intellectual and temperamental as it is geographic.

And it is erotic. Olive, we might say, exteriorizes an ambivalence that, for James, would only grow more acute. The novel intimates why James would, in later years, find himself disinclined to embrace the languages of sexual self-nomination that, after Wilde, might have been available to him, should he have cared to employ them. The matter with these languages, at least from the anticipatory perspective of *The Bostonians*, is perhaps not their self-exposing explicitness, or their self-entrapping specification, or even their largely punitive origins and intent (in medical languages of pathology and legal languages of criminality). In *The Bostonians*, he sketches out something like the impossibility, or near impossibility, of the very notion of a *new identity*, a newly-minted category of being, for anyone tuned to temporality in the way James is. (Just so, according to an understanding of queer time as characteristically attuned to derangements of linearity and generational progression, James's temporal disposition would have to figure as, finally, normative.[29]) The hunger for a ratifying precedent—which, hardly incidentally, gives rise to Wilde's famous in-trial soliloquy about the historical venerability of the love that dare not speak its name—sits painfully and uneasily alongside whatever yearning for recognition, articulacy, or simple relief might be sought in some *emergent* sodality, some *new* language, anchored in the acknowledgement of things that fall aslant of heterosexuality.

Reverence for precedent pushes against those yearnings for the relief of something like a new identity; as *The Bostonians* also makes excruciatingly clear, it does not satisfy such yearnings or diminish their intensity. Part of what is singular about *The Bostonians* is the kind and degree of its attention to how acutely one might suffer, in one's ambivalent longing for the unprecedented and the not-fully emerged, not the indignity of naming but the condition of namelessness. It is in this respect that *The Bostonians* is not only a novel of sexual history but also one that (again like *The Blithedale Romance*) uses the template of the erotic to adumbrate questions that promiscuously cross politico-historical registers. For in its interrogations of the viability of what is without precedent, *The Bostonians*—whatever its trappings—is also an especially acute novel of Reconstruction, or of its failure. The book wonders searchingly how the nation might clear space within itself for something unprecedented, without that new emergence descending into cheap and unenlivening novelty. The unprecedentedness of Olive's desire, in other words, offers James a way to think about, and worry over, a chief dilemma of Reconstruction, which concerns precisely the carving-out, in the postwar nation, of a place for the truly and massively unprecedented—an emancipated free black *citizenry*.[30] That the Civil War is the backdrop for the novel's operatic rivalries is no merely formal conceit.

And it is with those rivalries, and their irresolution, that the novel concludes, with an eye toward the dilemmas of the unprecedented that have marked the whole of its trajectory, and for which Olive has been so keen a register. For her, the in-between time anatomized by the novel, as languages of sexual specification move nearer and nearer a broad legibility, has come to seem in most respects like a sharpening of the world into bad options. If, in the terms of the novel, the emergent is unviable, namelessness is scarcely endurable. By the time James comes to write his letter to Annie Fields about the unspeakable past that is lost now to those who did not live through its strange epistemologies, he had adapted himself to an almost wistful longing for the forms of secrecy and occult knowledge that lost past engendered. But Olive Chancellor, with her fearful power of suffering and her fierce yearning, recalls to us the anguish such nostalgia pushes to the margins. We can leave her where James does, at the center of a "quick, complete, tremendous silence," her greeting as she takes the podium in the crowded hall in Verena's place: "Every sound instantly dropped, the hush was respectful, the great public waited, and whatever she should say to them (and he thought she might indeed be rather embarrassed), it was not apparent that they were likely to hurl the benches at her. Ransom, palpitating with his victory, felt now a little sorry for her, and was relieved to know that, even when exasperated, a Boston audience is not ungenerous" (*B*, 349). The novel declines to suggest how Olive fills that silence. For our part we can only wonder whether the languages that would in fact develop around the desire for a union of soul with another woman would be habitable for her. James's own trajectory, from 1886 to his 1914 letter to Annie Fields, suggests not. But here, at least, the silence that envelops Olive is, as Gustavus Stadler helps to remind us, "not ungenerous." It makes allowances.[31] Olive's embrace of feminism and reform, propelled by a yearning that outpaces her ambivalences, intimates the possibility of a different relation to those languages than the one James would come to—not necessarily free of disquiet or misgiving, but harboring perhaps a different design on the future.

Coda

The Turn

The Wilde trials, which unfolded in the spring of 1895, were gripping public theater. Henry James was among the captivated. Wilde and the scene surrounding him struck James, as he would aver in a letter to Edmund Gosse, as

> hideously, atrociously dramatic & really interesting—so far as one can say that of a thing of which the interest is qualified by such a sickening horribility. It is the squalid gratuitousness of it all—of the mere exposure—that blurs the spectacle. But the *fall*—from nearly 20 years of a really unique kind of "brilliant" conspicuity . . . to that sordid prison-cell & this gulf of obscenity over which the ghoulish public hangs & gloats—it is beyond any utterance of irony or any pang of compassion! He was never in the smallest degree interesting to me—but this hideous human history has made him so—in a manner.[1]

It is easy enough to read James's wrought fascination as the mark of that rich ambivalence with which his work, particularly his later work, is so replete: an ambivalence, as we have seen, about possibilities for sexual naming, identification, and legibility that the Wilde trials, with their lurid interplay of "exposure" and occlusion, explicitness and indirection, could only exacerbate.[2] Following the trail of those ambivalences, over several chapters I have been especially interested in describing the trials and their aftermath as the occasion, for many in their penumbra, for a special kind of loss. My claim has been that one legacy of the transformations in sexual ordering the Wilde trials can be seen to exemplify—I have been calling that transformation, with tendentious insistence, the advent of "modern" sexuality—is an *estrangement*, a steady making-strange, of ways of imagining sex otherwise: outside of solidifying taxonomies of hetero and homo, and in configurations unauthorized by those identities and their codings of the body's capacities for pleasure, perturbation, and attachment more generally. Borrowing from the literature of the period, with its often errant and extravagant imaginings, and borrowing, too, from contemporary queer scholars like Christopher Castiglia and Molly McGarry, I have been interested in assembling something like an archive of uncreated futures, of possibilities that would not, in the end, eventuate into being.[3]

And yet it would surely be a mistake to imagine that the Wilde trials, whatever the horror of their outcome for Wilde himself or the fear that newly prosecutorial regard for erotically nonnormative people would incite, issued only in constraint, diminution, and loss. We need only think again of a man like J. A. Symonds, Whitman's decades-long interlocutor, to be reminded of the affordances that might be found, at least by some, in the very modes and styles of sexual imagining that to others offered so little traction or promise. (Symonds is precisely the sort of figure that Foucault has in mind in his famous passage, in volume one of *The History of Sexuality*, on homosexuality and "reverse" discourse.[4]) It is from the seeds of German sexology, after all, that Symonds grows not only a defense of a homosexuality he is unafraid to name but a wider ratification, an ampler claim for dignity, that would itself flower over the next century into much broader and more radical claims. And while depictions of twentieth-century queer history as a steady movement from dispersal to mutual legibility, from invisibility to articulacy, from solitude to politics, may indeed be partial and in many pressing respects misbegotten, still its basic premise—that a newly emerging homosexuality offered new possibilities for queer life—is hardly without merit.[5] The becoming-legible of homosexual *identity*, whatever its confinements and however unequally distributed its benefits, plainly made the world more rather than less habitable for some, richer in possibility, wider, freer.

Still, I would want to remark again, with a nod back to Hawthorne, that not every kind of freedom is a cure for terror. So by way of conclusion, and in hopes of describing a bit more precisely something of what the transformations wrought in and around the trials might have felt like on the ground, I want to return to the figure with whom this study began and who has served, throughout, as a kind of touchstone: Henry James. For James, as we have seen, it is the inarticulability, the shaming namelessness, of same-sex desire that, at least at one early moment in his career, is the cause of great and disfiguring pain—such is the case of Olive Chancellor in *The Bostonians*. But then, years later, *after* the atrociously dramatic and really interesting trials of Oscar Wilde, in both his letter to Annie Fields and in the signature attenuations of his fiction, James comes to describe a markedly different, not uniformly *un*pleasurable style of illegibility to and within codifications of intimate attachment. (We might think here of Kevin Ohi's exacting reading of James's style and "its systematic challenging of the presumption that desire can be, or ought to be, represented."[6]) Between just these poles—a wariness of the inarticulability of same-sex love, and a wariness of the newly available terms in which it might be avowed—we have seen James, and others, navigate their way. And yet in the *immediate* aftermath of Wilde's terrible apotheosis, the story is different still. There and then, James seems to me to experience something located in a different register of affect altogether, something reducible neither to the pains nor the pleasures, the anguish nor the delight, of illegibility. What the transformations in sex and sexual meaning around Wilde most feel like to James, I want to suggest, is terror.

In *The Turn of the Screw*, his famously lurid ghost story from 1898, James asks us to imagine what it would be like to inhabit a time and place in which the signs of a specifically sexual signification, a specifically sexual intention or affect or impulse, supersaturate the lifeworld. Considering the moment of the emergence of psychoanalysis, which itself happens to coincide with both the Wilde trials and James's tale, Adam Phillips writes, "In psychoanalysis the supernatural returns as the erotic"[7]—a phrase irresistibly suggestive when taken up in relation to James's fin-de-siècle story of visitation. By way of bringing these many readings to anchor, then, I want to take up *The Turn of the Screw*, first in the hope of specifying exactly how this confusion of tongues, between ghosts and lovers, parents and seducers, desire and terror, might come into meaning late in the century. Ringing changes on Eve Sedgwick's reading of the Gothic as the quintessential genre of homosexual panic, I want briefly to suggest that James's Gothicism in *The Turn of the Screw* describes less the fearfulness of male proximity than the terror of a world in which the signs of sexual meaning so proliferate that, as Shoshana Felman argued in a seminal deconstructive essay from 1977, the least effort at determinative interpretation devolves almost immediately into an interminable paranoiac spiral.[8] And I want to use the story, too, as an occasion to meditate on some of the problems of historiography—on the idea, say, of a turning point, a paradigm shift or moment of stark rupture, in sexual history—that have stood behind and in many respects energized all the readings I have attempted thus far. James's tale brings such problems into vivid relief not least, I think, by posing them in terms so extreme, so supercharged with dire possibility. Or, to put it another way, James's story invites us to ask: If at the turn of the twentieth century the supernatural returns as the erotic, is sexuality thus the name of the madness—the possibly murderous madness—proper to an emerging modernity?

What ails the governess? For years this was the anchoring question in approaches to *The Turn of the Screw*. "At least since Edmund Wilson popularized the possibility that the governess is sexually repressed, we have been, without fail, invited to ask ourselves whether the ghosts are real or . . . hallucinations," Ellis Hanson appositely observes. "You can pick sides in the debate if you want," he goes on, "but you will always lose."[9] But diagnosis, as James knows as well as Hanson, is a virtually irresistible provocation. His "little fiction," James tells us in his preface to the tale, "rejoices . . . in a conscious provision of prompt retort to the sharpest question that may be addressed to it."[10] Very much like one of Freud's contemporaneous hysterics, the governess has a story that veritably pleads for interpretation, for a curative retelling.[11] (Just so, her story comes to us multiply framed by repetitions—as a retelling of a story told to our narrator by Douglas, which is a story she gave to Douglas years before—all of which suggest how the impossibility of any ambiguity-banishing destination for the story produces only, just as Felman notes, further provocation to exegesis.) One version of that story goes like this: in the middle of the nineteenth century, an unworldly young woman— "the youngest of several daughters of a poor country parson"—at the age of twenty takes a job as a governess (*TS*, 149). Her task is to care for two orphaned children, Miles and Flora, the charges of a bachelor uncle who lives in London and wishes, above all else, not to be troubled by these unfortunate relations. For this young woman the situation is in several respects peculiar: her employer, "a gentleman, a bachelor in the prime of life . . . a figure that had never risen, save in a dream of an old novel, before a fluttered and anxious girl out of a Hampshire vicarage" (*TS*, 149)—this employer sends her to live with the children quietly and peaceably, at his expense, in the old country home, in distant, desolate Essex. Despite her very real trepidations, the anxious girl out of Hampshire takes the job, and she does so, we are given to know, at least in part because of "the seduction exercised by the splendid young man," her employer, the bachelor who lives in Harley Street (*TS*, 151). "He struck her, inevitably, as gallant and splendid . . . she saw him all in a glow of high fashion, of good looks, of expensive habits, of charming ways with women" (*TS*, 149). To Essex, then, she goes.

There in Essex, in the nearly empty old estate over which, in the absence of the bachelor, she holds a peculiar kind of command, the governess's story deepens dramatically:

> In the first weeks the days were long; they often, at their finest, gave me what I used to call my own hour. . . . I liked it best of all when, as the light faded—or rather, I should say, the day lingered and the last calls of the last birds sounded, in a flushed sky, from the old trees—I could take a turn into the grounds and enjoy, almost with a sense of property that amused and flattered me, the beauty and dignity of the place. It was a pleasure at these moments to feel myself tranquil and justified; doubtless, perhaps, also to reflect that by my discretion, my quiet good sense and general high propriety, I was giving pleasure—if he ever thought of it!—to the person to whose pressure I had responded. What I was doing was what he had earnestly hoped and directly asked of me, and that I *could*, after all, do it proved even a greater joy than I had expected. I daresay I fancied myself, in short, a remarkable young woman and took comfort in the faith that this would more publicly appear. Well, I needed to be remarkable to offer a front to the remarkable things that presently gave their first sign. (163–64)

For Freud, whose first major theoretical statements about psychoanalysis are virtually contemporaneous with this story, it was above all else sexuality that, in Phillips's words, stood in as one of the "new, scientifically prestigious words for the occult, for that which is beyond our capacity for knowledge."[12] One now-famous reading of the story, and of this passage particularly, follows from just these premises. James's governess is fantasizing here about meeting the master, the bachelor she admired and to whose seduction she had succumbed. Instead, she sees something else. "He's a horror," she will later say (*TS*, 172). According to the Freudian reading pioneered by Edmund Wilson, the governess is plagued not by ghosts but by her own wishes, and whither they lead. That is, imagining herself as the mistress of the grounds, as she does here, also means imaging herself in relation to the bachelor in new ways. She sees herself, in James's ripe terms, "giving pleasure" to the master. (Then, in case we have missed the implication, she offers her "faith" that her pleasuring-giving "would more publicly appear," in which turn of thought we might well hear a fantasy of impregnation.) The appearance of Peter Quint, at this moment precisely, suggests that she is at once attracted by those imaginings and repulsed by them, fearful of the part of herself that entertains such manifestly transgressive desires. Accordingly, she transforms her wish to meet the bachelor into a threat, a force of uncertain origin that is menacing to her safety, her propriety, eventually her very decency. The ghost of Peter Quint, that is, is the realization less of her wish for some transgressive encounter with the bachelor than of her fear of that wish—of its strength, and her sense of herself as threatened by it.

Even in the skeletal outlines of this wholly standard reading—standard after Wilson's Freudian intervention, the passionate resistance to it, and its deconstructive synthesis in Felman's essay[13]—we can see why the tale would be irresistible both to Freudians and to scholars of turn-of-the-century sexuality more generally. Beyond the ample provision it makes for more and less clumsy symptomatic reading (of phallic towers, vaginal mud holes, and the like), the tale offers to psychoanalytically-invested readers richer and more elemental kinds of confirmation. To say for instance that the governess has wishes by which she feels threatened, wishes that she cannot countenance and that she refuses to acknowledge as wishes, but only as a mysterious sense of dread, is to return to the very cornerstone of Freud's work. It suggests, of course, the idea of the *unconscious*, that reservoir of all the wishes by which people—who because they are so prolifically variable, because they wish in so many multiplying, self-contradicting ways—feel so threatened, so unsettled, that they refuse to grant them even a hearing in conscious life; a name, that is, for the occult parts of ourselves. (About what he would later describe as the "discovery" of the unconscious, on which the analytic science he founded would be built, Freud wrote to Wilhelm Fleiss, "Do you suppose that some day on this house one will read on a marble tablet: 'Here revealed itself, on 24 July 1895, the secret of the dream to Dr. Sigm. Freud.'"[14])

And yet the tale is plainly about more than the bare fact of the unconscious, of the self's excess of and illegibility to itself, or even about the central place of desire in these dynamics. Not least by virtue of its insistent troping of supernatural horror and unspeakability—in a word, its Gothicism—the story has been understood in differently suggestive terms. Neill Matheson, for instance, frames the matter thus: "The story's casting of sexuality in the mode of Gothic terror and its thematizing of the fear of going public are responses to the climate of anxiety surrounding nonnormative sexuality in England in the 1890s, embodied for James (and many others) by the sensational trials of Oscar Wilde for 'indecency' in 1895, three years before the story's publication."[15] Again, one does not struggle to note the echoes: think of the governess's vision of herself as mistress of the grounds and her desire to please the master in that role. These desires are at once erotically transgressive and *class*-transgressive, a desiring above her station. Indeed, the story constantly returns to this slippage, to the way each form of transgressive desire comes to signify the other—which is only one of the ways the scandal around Wilde, wherein his contact with men of lower rank were read as indices of a sexually nonnormative character, find rich resonance in James's tale. An insoluble blurring of class and sexual transgressions, a scandalized obsession with what can and cannot be spoken, a remorseless hunting for signs of an undisclosed but presumptively injurious depravity: between the tale and the trials are points of connection, ranging from the detailed to the broadly thematic, numerous enough to make a historical-minded reader blush with a pleasure no less keen than that of the Freudian reader awash in the tale's overripe figures.

If Matheson is right that James's story responds to the "climate of anxiety" around Wilde's trials it also helps us, I think, to understand a bit more precisely the nature and quality of that fear. Consider the way the story figures interpretive instability as a kind of sexual panic, and vice-versa. Writ large across the whole of the tale is a fascination with the contagiousness, the ungovernableness, of those signifiers in which there resides the least possibility of erotic content. This is much of the point of the reading offered by Felman, who outpaces Freudian no less than anti-Freudian readings by noting how both, in their efforts at interpretive mastery, *repeat* the very madness that afflicts the governess by, in essence, enacting it. To take only one of many examples, here are the governess and Mrs. Grose discussing the letter they have just received informing them that young Miles has been dismissed from school. "Is he really bad?" the governess asks Mrs. Grose.

> The tears were still in her eyes. "Do the gentlemen say so?"
>
> "They go into no particulars. They simply express their regret that it should be impossible to keep him. That can have only one meaning." Mrs. Grose listened with dumb emotion; she forbore to ask me what this meaning might be; so that, presently, to put the thing with some coherence and with the mere aid of her presence to my own mind, I went on: "That he's an injury to the others." (*TS*, 158)

The governess goes on to frame Miles's alleged wickedness with a great array of connotations (injuriousness, false innocence, impossible youth) that doggedly refuse to realize themselves as the denotations (sexual precocity, masturbation, homosexuality) they nevertheless suggest. She moves in this way from a broad intimation of "badness" to an implication that vacillates teasingly between the loosely specifying and infinitely open-ended. There are "no particulars"—only hints and intimations, signs to be wrung dry of significance—but *"one meaning."*

In Felman's account, it is reading itself, the very compulsive reading and rereading the story prompts, that sponsors a movement toward what she calls the "killing within literature that which makes it literature—its reserve of silence, that which, within speech, is incapable of speaking." The story for her is most deeply an allegory of its own unreadability, a kind of deconstructive textbook study in the instability of language and "the threatening power of rhetoric itself." Which is to say, too, that it is for Felman a story of the *manias* of interpretation—what Hanson calls the "panicky chain reaction of erotic speculation"[16]—that unreadability seems to generate. She notes for instance how the ruthless logic of the story's rhetoric links tightly together efforts to "grasp" the meaning of its events—which is how the governess describes her own efforts at determinative interpretation—to that final, fatal "grasp" with which the governess appears to kill young Miles. "Meaning itself," she writes, "thus unavoidably becomes the outcome of an act of violence."[17]

Nothing about Felman's rhetorical reading seems to me to disqualify Matheson's sense of the tale as keenly responsive to the "climate of anxiety" generated by the Wilde trials. Indeed, the two strands of reading might better be understood to ratify one another. The interpretive mania Felman diagnoses may be proper to the problem of language as such, to "rhetoric itself," as she says. But it comes to interest James in *The Turn of the Screw*, just as Matheson suggests, as a problem of sexual meaning generally and a style of sexual interpretation (unresting, suspicious, elementally prosecutorial) in particular. Felman's rigorously deconstructive reading, in other words, might well strike us as strangely, suggestively *historical*: a singularly close accounting of the fate of sexual meaning in the near aftermath of a trial that crystallized major conceptual recalibrations in the field of intimate attachment, and came with its own readerly instigations and proliferating interpretive mandates. *The Turn of the Screw* is a story about the *contagion* of sex: about the spirals of interpretive mania that follow from the emergence of "sex" as exactly what the Wilde trials sought to make it—an illicit secret of the self—and from the subsequent inducement to scour *every* attachment for the smallest trace, the slenderest possibility, of contamination by desire.

That search, James insists, can come to captivate an interpretive disposition toward the whole of the world, and when it does, it is exquisitely hard to disentangle from madness. If the tale makes anything clear, it is that to search with such frantic, paranoiac urgency for sex is necessarily to find it, or its uncanceled possibility, absolutely everywhere, especially in the places it is most passionately prohibited (in the vicinity of children, for instance). The insatiable will to interpret that is both the story's subject and chief effect, in other words, is less the cure for than the content of the "madness" it narrates. Hence the story's Gothicism, its "climate," to use Matheson's word, of claustrophobic fear. But the paranoia of the Gothic here cuts in many ways. It functions not only in respect to the fear of same-sex proximity that, as Eve Sedgwick observes, is one of the genre's hallmarks. In *The Turn of the Screw*, it gathers up, instead, a fear of *every possible avenue of sexual impropriety*, including that between men and men, women and women, women and men, masters and servants, children and adults, children and other children, and many another besides. That the terror infects the whole of the relational field, in an infinitely multiplying series, is much of the point, from the very first notes of the work. ("If the child gives the effect another turn of the screw, what do you say to two?" [*TS*, 145].) For when the possibility of transgression, even of the direst sort, travels under the sign of affective dispositions, attentions, and investments that are themselves indistinguishable from the most normative and even compulsory relations (parent, friend, employee, guardian) the result, according to the tale, is a frenzy of terror-stricken paranoia that nothing this side of the grave can bring to rest—and, it turns out, not even that.

As if methodologically in spite of itself, then, Felman's seems to me among the acutest historical readings of the tale we have, one that allows us to read the Wilde trials as well, and to understand their most immediate effects to have conjoined, in the realm of sex, fear, mania, and an almost unbearably intensified imperative to interpret. If the story describes James's initial reckoning with the newly emerging world of post-Wildean "modern" sexuality, small wonder that, in his letter to Annie Fields, we find him lamenting the passing of a sphere of intimate relation organized otherwise. Whatever the illegibilities of that earlier model, it would seem at least to be freer, not only from punitive medico-legal terms of sexual personhood, but from a whole "climate" of quasi-terroristic interpretive mania. For the trials help to invent and make publicly legible not just an identity, with *its* possibilities and entrapments. They generate, too, a mode of reading, a strategy for the deducing, from a set of scattered and unjoined details, the legibility of a *type*, bound into coherence and specified by the sexuality understood to traverse and invest those details, to serve as their secret referent and point of conceptual coherence.

Of course, as the prominence of Freudian readings of *The Turn of the Screw* suggests to us no less forcefully than Foucault's introductory volume of *The History of Sexuality*, the modernity of this "modern" sexuality emerging at the century's end, inasmuch as one of its ground notes is indeed a sweeping and elementally paranoiac interpretive disposition toward intimate life, owes much to the author who also, in Foucault's phrase, possessed "the most famous ears of our time."[18] Freudian psychoanalysis, in other words, is a science of more-than-a-little paranoiac interpretation, at the root of which is sexuality—a discourse that, as Foucault so famously and persuasively argues, invents "sexuality" as an obscure, self-saturating but deviously extraempirical aspect of being, requiring because of that very obscurity an especially tenacious effort, typically by accredited "experts," to coax and cajole it out into speech. We need think only of Freud's famous moment of braggadocio from *Dora*: "When I set myself the task of bringing to light what human beings keep hidden within them," he writes, "not by the compelling power of hypnosis, but by observing what they say and what they show, I thought the task was a harder one than it really is. He that has eyes to see and ears to hear may convince himself that no mortal can keep a secret. If his lips are silent, he chatters with his finger-tips; betrayal oozes out of him at every pore."[19] The matter here is not merely the one that Felman dutifully points out, that psychoanalysis as method is often implicated in the ailments—maladies of knowing and unknowing, reading and refusal—it seeks to cure.[20] For Foucault the more crucial point is that Freud, by presuming that human urge to "keep hidden" the depths of selfhood, makes sex into the great, most potent and bottomlessly revelatory secret of ourselves, for which one must accordingly hunt with exactly the merciless exhaustiveness that so deranges the governess. In doing so, he helps to establish the analytic grammar according to which the sweeping coordinations of modern sexuality—the joining of disparate aspects of being in a bounded whole called "sexuality"—could be accomplished.

Throughout this book, I have been interested in exploring the losses entailed in the advent of what I have called modern sexuality, and in the alternate conceptions of the domain of sexuality—of the forms sex could yet take—that a range of authors dreamed into being in the moments leading up to its emergence, for which Wilde's spectacular trials can stand as a convenient emblem. It is not difficult, after Foucault, to grasp the ways Freud is implicated in that emergence, or to understand how Freud's, more than anyone else's, might be understood to be *the* face of modern sexuality, whatever the qualifications, revisions, deconstructions, and reelaborations that have followed him. Indeed, *The Turn of the Screw* seems to fold neatly together a post-Wildean prosecutorial interpretive disposition with a style of sexually-suspicious symptomatic reading in which, from this vantage, we can easily identify the outlines of what would come to be codified as Freudian psychoanalysis. If the modern turn of sexuality entails a number of losses, as I have tried to suggest, then Freud might plausibly be seen as one of the most culpable agents in speeding the extirpation of those looser, errant possibilities.

I have little appetite for the defense or prosecution, the praise or the burial, of Freud on this score. I would want to insist, though, that these convergences—the prosecutorial, the sexually-specifying, the furiously paranoiac—are not the sole Freudian legacies with which we are left to contend, or the only ways Freud might yet be essential to the telling of the history of sexuality both before, and in its transition into, its modern apotheosis. I am interested, instead, in sketching out a different paradox, one rooted in the capaciousness, at once troubling and intriguing, of Freud's understanding, not so much of what sex is or even of what sex might be, but of what might be sex. On this score, there is an especially telling moment in Freud's *Three Essays on the Theory of Sexuality* when, as he is working to specify what is sexual in children's affective lives, he avers, rather remarkably, "that all comparatively intense affective processes, including even terrifying ones, trench upon sexuality."[21] In certain ways, this is the *omphalos* of the Freudian interpretive disposition, the point on which followers like Jung and Adler would heretically depart from him: it marks Freud's eagerness to trace all the disturbances of personhood forceful enough to invite psychoanalytic intervention back to a sexuality that is thus rendered, as if by a rhetorical and definitional sleight of hand, vastly explanatory. (If it is of affective significance to the organism, Freud implies, it must be sexuality.) The supersaturation of personhood Foucault describes as an effect of the new technologies of modern power—the invention of sexuality as a switching-point for a wildly heterogeneous array of administrative investments, incitements, regulations, maximizations, and instrumentalizations—in this way dovetails all too seamlessly with a medical dispensation in which, in the vulgar iteration, *everything is sexual.*

Perhaps. But Freud's premises work in other ways, not free of the administrative overcodings Foucault isolates, surely, but operative in different registers as well. For Leo Bersani, for instance, it is Freud—in fact the Freud of the *Three Essays*—who most enables us to see that desire might be, in the famous phrase, "self-shattering," how it might name the self's strange compulsion to pursue intensities of sensation that actually erode the structures that make it legible *as* a self. Desire in this key is forever inducing a dissipation of the very coherent selfhood upon which disciplinary power depends.[22] This is one story, one strong critical narrative, that brings *together* Foucault and Freud. And there are others. Consider again the architecture of the homo/hetero distinction, the sharpness and rigidity of which the Wilde trials could only make the more urgent (not just for the sexually nonnormative but, as Sedgwick argued both in *Between Men* and *Epistemology of the Closet*, for *all* people who sustain any one among the socially necessary, but now highly fraught, kinds of relation to persons of the same sex). That architecture depends not only on a sexually-specifying understanding of personhood, wherein disparate aspects of being (gender performance, sexual preference, taste, education, bodily style, etc.) would be made coordinate with one another under the sign of a sexuality, homo or hetero or otherwise. It devolves, too, upon an understanding of human intimacy, of attachment itself, as cleanly divisible into discrete *kinds*, differentiated by the presence or absence of desire. To be heterosexual in such a scheme is not to desire every person of the opposite sex but, categorically, *no one* of the same sex—to be capable of an attachment to persons of the same sex that is scrupulously free of desire. The clarity of hetero- and homosexual identities, that is, requires the notion of a quality of attachment *purged of desire*, utterly free of contamination by sex. It is just this need that makes for the paranoia of the Gothic in Sedgwick's account as well as in James's tale.

Freud will have none of this. There is in the Freudian cosmology no attachment untinctured by desire, and no possibility of one—which is part (though only part) of why Freud would resist, as he puts it in a footnote added in 1915 to *Three Essays*, "any attempt at separating off homosexuals from the rest of mankind as a group of special character."[23] The coherence of the hetero/homo distinction on which a post-Wildean modern sexuality turns is thus at once provided for, *and also radically undermined*, by a Freudian imagining of desire as the ground note of all human attachment. In an atmosphere everyday more overheated by the drive to expunge from same-sex attachments the least damning trace of sex—a drive in which phobic violence against the nonnormative figures prominently—Freud offers only refusals.

This interruption of the coherence of separable homo- and heterosexual identities is of course not uniform in effect. It could also be understood, for instance, as a conceptual framing that is elemental to the *undecidability* of affect that makes homophobia so powerful a social tool. (Never to know what could be sex is, in a social world organized increasingly by a phobic policing of attachment, to be forever and insolubly vulnerable.) No amount of reframing of Freudian premises can solve this paradox. But Freud's insistence in *Three Essays* upon the way all forceful affective processes "trench upon sexuality" makes other sorts of provisions as well, and these, I think, are nearer to the imaginative efforts we have been tracking thus far, of authors who both precede and are contemporaneous with him. For what I have described as Freud's refusal is at base a refusal to quarantine sex, or sequester it: a resistance to the portioning off of a set of affects or investments understood to be sexual from the rest of the person's life. It is, in other words, the mark of a striking and potentially useful sort of agnosticism about what might prove to be sex. If in the *Three Essays* we find Freud struggling mightily—and with, at moments, a laughable incoherence[24]—to return the sexuality he had postulated in the first two essays back to the strict and narrow parameters of heterosexual reproduction, that very struggle attests to how thoroughly sex itself is for Freud without a priori content, how unpredetermined the forms it might take actually are.

It is on this ground that I would make a case for the utility of the Freudian legacy, precisely in the theoretical strength and complexity it invests in the notion of sex as something unpredetermined, without forms and parameters that can be known in advance. For it is here, I think, that Freud touches the strand of queer theory to which this book is most indebted and to which it has most wished to contribute. The recent turn in queer studies to temporality, which has so enlivened the ways that we think about history as an object and explanatory rubric, has also, in its attentions to the exquisite vulnerability of sex and sexual knowledge to the epistemology of *futures* both imagined and longed for, given to us new ways to be interested in, for instance, the implications of Sedgwick's point that "no one *can* know *in advance* where the limits of gay-centered inquiry are to be drawn"; or in what Dana Luciano describes as "the non-given status of sex as such"; or in José Muñoz's exploration of "doing away with feminism, queerness, and race as epistemological certitudes"; or in the whole problematic that Elizabeth Freeman frames wonderfully in an essay called "Still After," when she asks, "Wasn't my being queer, in the first instance, about finding sex where it was not supposed to be, failing to find it where it was, finding that sex was not, after all, what I thought it was? As a model for doing queer theory, does not that rely on the capacity to be surprised, not only by radical transformations but also by the embarrassing reappearance of the ordinary or the over?"[25] From the determination to approach sex as something not known in advance—not circumscribed in an already-given set of acts or affects, or for that matter an already-given set of disruptions, displacements, and inarticulabilities[26]— there follows, as all these theorists demonstrate, a series of potentially revelatory shifts in critical perspective. One comes into a sense of sex as, for instance, an unfinished project, a set of possibilities constrained but unpredetermined by locally available terms and modes of expression; or as comprised of dispositions and affects that might not know themselves *as* sex in any but retrospective appraisals; or as the point of entry for a host of constraints and subjections but also for varieties of *surprise*, of uncertainty, of intensities that are forever unwriting the codes by which we become legible to ourselves, our present tense, and our imagined future. All of this has helped to dislodge the inclination to read moments of the past, and particularly the sexual past, in lockstep coordination with their contextual determinations, and has sponsored in turn a desire to explore some counter-moves: to *touch* the past, for example, in identification and desire, or for that matter (as Heather Love's work shows) in anguish and shame; or to grant something of the past's alterity to the present tense, but to approach that alterity as itself something unstable and incomplete, fissured by points of connection and continuity.[27]

Only one of the possibilities that emerges from these altered critical dispositions, and that has made queer temporality scholarship particularly important to my work here, is a sense of the past not as locked in a kind of intractable illegibility to present-tense apprehension, but as a scene of different kinds of possibility. For me, those different possibilities have been most meaningful as ways of imagining sex otherwise, of figuring intimacy in terms and forms aslant those of the normative, the legible, even the articulable. My goal has been to look at the writings of a handful of authors and, from that, to assemble an archive of lost possibilities, hard to make legible in our own moment but valuable not least for their *obliquity* to our own terms of imagining. And that effort has seemed to me enabled—paradoxically, it is true—by aspects of the very Freudianism whose ascendance works such dramatically different effects in the moment James writes *The Turn of the Screw*.

But to suggest as I have that "modern" sexuality does entail a new kind of emergence, that the Wilde trials might be understood to emblematize a *turn*, is not to insist on some absolute difference, to deny (to take one example) Sedgwick's point from *Epistemology of the Closet* about the "unrationalized" overlapping of historically concurrent systems of sexual signification, and even less to render the past inaccessible to our touch, be it undertaken in delight, in sorrow, or in any of the unstable admixtures of affect that travel under no one name.[28] It is only according to all-or-nothing logics, in other words, that an interest in the alterity of the past reads as a kind of radical othering, of the sort for which a cultivated anachronism might seem to be the queerest cure.[29] Thinking of the past as a scene of broken-off futures, of possibilities skewed toward inarticulacy by time's unfolding, has for me been an undertaking anchored in related but finally different allegiances and imperatives: less a desire to touch the past per se, be it erotically or melancholically, than to cultivate through the *friction* of such an exchange precisely that proliferation of only barely articulable intimate possibility, that expansion in the realm of what might be sexually habitable, that is at the very heart of what Michael Warner calls "the world-making project of queer life."[30] Warner's is one of the most moving descriptions I know of the lived effects of that project:

> Because gay social life is not as ritualized and institutionalized as straight life, each relation is an adventure in nearly uncharted territory. . . . There are almost as many kinds of relationship as there are people in combination. Where there are patterns, we learn them from other queers, not from our parents or schools or the state. Between tricks and lovers and exes and friends and fuckbuddies and bar friends and bar friends' tricks and tricks' bar friends and gal pals and companions 'in the life,' queers have an astonishing range of intimacies. Most have no labels. Most receive no public recognition. Many of these relations are difficult because the rules have to be invented as we go along. Often desire and unease add to their intensity and their unpredictability. They can be complex and bewildering, in a way

that arouses fear among many gay people, and tremendous resistance and resentment from many straight people. Who among us would give them up?[31]

Queer life, on this account, specializes in the multiplication of possibilities for intimate life, in a turbulent, risky, always-unsettled expansion of the roster of forms of connection in which one might find joy, solace, replenishment, and, not least, sexual pleasure. Such world-making seems to me rooted in, *allowed by*, an understanding of sex as without pregiven form or extension—rooted, that is, in precisely that attentive openness-to-surprise about what might prove to be sex that I have tried to ground my own approach to the sexual past. (Warner himself underscores as much, in ways that resonate with Sedgwick's and Luciano's and Freeman's remarks: "Were we to recognize the diversity of what we call sexuality with the kind of empathic realism in which many queers are unsurpassed, the result would not be separatism, and could not be, because it would give us no view of who 'we' are apart from the fact that there are a lot of nonnormative sexualities in the world."[32]) By this logic, what I have been calling the obliquity of the past with respect to the present tense, however fractured and multiply-invested we take that present to be, comes into meaning less under the rubric of radical alterity—some pure "otherness" we can only leave unmolested or imperiously overcode—than as an element in a more Deleuzian expansion, an alterity that is *additive*, a multiplication of differences in the absence of a single, stable standard of measure.

If I have been abidingly interested here in habitations of sex that fall aslant of modern codings of sexual subjectivity and embodiment—in the extensions of being Thoreau and Smith think their bodies make possible, say, or in the derangements of temporality into which Hawthorne and Dickinson feel their desires and anxieties propel them—it has been motivated in part by a desire to add those errancies, *as* errancies, in the grain of their obliquity, to the catalog, neither exclusive nor exhaustive, of what might be sex. Perhaps counterintuitively, close reading has seemed to me one especially strong way to bring such obliquities into sharp relief. Here again, I think of myself as especially indebted to Sedgwick. Considering the need to carve out within our theoretical frameworks a way to value "profound, complex variation" as a part of "not mere agnosticism, but more active potential pluralism on the heavily contested maps of sexual definition," she writes: "The shifting interfacial resistance of 'literature itself' to 'theory' may mark . . . the surface tension of this reservoir of unrationalized nonce-taxonomic energies."[33] That turn to the nonce tax-onomies close reading can so often disclose sounds, to my ears, especially resonant alongside Warner's account of intimacies grounded neither in "labels" nor "public recognition"; and her nod to the "interfacial resis-tance" of literature to systems of claiming speaks, too, to the friction, the pleasurable joining and unjoining, that anchors Freeman's rendering of queer historiography. Such at least is one way of suggesting how the his-toriographic and readerly ambitions that have motivated my work over these chapters might be seen to intersect with the processes of enlarge-ment, of accretion and expansion, that Warner would have us understand as integral to "the world-making project of queer life." Or as Kathryn Bond Stockton turns the point, zeroing in on the commerce between his-toriography and enlargement: "no matter what anyone claims for History as a record of origins, ends, authorities, and identities, even orthodox his-torical practice shows that we are in each moment simply adding to his-torical *spread*—adding more documents, findings, arguments. . . . History will just keep getting fatter."[34] I have not offered those efforts at addition as properly "utopian," due in part to a wish to sidestep the bifurcation of queer theory into optimistic/future-oriented and death-driven/antisocial camps, but also in respect to the qualities of loss and, indeed, terror that I have found, particularly in late-century authors' engagements with a sexually transforming world. My widest ambition instead has been to lay out just a few of what have seemed to me useful, usable terms according to which we might once more place the imaginative labors of a small handful of writers—Whitman, Thoreau, and Dickinson, Jewett and Douglas and Smith, Jacobs and Melville and Hawthorne, and finally James himself—within a project they at once could never have imagined and have always enabled: the making of a broader, richer, stranger queer world.

Notes

1. Henry James Papers (MS Am 1745.1 [16]), Houghton Library, Harvard University. I offer high thanks to Christoph Irmscher for bringing this letter to my attention. For more on Annie Adams Fields, see Irmscher's "On Henry James and Annie Fields," *Raritan* 26, no. 4 (Spring 2007): 155–79.

2. David Halperin, *How to Do the History of Homosexuality* (Chicago: University of Chicago Press, 2002), 17.

3. Ed Cohen's *Talk on the Wilde Side: Towards a Genealogy of a Discourse on Male Homosexuality* (New York: Routledge, 1993) offers perhaps the most pointed and concise articulation of this position. Cohen reads the Wilde trials as a kind of capstone event, a mass-mediated spectacle of unprecedented reach that gathered into itself and solidified many of the movements *toward* the modern, sexologically inspired taxonomies of erotic life whose transforming advent, in the late nineteenth-century, Michel Foucault has theorized in such detail. These movements pointed toward the emergence of the "homosexual" as a new species of being, toward an understanding of sexuality as an aspect of subjectivity that harbors a special secret truth of self, binds together formerly distinct qualities of character and disposition, and requires much in the way of expert intervention to articulate, evaluate, harness, and turn to proper use. Cohen's work sets itself in dialogue not only with Foucault's *History of Sexuality, Volume 1*, but also with strong literary and historical scholarship from pioneering critics like (to name only a very few) Eve Kosofsky Sedgwick, Jeffrey Weeks, Carroll Smith-Rosenberg, Lillian Faderman, and David Halperin. See Sedgwick's *Between Men: English Literature and Male Homosocial Desire* (New York: Columbia University Press, 1985) and *Epistemology of the Closet* (Berkeley: University of California Press, 1990); Jeffrey Weeks's *Sexuality and Its Discontents: Meanings, Myths, and Modern Sexualities* (London: Longman, 1980); Smith-Rosenberg's *Disorderly Conduct: Visions of Gender in Victorian America* (New York: Oxford University Press, 1985); Faderman's *Surpassing the Love of Men: Friendship between Women from the Renaissance to the Present* (New York: Morrow, 1981); and Halperin's *One Hundred Years of Homosexuality: The Ancient World and Other Essays on Greek Love* (New York: Routledge, 1990).

4. See Foucault's *History of Sexuality*, vol. 1, *An Introduction*, trans. Robert Hurley (New York: Vintage, 1978). For a generous collection of some of sexology's key documents,

see *Sexology Uncensored: The Documents of Sexual Science*, ed. Lucy Bland and Laura Doan (Chicago: University of Chicago Press, 1998). See also Bland and Doan's *Sexology in Culture: Labeling Bodies and Desires* (Chicago: University of Chicago Press, 1998) and, for a broader range of reference, Thomas Laqueur's *Making Sex: Body and Gender from the Greeks to Freud* (Cambridge, Mass.: Harvard University Press, 1999).

5. For overviews of the question of evidence and the history of sexuality, see, along with those cited above, Halperin's concluding chapter in *How to Do the History of Homosexuality*; George Chauncey's introduction (as well as his "Note on Sources") to *Gay New York: Gender, Urban Culture, and the Making of the Gay Male World 1890–1940* (New York: Basic Books, 1994), 1–29, 365–70; and Leila J. Rupp's introduction to *A Desired Past: A Short History of Same-Sex Love in America* (Chicago: University of Chicago Press, 1999), 1–11.

6. As Eve Sedgwick wrote memorably in the introduction to *Epistemology of the Closet*, "to identify *as* must always include multiple processes of identification *with*" (61). Though the premise here has been the subject of wide-ranging theoretical dispute—the "antisociality" thesis, identified chiefly with critics like Leo Bersani and Lee Edelman, might be said to have its roots in a radical skepticism with respect to just this point—still the affiliative affordances of a claimed queer identity, so underscored by Sedgwick, have been at the center of much historical scholarship. For an especially keen account of that scholarly trajectory, and of a queer *yearning* for forms of affiliation not quite provided by one's historical circumstances, see Christopher Nealon's *Foundlings: Lesbian and Gay Historical Emotion before Stonewall* (Durham, N.C.: Duke University Press, 2001), especially 7–13. For a many-voiced consideration of antisociality, see the *PMLA* forum from 2006 entitled "The Antisocial Thesis in Queer Theory," with participants Robert L. Caserio, Lee Edelman, Judith Halberstam, José Esteban Muñoz, and Tim Dean, *PMLA* 121, no. 3 (2006): 819–28.

7. As Jonathan Ned Katz tells the story of nineteenth-century sexuality in his magisterial *Love Stories: Sex between Men before Homosexuality* (Chicago: University of Chicago Press, 2001), the movement toward the century's end is coincident with a movement toward greater and greater courage in self-exposure and self-nomination, more expansive and more articulate public advocacy (seen especially in early defenders of gay sexuality like Edward Peirce, John Symonds, and Edward Carpenter), and finally wider, if still truncated, freedom for queer people. In Jonathan Dollimore's pithy formulation, this is a movement "from pathology to politics." Again, Nealon's approach in *Foundlings* to this broadly progressivist telling of the story of the history of sexuality—a usefully skeptical one that attends to what I regard as the untimely longings of queer writers for modes of belonging not immediately available to them—informs my own throughout. See Jonathan Dollimore's *Sexual Dissidence: Augustine to Wilde, Freud to Foucault* (Oxford: Clarendon Press, 1991).

8. Nealon, *Foundlings*, 8. I borrow the term "earliness" from Nealon's account of American "physique culture" of the 1950s. "The silly utopias of muscle culture," he writes, "can serve, if we let them, as sketches for the movements of a sexuality that, because it is

never isolable in persons, is also open to a hopeful earliness *in* history" (139). That hopeful earliness in history, tracing out as it does a "perpetual becoming-historical" of sexuality that is saturated with attachments to as yet unforeclosed possibilities for future modes of being, seems to me an especially apt figure for the experience of sexuality in the specific flux that is the late-nineteenth century, before the concretization of modern taxonomies of sex but in the grips of a series of movements *toward* them.

9. Henry David Thoreau, *Walden*, ed. J. Lyndon Shanley (Princeton: Princeton University Press, 1971), 178.

10. For a fine account of "the problem of the indiscernible event," inflected strongly by the work of Alain Badiou, see Jonathan Elmer's "Babo's Razor; or, Discerning the Event in an Age of Differences," *Differences* 19, no. 2 (2008): 57, 54–81. Todd Haynes's *Velvet Goldmine* is only one testament to the unfinished business between Wilde and the worlds that would come after him.

11. See Eve Kosofsky Sedgwick, *Tendencies* (Durham, N.C.: Duke University Press, 1993), 57. For some of Sedgwick's especially suggestive work about Wilde, see, in *Tendencies*, "Tales of the Avunculate: Queer Tutelage in *The Importance of Being Earnest*" (52–72) and the opening strains of "Willa Cather and Others" (167–76).

12. Quoted in David Deitcher, *Dear Friends: American Photographs of Men Together, 1840–1918* (New York: Harry N. Abrams, Inc., 2001), 110.

13. Halperin, *How to Do the History of Homosexuality*, 42.

14. I am thinking here, in this emphasis on pausing, acceleration, and uneven development, of Elizabeth Freeman's work on what she calls "erotohistoriography." See *Time Binds: Queer Temporalities, Queer Histories* (Durham, N.C.: Duke University Press, 2010).

15. "Sex," we might say, would after Wilde become a kind of code for a series of dispositions and affects that had been available in at least loose distinction from one another. Close consideration of passions before Wilde affords us the chance to parse more exactingly states of being not *separate* from desire but only clumsily grasped by the broad sweep of a term like "sex." The work of *Tomorrow's Parties*, in this way, follows the lead of scholars like Lauren Berlant and Ann Cvetkovich, who in their attention to public feeling aim to establish a more discerning and fine-grained vocabulary to describe, for instance, the interstitial sorts of affects that taxonomies of sex after Wilde tend to obscure. I am thinking here, too, of Bruce Burgett's recent suggestion that there may be other, more errant and less codifiable "relations among bodies, their physical sensations, their modes of perception, and their sensual appetites" than can be named without remainder by the term "sexuality." See Bruce Burgett's "Sex, Panic, Nation," *American Literary History* 21, no. 1 (Spring 2009): 67–86, here 70.

16. See Luciano, *Arranging Grief: Sacred Time and the Body in Nineteenth-Century America* (New York: New York University Press, 2007), 9; Heather Love, *Feeling Backward: Loss and the Politics of Queer History* (Cambridge, Mass.: Harvard University Press, 2007); Molly McGarry, *Ghosts of Futures Past: Spiritualism and the Cultural Politics of Nineteenth-Century America* (Berkeley: University of California Press, 2008); José Esteban Muñoz, *Cruising Utopia: The Then and There of Queer Futurity* (New York: New York

University Press, 2009), especially 1–48; Christopher Castiglia, *Interior States: Institutional Consciousness and the Inner Life of Democracy in the Antebellum United States* (Durham, N.C.: Duke University Press, 2008); Sharon Marcus, *Between Women: Friendship, Desire, and Marriage in Victorian England* (Princeton: Princeton University Press, 2007); Bruce Burgett, "Sex, Panic, Nation"; Christopher Looby, "Strange Sensations: Sex and the Aesthetic in 'The Counterpane,'" in *Melville and Aesthetics*, ed. Samuel Otter and Geoffrey Sanborn (New York: Palgrave, 2011), 65–84; Jordan Alexander Stein, "*The Blithedale Romance's* Queer Style," *ESQ* 55, nos. 3–4 (2009): 211–36; and Freeman, *Time Binds*. For an especially trenchant survey of this new queer work, and of the scholarly trajectories from which it eventuates, see Freeman's introduction to the special issue she edited of *GLQ* entitled "Queer Temporalities," *GLQ* 13, nos. 2–3 (2007): 159–76.

17. Freeman, *Time Binds*, 120.

18. Lauren Berlant, *Cruel Optimism* (Durham, N.C.: Duke University Press, 2011), 123. The phrase is a part of Berlant's artful summary of Sedgwick's work: "Sedgwick seeks to read every word the subject writes (she believes in the author) to establish the avowed and disavowed patterns of his or her desire, and then understands those repetitions in terms of a story about sexuality that does not yet exist as a convention or an identity. That aim is what makes her writing so optimistic." In the concluding section of *Tomorrow's Parties*, I address more directly some of the forms that complex optimism might take.

19. José Esteban Muñoz frames the methodological stakes of this sort of attentive agnosticism with useful candor: "doing away with feminism, queerness, and race as epistemological certitudes," he writes, "would open a site of potentiality where these particularities exist as methodologies that free new meaning. *We cannot know in advance the politics prescribed by these critical modes, and we should not*" ("The Sense of Watching Tony Sleep," in *After Sex?: On Writing after Queer Theory*, ed. Janet Halley and Andrew Parker [Durham, N.C.: Duke University Press, 2011], 142–50, here 149–50, emphasis added).

20. He goes on: "Whether or not a couple had sex is a natural question to ask, but the answer will not allow us into the private meaning of their bond" (Caleb Crain, *American Sympathy: Men Friendship, and Literature in the New Nation* [New Haven: Yale University Press, 2001], 33).

21. Two of the most prominent works in this tradition would be Lee Edelman's *No Future: Queer Theory and the Death Drive* (Durham, N.C.: Duke University Press, 2004) and Judith Halberstam's *In a Queer Time and Place: Transgender Bodies, Subcultural Lives* (New York: New York University Press, 2005).

22. For a strident critique of historicist methodology and its suspect resistance to anachronism, see Carla Freccero, *Queer/Early/Modern* (Durham, N.C.: Duke University Press, 2006). On the Americanist side, this critique is given particularly strong expression in Valerie Rohy's *Anachronism and Its Others: Sexuality, Race, Temporality* (Albany: State University of New York Press, 2009). On erotohistoriography, see Freeman's "Time's Binds, or, Erotohistoriography," *Social Text* 84–85 (2005): 57–68, as well as her *Time Binds*. On the "touch across time," see Carolyn Dinshaw's *Getting Medieval: Sexualities and Communities, Pre- and Postmodern* (Durham, N.C.: Duke University Press, 1999), 21; see

also, in relation to Dinshaw, the canny parsings of historiographic problems in Valerie Traub, *The Renaissance of Lesbianism in Early Modern England* (New York: Cambridge University Press, 2002), especially 1–35.

23. This point follows from the account of the salience of taxonomies of hetero and homo in Thoreau's work at a moment far, far earlier than 1895 in Michael Warner's "Thoreau's Bottom," *Raritan* 11 (1992): 53–79. Salutary here, too, is Stephen Shapiro's "Sexuality: An Early American Mystery," *The William and Mary Quarterly* 60, no. 1 (January 2003): 189–92. Shapiro offers what he names a "tripartite historical schematization" that conceptualizes a movement from sexual acts to "sensual tendency" to, finally, the modern sense of sexual identity. Shapiro's parsing of premodern erotic life is useful not least for the way it deftly complicates any before/after schematization (191). My own interests lay less in establishing the pertinence of any of these domains than in tracking the multiple and uncoordinated movements *within* his middle category, that of "sensual tendencies," as they unfold in the long, last moment before the ascendance of modern sexual identity. For an especially strong deployment of Shapiro, see Christopher Looby, "Strange Sensations," 65–84.

24. See Kathryn Kent, *Making Girls into Women: American Women's Writing and the Rise of Lesbian Identity* (Durham, N. C.: Duke University Press, 2003). Kent argues that "modern lesbian identity has its roots in the United States not just or even primarily in sexology and medicalization but in white, middle-class 'women's culture,' distinguished in part by its central focus on the mother," and that "sentimental culture" provides an early groundwork for lesbian identity or what she calls protolesbian identity (1, 5). In a way that I have found instructive, the book aims also "to call into question the teleology of identity that assumes that identifications and desires automatically lead to identities" (2). This is especially pertinent in an era before the elements that compound sexual identity had been made quite so coordinate—before, that is, there was so determinate a sexual identity one might cathect. Kent's work also offers a fine parsing of readings of presexological female intimacy in the terms of "the rosy, undefinable 'female world of love and friendship' first delineated by Carroll Smith-Rosenberg and Lillian Faderman." Kent's angle of approach to Faderman and Smith-Rosenberg—critical but not ungenerous—follows from Lisa Moore's work in *Dangerous Intimacies: Toward a Sapphic History of the British Novel* (Durham, N.C.: Duke University Press, 1997). Related work on the question of American male friendship includes Crain's *American Sympathy* and Axel Nissen's *Manly Love: Romantic Friendship in American Fiction* (Chicago: University of Chicago Press, 2009).

25. McGarry, *Ghosts of Futures Past.*

26. See Colm Tóibín, *The Master* (New York: Scribner, 2004). Adam Phillips's essay "The Interested Party" reads as a nice corrective to this elementally condescending view of James, as does (in a different register) Eve Sedgwick's "Is the Rectum Straight?: Identification and Identity in *The Wings of the Dove*," in which she departs from Kaja Silverman's reading of James in *Male Subjectivity at the Margins*. See Adam Phillips, *The Beast in the Nursery: On Curiosity and Other Appetites* (New York: Vintage, 1998), 3–36, and Sedgwick's *Tendencies*, 73–103.

27. Stein, "*The Blithedale Romance's* Queer Style," 212 and 214.

28. Halperin, *How to Do the History of Homosexuality*, 88. For an especially strong critical use of Halperin, see Annamarie Jagose, *Inconsequence: Lesbian Representation and the Logic of Sexual Sequence* (Ithaca, N.Y.: Cornell University Press, 2002).

29. Halperin, *How to Do the History of Homosexuality*, 42.

30. Berlant, *Cruel Optimism*, 97.

31. For a related account of how Foucault's approach might be of different use to criticism than the routines of historicist practice quite fully allow, see Luciano's reading of Richard Brodhead, "disciplinary intimacy," and Foucault in *Arranging Grief*, 127–35.

32. Sedgwick, *Epistemology of the Closet*, 23.

33. See especially Virginia Jackson's splendid account of the erotics of Dickinson's writing in *Dickinson's Misery: A Theory of Lyric Reading* (Princeton: Princeton University Press, 2005).

34. Perry Miller, *Consciousness in Concord* (Boston: Houghton Mifflin, 1958), 90.

35. On this exchange (though read to different purposes than my own), see Katz, *Love Stories*, 272–87.

36. My sense of the theoretical liabilities of discursive contextualization as a mode of historicism is especially indebted to, and fortified by, work in Mark Seltzer's *Serial Killers: Death and Life in America's Wound Culture* (New York: Routledge, 1998) and James Chandler's *England in 1819: The Politics of Literary Culture and the Case of Romantic Historicism* (Chicago: University of Chicago Press, 1998), especially 135–51.

37. Simon Jarvis, "For a Poetics of Verse," *PMLA* 125, no. 4 (2010): 931–35, here 931.

38. Peter Coviello, *Intimacy in America: Dreams of Affiliation in Antebellum Literature* (Minneapolis: University of Minnesota Press, 2005), 16.

39. Kathryn Bond Stockton, *The Queer Child, or Growing Sideways in the Twentieth Century* (Durham, N.C.: Duke University Press, 2009), 52.

40. Wai Chee Dimock, *Through Other Continents: American Literature across Deep Time* (Princeton: Princeton University Press, 2006). On the temporal turn in queer studies, see Freeman's introduction to the special issue of *GLQ*, "Queer Temporalities," as well as "Queer and Not Now," her introduction to *Time Binds*, 1–19.

41. Nealon, *Foundlings*, 22.

42. "Great works," Adorno writes in *Aesthetic Theory*, "wait." (Or again, in more theoretically elaborate language: "Artworks draw credit from a praxis that has yet to begin and no one knows whether anything backs their letters of credit.") Theodor W. Adorno, *Aesthetic Theory*, ed. and trans. Robert Hullot-Kentor (Minneapolis: University of Minnesota Press, 1997), 40, 83. For a wonderful, carefully discriminating piece that elaborates on Adorno's sense of waiting, and on the contiguities and gaps between Frankfurtian and modern (as well as postmodern) dispositions toward the politics of history, see Christopher Nealon's "Camp Messianism, or the Hopes of Poetry in Late-Late Capitalism," *American Literature* 76, no. 3 (2004): 579–602. (Nealon himself draws extensively from Frederic Jameson's *Late Marxism: Adorno, or, The Persistence of the Dialectic* [New York: Verso, 1990].)

43. Friedrich Nietzsche, *The Will To Power*, trans. Walter Kaufmann and R. J. Hollingdale (New York: Vintage, 1968), 503; for related mediations on the untimely, see Nietzsche's *Untimely Meditations*, ed. Daniel Breazeale, trans. R. J. Hollingdale (Cambridge: Cambridge University Press, 1997), especially "On the Uses and Disadvantages of History for Life," 57–123. Elizabeth Grosz reads Nietzsche's investment in the possibilities of the *untimely* as part of his endeavor to write "for a future that the present cannot recognize." See Grosz's *In the Nick of Time: Politics, Evolution, and the Untimely* (Durham, N.C.: Duke University Press, 2004), 117. Benjamin's work in this critical vein is legible not only in the "Theses on the Philosophy of History" but also in "The Work of Art in the Age of Mechanical Reproduction," where he writes that, "One of the foremost tasks of art has always been the creation of a demand which could be fully satisfied only later." See *Illuminations*, ed. Hannah Arendt, trans. Harry Zohn (New York: Shocken Books, 1968), 237.

44. Lauren Berlant, *The Female Complaint: The Unfinished Business of Sentimentality in American Culture* (Durham, N.C.: Duke University Press, 2008), 24, 25.

45. Nealon, *Foundlings*, 180.

NOTES TO CHAPTER 1

1. Henry David Thoreau, *Walden*, ed. J. Lyndon Shanley (Princeton: Princeton University Press, 1971), 178. Cited hereafter as *W*.

2. The cannon of scholarship on Thoreau as a man interweaving the roles of naturalist and poet is vast. My own sense of this critical tradition is informed principally by F. O. Matthiessen, *American Renaissance: Art and Expression in the Age of Emerson and Whitman* (New York: Oxford University Press, 1941); Miller, *Consciousness in Concord*; Joel Porte, *Emerson and Thoreau: Transcendentalists in Conflict* (Middletown, Conn.: Wesleyan University Press, 1965); Charles R. Anderson, *The Magic Circles of Walden* (New York: Holt, Rinehart and Winston, 1968); Lawrence Buell, *Literary Transcendentalism: Style and Vision in the American Renaissance* (Ithaca, N.Y.: Cornell University Press, 1973) and especially Buell's *The Environmental Imagination: Thoreau, Nature Writing, and the Formation of American Culture* (Cambridge, Mass.: the Belknap Press of Harvard University Press, 1995); Stanley Cavell, *The Senses of "Walden"* (San Francisco: North Point Press, 1981); Sharon Cameron, *Writing Nature: Henry Thoreau's Journal* (New York: Oxford University Press, 1985); H. Daniel Peck, *Thoreau's Morning Work: Memory and Perception in "A Week on the Concord and Merrimack Rivers," the "Journal," and "Walden"* (New Haven, Conn.: Yale University Press, 1990); Alan D. Hodder, *Thoreau's Ecstatic Witness* (New Haven, Conn.: Yale University Press, 2001); and David M. Robinson, *Natural Life: Thoreau's Worldly Transcendentalism* (Ithaca, N.Y.: Cornell University Press, 2004).

3. Henry David Thoreau, *Journal*, vol. 4, *1851–1852*, ed. Robert Sattelmeyer, Leonard N. Neufeldt, and Nancy Craig Simmons (Princeton: Princeton University Press, 1992), 137. Quotations from the journal come from the Princeton editions of *The Writings of Henry D. Thoreau*, ed. Elizabeth Hall Witherell, et al. *Journal* appears in eight volumes to date.

Internal citations—cited as *J* hereafter—will be followed by the volume number in Roman numerals, a colon, and the page number. (I will not be citing, as some others have, according to the number of the manuscript volume of Thoreau's journal.)

4. "If *Walden* is that book which tries to achieve deep sympathy with man and with nature, to retrieve what Thoreau has learned in isolation and to socialize it for us, it tells us two finally incompatible stories—of rapture at the natural world, of rage at the social one." In this way, Cameron suggests, "*Walden* suffers diversion from its own best subject: Thoreau's unmediated relation to nature." The journal, Cameron argues, works to cure this diversion (*Writing Nature*, 29).

5. Cameron writes sharply about the journal as motivated by Thoreau's disquiet with respect to the ways *Walden*, over which he labored for many years, would render nature problematically legible. On the period of strain with Emerson, see especially Porte, *Emerson and Thoreau*; see also Robert D. Richardson Jr.'s biography *Henry Thoreau: A Life of the Mind* (Berkeley: University of California Press, 1986) and Harmon Smith, *My Friend, My Friend: The Story of Thoreau's Relationship with Emerson* (Amherst: University of Massachusetts Press, 1999).

6. Cameron provides a comprehensive reading of the journal, attempting in effect to rescue it from Perry Miller's occasionally sweeping dismissiveness in *Consciousness in Concord*. ("Miller does not so much discuss the *Journal*," Cameron avers, "as chastise Thoreau for writing it" [158].) As a result of both Cameron's intervention and of the continuing publication of new volumes of the journal in the Princeton series, strong and newer work that takes the journal as significant in its own right—and not as simply an addendum to *Walden*—has appeared. As Alan D. Hodder has it, "In recent years, the journal has increasingly taken center stage in much of the best critical writing on Thoreau, and by virtue of this recent work, we now have a much better idea of the character and contributions of this distinctive record" (*Thoreau's Ecstatic Witness*, 250). See especially Peck, Hodder, and Robinson.

7. Or, as he puts it in the "Wednesday" section of *A Week*, "In my experience, persons, when they are made the subject of conversation, though with a friend, are commonly the most prosaic and trivial of facts" (Henry David Thoreau, *A Week on the Concord and Merrimack Rivers*, ed. Carl F. Hovde et al [Princeton: Princeton University Press, 1980], 260).

8. Ralph Waldo Emerson, "Experience," in *Ralph Waldo Emerson*, ed. Richard Poirier (New York: Oxford University Press, 1990), 232.

9. This phrase (and the cadence of my title) is borrowed from a talk of Christopher Nealon's, "Disappointment, or, Western Marxism and Queer Theory" (Cornell University, 2 April 2005), and the idea is inflected by a reading of his *Foundlings*, and of his essay "Camp Messianism."

10. My own sense of this epoch, of Thoreau's place in it, and of the methodological dilemmas that attend its telling is shaped significantly by Warner's "Thoreau's Bottom," as well as his "*Walden*'s Erotic Economy," in *Comparative American Identities*, ed. Hortense J. Spillers (New York: Routledge, 1991), 157–74. A sense of Thoreau's pervasive expectancy,

though read in contexts other than the sexual, can be found in Miller, *Consciousness in Concord* ("Anticipation, as conceived in these lonely years, became for Thoreau a consolation," 107), and in Peck, *Thoreau's Morning Work*, especially 3–21.

11. For histories of sexuality in America before the solidification of sexological taxonomies like heterosexuality and homosexuality, see Smith-Rosenberg *Disorderly Conduct*; John D'Emilio and Estelle Freedman, *Intimate Matters: A History of Sexuality in America* (New York: Harper and Row, 1988); Leila J. Rupp, *A Desired Past*; Jonathan Ned Katz, *Love Stories*; Caleb Crain, *American Sympathy*; and Kathryn R. Kent, *Making Girls into Women*.

12. "I write," Nietzsche says in *The Will to Power*, "for a species that does not yet exist" (503). Or again, in a different key, from "On the Uses and Disadvantages of History for Life": "History belongs above all to the man of deeds and power, to him who fights a great fight, who needs models, teachers, comforters and cannot find them among his contemporaries" (67). Elisabeth Grosz describes this style of Nietzsche's historicism (in terms that suggest how important his work would be to Walter Benjamin) as the desire "to write for a future that the present cannot recognize" (*In the Nick of Time*, 117).

13. Miller, *Consciousness in Concord*, 81. On nineteenth-century bachelorhood and its sexual meanings and possibilities, see E. Anthony Rotundo, *American Manhood: Transformations in Masculinity from the Revolution to the Modern Era* (New York: Basic Books, 1993); Vincent Bertolini, "Fireside Chastity: The Erotics of Sentimental Bachelorhood in the 1850s," *American Literature* 68 (December 1996): 707–38; and Bryce Traister, "The Wandering Bachelor: Irving, Masculinity, and Authorship," *American Literature* 74 (March 2002): 111–37.

14. Henry Abelove, "From Thoreau to Queer Politics," in Abelove, *Deep Gossip* (Minneapolis: University of Minnesota Press, 2003), 35.

15. Abelove summarizes the exchange nicely: "This passage is, of course, a representation of seduction. Thoreau is figured as the seducer. He has the very Greek book. He puts it into the young man's hands, while they are secluded together at a remote cabin in the woods. The young man is figured as the object of the seduction. . . . As for the reading the two of them share, it is highly suggestive. For according to a famous and long-standing tradition of interpretation, Achilles was the lover of Patroclus" (*Deep Gossip*, 36).

16. Thoreau, *A Week*, 263, 266, 269–70.

17. Thoreau, *A Week*, 272.

18. Miller, *Consciousness in Concord*, 90.

19. Michael Warner, "Thoreau's Bottom," 61, 54. Warner's readings here and in "*Walden*'s Erotic Economy" both serve to orient critics less toward the decisive invention of hetero- and homosexuality at the end of the century than toward the gradual processes—extensive and unsystematized and operative well before 1895—that would later produce the emergence of what we think of as "modern" sexuality. But the essays do more than this. They provide as well a useful rebuke to those critics who read Thoreau as elementally detached from the pressures, and the ethical demands, of history. On Warner's account, history—more particularly, a liberal individualism shaped by a burgeoning market capitalism—is what mediates quite decisively between Thoreau and the body he wants,

whose expansive satisfactions he can intuit but not quite realize. He is not out of history: history (as Jameson has it) is for Thoreau what *hurts*, what will not yield up to him the ampler and more sensually attuned body he dimly feels and achingly desires. See Frederic Jameson, *The Political Unconscious* (Ithaca, N.Y.: Cornell University Press, 1981), 102.

20. On market capitalism and Thoreau's resistances to an instrumental self-relation, see the whole of Warner's "*Walden*'s Erotic Economy." "The self-regard he longs for," Warner writes, is "contemplative rather than instrumental" (161).

21. Henry David Thoreau, "Chastity & Sensuality," in *Collected Essays and Poems*, ed. Elizabeth Hall Witherell (New York: Library of America, 2001), 332. Thoreau's caustic responses to heterosexuality are not rare. In another occasional essay, this one entitled "Love," he writes, "If common sense had been consulted, how many marriages would never have taken place; if uncommon or divine sense, how few marriages such as we witness would ever have taken place!" (*Collected Essays*, 325).

22. Milette Shamir, *Inexpressive Privacy: The Interior Life of Antebellum American Fiction* (Philadelphia: University of Pennsylvania Press, 2008), 213. Shamir, whose book takes up the tension in antebellum writing "between the desire to express the self and the desire to find reprieve from self-expression, between the social imperative to invade the architectured self and the wish to carve out a chamber of 'radical privacy' within it," offers, along with Warner, one of the very strongest readings of the vexations of intimacy in Thoreau, particularly as mediated by an ascendant, if fractured, liberal ideology of privacy (*Inexpressive Privacy*, 8). My own account reads homoeroticism more as an intriguing, if unfulfilled, promise for Thoreau than, as Shamir has it, one of the "obstacles" he must negotiate as he "seeks a path of emotional connectedness that will bypass the strictures imposed on bounded manhood" (*Inexpressive Privacy*, 212); still, I take her work to be exemplary in its attention to Thoreau as a writer not foreswearing the realm of the intimate as much as seeking relief from the terms and logics in which intimacy is available to him.

23. I am thinking here of Jane Bennett's searching account (itself inspired by Thoreau) of "the extent to which human being and thinghood overlap, the extent to which the us and the it slip-slide into each other." See Jane Bennett, *Vibrant Matter: A Political Ecology of Things* (Durham, N.C.: Duke University Press, 2010), 4. That overlap, I have been suggesting, both intrigues Thoreau and, in its nonseamlessness or nontotality, frustrates him with respect to other people. The vibrant, vital being of his *own* body is one place where he experiences the possibility of overcoming that frustration.

24. Thoreau, *A Week*, 268.

25. Luciano, *Arranging Grief*, 9.

26. Thoreau, "Chastity & Sensuality," 332.

27. One thinks here, too, of Lauren Berlant's trenchant observations about the political valence of what she calls "uncommitted emotions" ("disbelief" is her post-'04 reelection example), which she suggests are often mistakenly deemed "apolitical, even blockages to the political." Such emotions, "which veer away from commitments to an object choice in an available political world," involve in her reading not apathy but a "stopping and looking

around while full of unacted-on sensation related to refusing a consensual real." These distinctions are suggestive, I think, for thinking about Thoreau, whose own consistent refusals of a consensual real—he will not be shipwrecked on this vain reality—have often been mistaken for a particularly narcissistic brand of ahistorical quietism. See Berlant, "Unfeeling Kerry," *Theory & Event* 8, no. 21 (2006), as well as Nealon's Adorno-inflected reading of the political valences of the pause, of *waiting*, in his "Camp Messianism."

28. Peck grasps something of this dynamic when he writes of "Thoreau's awareness of . . . a severely arhythmical relation between the time of consciousness and the world's time" (*Thoreau's Morning Work*, 5). Expanding our reading of Thoreau's resistances to the market logics of the midcentury, we might note that the increasingly capitalized modernity Thoreau wishes to resist embodies itself not least as, precisely, a mode of *temporality*: the temporality Marx and Benjamin, to name only two, would identify with an unassimilable rapidity of motion and change, the hurried-up time of industrial production, urban flux, and commodity obsolescence. Sex offers Thoreau a mode of experience that works in resistance to the self's captivation, its overcoding, by market temporalities. For an especially fine reading of the temporalities of sex in its relation to the temporalities of antebellum American capital, see Dana Luciano's *Arranging Grief*.

29. Cameron, *Writing Nature*, 90, 102. She argues that throughout the journal Thoreau labors to effect as comprehensive and rigorous an erasure of the human from his writing as is feasible, the better to approach the writing of nature in its profound otherness from the human, but she also observes that Thoreau does so without abandoning the idea of an audience, suggesting that in the journal Thoreau presupposes "that his connection to us, apparently inviolate, will endure his death" (*Writing Nature*, 100). This quasi-Whitmanian sense of connection to unborn others recalls, I am arguing, less the ecstatic overcoming of physical boundaries to intimacy and passion than the projection of the self into a future where its desires might find an articulacy and even a fulfillment—an "entireness"—that the present cannot afford them.

30. On possessive renderings of sexuality, and the resistance to them, see especially Guy Hocquenghem's *Homosexual Desire*, trans. Daniella Dangoor (1972; Durham, N.C.: Duke University Press, 1993); see also Nealon, *Foundlings*, especially 177–82.

31. Quoted in Deitcher, *Dear Friends*, 110.

32. David Halperin stresses this point, as we have seen, especially strongly: "The history of sexuality, as Foucault conceived it, then, is not a history of the representations, categories, cultural articulations, or collective and individual expressions of some determinate entity called sexuality but an inquiry into the historical emergence of sexuality itself, an attempt to explain how it happened that in the eighteenth and nineteenth centuries sexuality gradually came into existence as a conjunction of strategies for ordering social relations, authorizing specialized knowledges, licensing expert interventions, intensifying bodily sensations, normalizing erotic behaviors, multiplying sexual perversions, policing personal expressions, crystallizing political resistances, motivating introspective utterances, and constructing human subjectivities" (*How to Do the History of Homosexuality*, 88).

The matter is, of course, not that there is nothing interesting, or intellectually useful, about reading Thoreau in relation to the emerging medical, legal, pedagogical, religious, commercial, or journalistic languages that had in his time come to concern themselves more and less directly with the matter of sex. To take only the nearest example: the male purity movement, with its medico-psychological emphases on onanism's grave threat to the integrity of the self, surely provided Thoreau an important conceptual vocabulary, however idiosyncratically he would inhabit it. But my work here does not presume that such discourses "produced" sexuality, and it offers this refusal not least because the writers of the era (as I argued in the introduction) labored so strenuously, and variously, to evade just such codifications and to imagine sexuality in frameworks other than the given. Their "exemplarity" is in large measure a function of a kind of false retrospect. On onanism, anti-onanism, and its multiple contexts, see the essays collected in *Solitary Pleasures: The Historical, Literary, and Artistic Discourses of Autoeroticism*, ed. Paula Bennett and Vernon A. Rosario II (New York: Routledge, 1995). On onanism as a post-Enlightenment malady, a species of autonomous individualism gone recklessly awry, see Thomas Laqueur, *Solitary Sex: A Cultural History of Masturbation* (New York: Zone Books, 2003); relatedly, on onanism as linked to a tendency to "reverie," see G. J. Barker Benfield, *The Horrors of the Half-Known Life: Male Attitudes toward Women and Sexuality in Nineteenth-Century America* (New York: Harper and Row, 1976).

33. Richardson Jr., *Henry Thoreau*, 58.

34. My sense of biopower here comes most directly from Foucault's *History of Sexuality, Volume 1*, though it is inflected too by Giorgio Agamben's *Homo Sacer: Sovereign Power and Bare Life*, trans. Daniel Heller-Roazen (Stanford, Ca.: Stanford University Press, 1998), and, in respect to nineteenth-century America, by Luciano's linking of biopower to temporality in *Arranging Grief*.

35. For a sharp account of the use of women as emblems of market capital, see Gillian Brown, *Domestic Individualism: Imagining Self in Nineteenth-Century America* (Berkeley: University of California Press, 1990). On modes of defensive projection in Hemingway and others, see Toni Morrison, *Playing in the Dark: Whiteness and the Literary Imagination* (New York: Vintage, 1992).

36. Michael Warner, *The Trouble with Normal* (Cambridge, Mass.: Harvard University Press, 1999), 168. Warner's acute skepticism with respect to the turn in national queer politics toward "a new form of post-liberationist privitization" seems to me to have been fortified by his rich engagements with figures like Thoreau and Whitman.

37. Shamir, *Inexpressive Privacy*, 213. Shamir goes on in the passage, "But, as [Candace] Vogler claims, 'not all intimacies are affairs of the self and . . . the fact that some intimacies are *not* affairs of the self is what makes people want them.'"

NOTES TO CHAPTER 2

1. Quoted in Roy Morris Jr., *The Better Angel: Walt Whitman in the Civil War* (New York: Oxford University Press, 2000), 236. Morris comes by these stories through the work

of Charley Shively, in his edited collection *Calamus Lovers: Walt Whitman's Working Class Camerados* (San Francisco: Gay Sunshine Press, 1987) and his *Drum-Beats: Walt Whitman's Civil War Boy Lovers* (San Francisco: Gay Sunshine Press, 1989).

2. Shively, *Drum-Beats*, 217, 216, 215, 221.

3. From Whitman's *Specimen Days*, quoted in Walt Whitman, *Poetry and Prose*, ed. Justin Kaplan (New York: Library of America, 1996), 713. Cited hereafter as *PP*.

4. Walt Whitman, *The Correspondence*, vol. 1, *1842–1867*, ed. Edwin Haviland Miller (New York University Press, 1961), 59.

5. Whitman, *Correspondence*, 68, 70.

6. Walt Whitman, *Memoranda During the War*, ed. Peter Coviello (New York: Oxford University Press, 2004), 103.

7. Hence Whitman's insistence that "the special meaning of the 'Calamus' cluster . . . mainly resides in its political significance": desire, as he portrays it there, is what *makes* national coherence, inasmuch as nationness is for him, at its root, an especially ardent kind of connectedness among strangers (*Poetry and Prose*, 1035).

8. Walt Whitman, *Leaves of Grass, 1860: The 150th Anniversary Facsimile Edition*, ed. Jason Stacy (Iowa City: University of Iowa Press, 2009), 366.

9. Betsy Erkkila, *Whitman the Political Poet* (New York: Oxford, 1989); Shively, *Drum-Beats*; Robert Leigh Davis, *Whitman and the Romance of Medicine* (Berkeley: University of California Press, 1997); Max Cavitch, *American Elegy: The Poetry of Mourning from the Puritans to Whitman* (Minneapolis: University of Minnesota Press, 2007); and Michael Warner, "Civil War Religion and Whitman's *Drum-Taps*," in *Walt Whitman: Where the Future Becomes Present*, ed. David Haven Blake and Michael Robertson (Iowa City: University of Iowa Press, 2008), 81–90. My sense here of what we might call Whitman's erotic nationalism is informed by other readings as well—Michael Moon's *Disseminating Whitman* (Cambridge, Mass.: Harvard University Press, 1990); Vivian R. Pollack's *The Erotic Whitman* (Berkeley: University of California Press, 2000); Mark Maslan's *Whitman Possessed: Poetry, Sexuality, and Popular Authority* (Baltimore, Md.: Johns Hopkins University Press, 2001); and especially Moon's "Solitude, Singularity, Solidarity: Whitman vis-à-vis Fourier," *ELH* 73, no. 2 (2006): 303–23—though I am perhaps most aligned with Davis's understanding in *The Romance of Medicine* of the critical history of Whitman's war years. Appraisals, he rightly notes, have tended to be divided between those emphasizing "the failure of America's democratic experiment," as exemplified by the war, and those that stress an "optimistic strain." Davis himself follows the latter path, arguing that Whitman "also discovered sexual and political promise in [the war] . . . and he faced the uncertainty of a deferred or conflicted Union with much greater hope than is usually recognized" (*Romance of Medicine*, 152). My own reading differs from Davis's not least in stressing the often eerie simultaneity of Whitman's devastation and his exuberance, though like him I think that whatever relief from despair Whitman finds after the war gathers in the new possibilities he discovers there for sex and eroticized sociability.

10. For an expanded reading of "Calamus" in this vein, see Coviello, *Intimacy in America*, as well as Moon, "Solitude, Singularity, Solidarity."

11. Cavitch, *American Elegy*, 236–44; Warner, "Civil War Religion," 86.

12. For more on "the unrepresentable traces of war" in *Memoranda*, see Timothy Sweet, *Traces of War: Poetry, Photography, and the Crisis of the Union* (Baltimore, Md.: Johns Hopkins University Press, 1990), 48.

13. Shively, *Drum-Beats*, 107, 138, 139, 173, 206, 144.

14. Shively, *Drum-Beats*, 144.

15. Shively, *Drum-Beats*, 191.

16. Alcott, *Hospital Sketches*, in *Alternative Alcott*, ed. Elaine Showalter (New Brunswick, N.J.: Rutgers UP, 1988), 41. Ed Folsom notes precisely this phenomenon in the archive of photographs of Whitman, observing that "Instead of documenting his biological family . . . Whitman chose to construct a very different kind of family, one in which he could coterminously occupy the place of father and mother, wife and husband, lover and friend" ("Whitman's Calamus Photographs," in *Breaking Bounds: Whitman and American Cultural Studies*, ed. Betsy Erkkila and Jay Grossman [New York: Oxford UP, 1996], 193–219, 194).

17. "Statistics enabled detachment and psychically rewarded the habit of quantification that had emerged in the course of market revolution as a national characteristic" (Cavitch, *American Elegy*, 239).

18. On this point, see especially Michael Moon and Eve Kosofsky Sedgwick's suggestive essay taking up "the traces of the poet's incestuous practice" ("Confusion of Tongues," in *Breaking Bounds*, 23–28, here 28). On the vexed intertwinings of parental, fraternal, and erotic relation in Whitman's Civil War life, see also Robert Roper's *Now the Drum of War: Walt Whitman and His Brothers in the Civil War* (New York: Walker Books, 2008).

19. Foucault, *History of Sexuality*, vol. 1, 111.

20. I am thinking of course of Edelman's pathbreaking work in *No Future*.

21. Halberstam, *In a Queer Time and Place*, 5.

22. Stockton, *Queer Child*, especially 11–17.

23. On seriality, see Moon, "Solitude, Singularity, Solidarity." Related here as well are Elizabeth Fenton and Valerie Rohy's wonderfully suggestive remarks on presidency and succession as themselves modes of imagining time and futurity that complicate "the trope of heteronormative familiarity." See their "Whitman, Lincoln, and the Union of Men," *ESQ* 55, nos. 3–4 (2009): 237–67, here 245. See also Freeman, *Time Binds*, 167.

24. As Freeman puts it concisely in *Time Binds*, "'Generation,' a word for both biological and technological forms of replication, cannot necessarily be thrown out with the bathwater of reproductive thinking" (65). Or to put this another way: though homophobia may characteristically route its visions of the future through the banalized image of the child, it does not follow that invocations of children, or the future, or even children as the future, are all themselves irreducibly homophobic.

25. Walt Whitman, *The Correspondence*, vol. 5, *1890–1892*, ed. Edwin Haviland Miller (New York: New York University Press, 1969), 73.

26. Michael Robertson, *Worshipping Walt: The Whitman Disciples* (Princeton: Princeton University Press, 2008), 161.

27. Horace Traubel, *With Walt Whitman in Camden*, vol. 1 (Boston: Small, Maynard, 1906), 76.

28. John Addington Symonds, *The Letters of John Addington Symonds*, vol. 3, ed. Herbert M. Schueller and Robert L. Peters (Detroit: Wayne State University Press, 1969), 819.

29. Sedgwick, *Between Men*, 204. Strong rehearsals of the correspondence between the two men appear in *Between Men*, Robertson's *Worshipping Walt*, as well as Jonathan Ned Katz's *Love Stories*, especially 257–87.

30. Robertson, *Worshipping Walt*, 159.

31. Very recently, Betsy Erkkila made a related point: "Given the languages of paternal, maternal, and familial affection in which Whitman carried on his relationships and correspondence with Fred Vaughan, Peter Doyle, Harry Stafford, and some of the soldiers he met during the war, including Tom Sawyer and Lewis Brown, one might argue that Whitman was thinking [in his response to Symonds] of some of the 'illegitimate sons' he adopted, fathered, and mothered over the course of his life" (*Walt Whitman's Songs of Male Intimacy and Love* [Iowa City: University of Iowa Press, 2011], 148). In my reading, Whitman is thinking less of the "sons" than of the children that, through them, he has parented. My work here could be said to involve a close explication of the logics—historical, textual—by which one might imagine such a vision of Whitman's patrimony.

NOTES TO CODA: A LITTLE DESTINY

1. Thoreau, "Chastity & Sensuality," in *Collected Essays*, 332.

2. Thoreau, "Chastity & Sensuality," in *Collected Essays*, 332.

3. For an exhaustive account of the varieties of futurity on offer in "classic American literature"—a category he forms with deliberate and critical capaciousness—see Mitchell Breitwieser, *National Melancholy: Mourning and Opportunity in Classic American Literature* (Stanford, Ca.: Stanford University Press, 2007), 1–56.

4. Dana Luciano, "Touching, Clinging, Haunting, Worlding: On the Spirit Photograph," lecture given at Bowdoin College, 1 May 2010. I am thinking here, too, of Lauren Berlant's considerations of the possibilities of a "political art whose aim is not a refunctioning of the political but *a lateral exploration of an elsewhere that is first perceptible as an atmosphere*" (Berlant, *Cruel Optimism*, 20, emphasis added).

5. *Open Me Carefully: Emily Dickinson's Intimate Letters to Susan Huntington Dickinson*, ed. Ellen Louise Hart and Martha Nell Smith (Ashfield, Mass.: Paris Press, 1998), 33. Cited hereafter as *OMC*. Like everyone else who studies Dickinson, I have benefited enormously from the Dickinson Electronic Archive (as well, of course, from Thomas H. Johnson and Theodora Ward's edition of the letters). I quote here, though, from the letters as arranged in Hart and Smith's collection to mark how formative their scholarly framing, both of the letters and of Dickinson's relation to Susan, has been for my own work.

6. Thoreau, *A Week*, 272.

7. For a good assessment of that tradition, and a strong account of the correspondence itself, see Marietta Mesmer, *A Vice for Voices: Reading Emily Dickinson's Correspondence* (Amherst: University of Massachusetts Press, 2001).

8. To cite only a few expert parsings of these and related matters in Dickinson's poetry, see Sharon Cameron *Choosing Not Choosing: Dickinson's Fascicles* (Chicago: University of Chicago Press, 1992); Susan Howe, *The Birth-mark: Unsettling the Wilderness in American Literary History* (Middletown, Conn.: Wesleyan University Press, 1993); Heather McHugh, "What Dickinson Makes a Dash For: Interpretive Insecurity as Poetic Freedom," in McHugh, *Broken English: Poetry and Partiality* (Middletown, Conn.: Wesleyan University Press, 1993), 101–14; and Jackson, *Dickinson's Misery*.

9. From 12 March, 1853:

> All life looks differently, and the faces of my fellows are not
> the same they wear when you are with me. I think it is this,
> dear Susie; you sketch my pictures for me, and 'tis at their
> sweet colorings, rather than this dim real that I am used, so
> you see when you go away, the world looks staringly, and I
> find I need more vail. (*OMC*, 45)

10. See Jackson's reading of this letter in *Dickinson's Misery*, 118–26. Jackson contends, "It is a letter *about* reading literary texts, and finally about not wanting to be read in the way those were read" (123). For Dickinson, she painstakingly shows, writing's devolution to literature makes for an overcoding by convention—the not-always-enlivening convention whose name is *literature*. And so, "In order to keep the pathos of life's appropriation by literature from becoming the pathos *of* literature, Dickinson makes it into something else" (123). But the anxiety Jackson pinpoints, I am arguing, is different—is separable—from the case Dickinson makes *for* writing, for the fragile but sustaining private world, set obliquely alongside the dim real of everyday language and everyday time, that written correspondence constructs for herself and Susie to inhabit.

11. The phrase "trembling before history" comes from Warner's "Civil War Religion and Whitman's *Drum-Taps*," 88.

NOTES TO CHAPTER 3

1. Jameson, *The Political Unconscious*, 102.

2. The phrase "the female world of love and ritual" belongs to Smith-Rosenberg (see *Disorderly Conduct*). The distinction is uncertain in light of the sharp turn, in the 1990s, in Jewett criticism. Strong feminist recoveries of Jewett (recoveries from a belittling sense of her as a finally "minor" talent) by Josephine Donovan, Marcia McClintock Folsom, Elizabeth Ammons, Sarah Way Sherman, Marjorie Pryse and others gave way to stinging rebukes, largely on the ground of Jewett's complicity in imperial/racist exclusions and hardening class divisions, by scholars like Amy Kaplan, Ammons herself, Sandra Zagarell, and, perhaps most forcefully, Richard Brodhead. An excellent, ample

account of these disputes—which reads the politically critical moment as following upon an earlier "utopian moment"—appears in Karen L. Kilcup and Thomas S. Edwards, "Confronting Time and Change: Jewett, Her Contemporaries, and Her Critics," in *Jewett and Her Contemporaries: Reshaping the Canon*, ed. Kilcup and Edwards (Gainesville: University of Florida Press, 1999), 1–27. For an attempt to intervene in these clashes, and to mitigate a bit the sweeping dismissals of critics like Brodhead while taking seriously the substance of their critiques, see also Marjorie Pryse's "Sex, Class, and 'Category Crisis': Reading Jewett's Transitivity," in *Jewett and Her Contemporaries*, 31–62. A strong earlier account of these emerging divisions (which casts them as a conflict between "celebratory" and "historical" approaches to Jewett) appears in June Howard's "Unraveling Regions, Unsettling Periods: Sarah Orne Jewett and American Literary History," *American Literature* 68, no. 2 (1996): 365–84. See also Josephine Donovan, *New England Local Color Literature: A Woman's Tradition* (New York: Frederick Ungar, 1983); Marcia McClintock Folsom, "'Tact Is a Kind of Mind-Reading': Empathic Style in Sarah Orne Jewett's *The Country of the Pointed Firs*," *Colby Library Quarterly* 18, no. 1 (1982): 66–78; Sarah Way Sherman, *Sarah Orne Jewett: An American Persephone* (Hanover, N.H.: University Press of New England, 1989); and Elizabeth Ammons, *Conflicting Stories: American Women Writers at the Turn of the Twentieth Century* (New York: Oxford University Press, 1991). For the anti-utopians, see Amy Kaplan, "Nation, Region, and Empire," in *Columbia Literary History of the United States*, ed. Emory Elliott (New York: Columbia University Press, 1988), 240–66; Richard Brodhead, *Cultures of Letters: Scenes of Reading and Writing in Nineteenth-Century America* (Chicago: University of Chicago Press, 1993); and Ammons, "Material Culture, Empire, and Jewett's *Country of the Pointed Firs*," in *New Essays on "The Country of the Pointed Firs*," ed. June Howard (New York: Cambridge University Press, 1994), 81–100.

3. Heather Love, "Gyn/Apology Sarah Orne Jewett's Spinster Aesthetics," *ESQ* 55, nos. 3–4 (2009): 305–34, here 310 and 313.

4. Nealon, *Foundlings*, 13.

5. Brodhead, *Cultures of Letters*; Ammons, "Material Culture." See also Sandra Zagarell, "*Country's* Portrayal of Community and Exclusion of Difference," as well as Susan Gillman, "Regionalism and Nationalism in Jewett's *Country of the Pointed Firs*," both in June Howard's *New Essays on "The Country of the Pointed Firs*" (39–60, 101–18), for iterations of the critical/anti-utopian perspective on Jewett.

6. On wounding as historical model, and the problems with that paradigm, see especially Seltzer's work on "Wound Culture" in *Serial Killers*, 253–92. See also Wendy Brown, *States of Injury: Power and Freedom in Late Modernity* (Princeton: Princeton University Press, 1995).

7. Dana Luciano, "Geological Fantasies, Haunting Anachronies: Eros, Time, and History in Harriet Prescott Spofford's 'The Amber Gods,'" *ESQ* 55, nos. 3–4 (2009): 269–303, 298.

8. Sarah Orne Jewett, *The Country of the Pointed Firs*, ed. Alison Easton (New York: Penguin, 1995), 26. Cited hereafter as *Firs*. Easton's edition reprints *Firs* as published in

book form between 1896 and Jewett's death in 1909 (before, in later editions, additional Dunnet Landing stories were added).

9. See Judith Fetterley, "Reading *Deephaven* as a Lesbian Text," in *Sexual Practice/ Textual Theory: Lesbian Cultural Criticism*, ed. Susan J. Wolfe and Julia Penelope (Cambridge: Blackwell, 1993), 164–83; Kate McCullough, *Regions of Identity: The Construction of America in Women's Fiction* (Stanford, Ca.: Stanford University Press, 1999); Judith Fetterley and Marjorie Pryse, *Writing Out of Place: Regionalism, Women, and American Literary Culture* (Urbana: University of Illinois Press, 2003); and Marcus, *Between Women*. Earlier accounts of queer possibility in Jewett can be found in Josephine Donovan's "The Unpublished Love Poetry of Sarah Orne Jewett," *Frontiers: A Journal of Women Studies* 4 (January 1980): 26–31, as well as her "Nan Prince and the Golden Apples," *Colby Library Quarterly* 22, no. 1 (March 1986): 17–27; and in Faderman's *Surpassing the Love of Men*, 190–203. Though it appeared too late for me to address it here, I want to note too how much I admire Sarah Ensor's "Spinster Ecology: Rachel Carson, Sarah Orne Jewett, and Nonreproductive Futurity," *American Literature* 84, no. 2 (2012): 409–35. Ensor's deft reading of nonheteronormative futures resonates with my own concerns about the dialectics of sociability and antisociality in Jewett.

10. Stein, "*The Blithedale Romance*'s Queer Style," 212.

11. Marcus, *Between Women*, 21.

12. Freeman, *Time Binds*, 117. I am inspired throughout this chapter by Freeman's and Luciano's meditations on Jameson's pronouncement, as well as those of Lauren Berlant in "Two Girls, Fat and Thin" in *Cruel Optimism*, 121–59.

13. This pairing, of pleasure and justice in the mode of historiography, follows directly from Luciano's arguments. Meditating on what Wendy Brown, following the Derrida of *Specters of Marx*, calls "a noncontemporaneous idiom for justice," Luciano writes that "the challenge we confront is to find ways to think . . . differing manifestations of violence together toward the development of an idiom of justice for histories of trauma, sexual and otherwise—one that would not foreclose or deny the deployment of sexual and corporeal pleasure as part of what 'justice' might mean" ("Geological Fantasies," 297).

14. For more on stylistic tact, see Folsom, "Tact Is a Kind of Mind-Reading."

15. Like many another, I have had my sense of the reach and the utility of the Deleuzian notion of "assemblage" sharpened considerably by the work of Jasbir Puar. See her *Terrorist Assemblages: Homonationalism in Queer Times* (Durham, N.C.: Duke University Press, 2007). Jane Bennett, also, takes up "assemblage" in relation to the vitality of objects—a matter, as we shall see, precious to Jewett—in her *Vibrant Matter*. My use of "assemblages" to describe the formations made by a deterritorialized, nonmatrimonial love is informed by, and indebted to, their strong uses of Deleuze.

16. Pryse writes suggestively about the timing of that emergence with respect to Jewett, noting that "Jewett herself, writing during the transition to modernism, reflects a concern with categories—especially . . . with the categories of sex and class—even though much of her work appears to resist the very concept of category" ("Sex, Class, and 'Category Crisis,'" 40). Her thoughts on Jewett's likely awareness of what she calls "modernist

categories of sexuality" (42) are indebted to Josephine Donovan's "Nan Prince and the Golden Apples," where Donovan argues that Jewett, having traveled to Europe in 1882, the year of the appearance of Krafft-Ebing's *Psychopathia Sexualis*, and having access as well both to her father's medical library and to his conversation, would have been aware of the emerging taxonomies of German sexology, and would have rejected them. The degree of Jewett's engagement with those nascent categories interests me less here than the work she does in the space of their uncompleted emergence.

17. Elizabeth Ammons, "Jewett's Witches," in *Critical Essays on Sarah Orne Jewett*, ed. Gwen L. Nagel (Boston: G. K. Hall & Co., 1984), 165–84, here 177. "Mrs. Todd," Ammons writes, "is directly linked to the world of witchcraft: she cuts herbs by moonlight for charms, dispenses secret concoctions after sundown, stands majestically encircled by the black and gray braids of her homespun rug" (176).

18. Bill Brown, *A Sense of Things: The Object Matter of American Literature* (Chicago: University of Chicago Press, 2003), 88.

19. On abortion in the nineteenth century, see Carroll Smith-Rosenberg, *Disorderly Conduct*, especially "The Abortion Movement and the AMA, 1850–1880," 217–44.

20. Pryse, "Sex, Class, and 'Category Crisis,'" 40.

21. Brown, *Sense of Things*, 81–124, 83, 85. His work picks up on notes struck earlier by Folsom as well as Brodhead.

22. I am informed here by the theoretical frameworks offered in Jane Bennett's *Vibrant Matter*, as well as by the work of the "Interspecies" special issue of *Social Text* (29, no. 1 [Spring 2011]) edited by Julie Livingston and Jasbir K. Puar. (See in particular their comments on "animal studies" from their introduction to the volume, 3–14.)

23. Rohy, *Anachronism and Its Others*, 57. My work here on object-love in Jewett, which takes those loves to register both losses of possibility *and* the expansive diffusion of affect freed from its confinement in matrimony, rhymes with Rohy's reading of "overinvestment in objects" in Jewett in the terms of "fetishism's double attitude toward loss" (*Anachronism and Its Others*, 57, 49–59). See also Luciano's related remarks on "unconventional couplings—with paintings, landscapes, worlds" in Spofford, and on the way they "point toward a Deleuzian conception of sexuality as unleashing and enabling transformative becomings, eschewing imitation and identification" ("Geological Fantasies," 286).

24. Love, "Gyn/Apology," 310.

25. Love, "Gyn/Apology," 305, 326.

26. Brown, *Sense of Things*, 99, 109–10.

27. On the entanglement of class and queerness in Jewett, see especially Pryse, who writes, "The pathologization of same-sex love at the end of the nineteenth century supported the privilege of the emerging class of white male doctors with medical specialties who practiced in urban centers," suggesting deftly the ways Jewett's class affiliations— so much the object of critique in an account like Brodhead's—are crossed, and made more intricate than such critiques quite allow, by her erotic affiliations ("Sex, Class, and 'Category Crisis,'" 55).

28. Quoted in Deitcher, *Dear Friends*, 110.

29. See, as exemplary in this vein of critique, Kaplan, "Nation, Region, and Empire"; Brodhead, *Cultures of Letters*; Zagarell, *"Country's* Portrayal of Community and Exclusion of Difference"; Gillman, "Regionalism and Nationalism in Jewett's *Country of the Pointed Firs*"; and Ammons, "Material Culture, Empire, and Jewett's *Country of the Pointed Firs.*" It is Ammons, for instance, who enjoins us to note "the subtle but clear protofascist implications" of the Bowden reunion near the conclusion of *Firs*, with its cavalcade of "all those white people marching around in military formation ritualistically affirming their racial purity, global dominance, and white ethnic superiority and solidarity" (97). Pryse's is an especially strong rejoinder to these critics' tendency to back away from the strands of subtle textual *relation* that tie Jewett's work to the imperialism surrounding her in the drive to describe her work *as* that imperialism in literary form, and to arraign it. See her "Sex, Class, and 'Category Crisis.'" An especially strident broadside against political critiques of Jewett appears in Josephine Donovan's "Jewett on Race, Class, Ethnicity, and Imperialism: A Reply to Her Critics," *Colby Quarterly* 38, no. 4 (December 2002): 403–16.

30. See for instance Barbara A. Johns suggestive remarks in "'Mateless and Appealing': Growing into Spinsterhood in Sarah Orne Jewett," in *Critical Essays on Sarah Orne Jewett*, ed. Gwen L. Nagel (Boston: G. K. Hall & Co., 1984), 147–65. But Johns writes aptly, too, when considering the "nightmare" destiny of a *Grey Gardens*-like figure like Miss Chauncey in *Deephaven*, that "Jewett's warning about the emotional starvation possible in single life is matched by her description of the violence possible in marriage" (152).

31. Bill Brown, *Sense of Things*, 124.

32. On what came to be understood as "the antisocial thesis"—the understanding of queer desire as what transpires at the place of the social's collapse, as that which marks its dissolving impossibility—see especially Bersani's work in *Homos* (Cambridge, Mass.: Harvard University Press, 1996), and Edelman in *No Future*. Both are salutary in the force of their refusal of bucolic visions of queer belonging, and in their accounts of the value of certain kinds of inadmissibility within, and elemental antagonism to, the coherence of the social. For a wider consideration of antisociality, see the *PMLA* forum "The Antisocial Thesis in Queer Theory."

33. Bill Brown, *Sense of Things*, 124.

34. Nealon, *Foundlings*, 23.

35. Johns, "Mateless and Appealing," 161. I think here of Michael Cobb's work on "the isolated figures of the 'single' who are misconstrued as lonely figures." He writes suggestively, "They might not be lonely—they might just want to be antisocial, they might just want to relate to others outside of the supreme logic of the couple, which has become the way one binds oneself to the social." Cobb deftly identifies here how what looks like a kind of queer antisociality might *also* express a hunger for a different kind, a different scene, of relationality—one that, like so much of Jewett's Dunnet Landing, is not wholly overcoded by "the supreme logic of the couple" (Michael Cobb, "Lonely," in *After Sex?* 207–20, here 217).

36. See again Edelman, *No Future.*

37. On "compearance" and a community knit together by an unshareable mortal singularity, that inoperative universalism, see Jean-Luc Nancy, *The Inoperative Community,* ed. Peter Connor, trans. Peter Connor, Lisa Garbus, Michael Holland, and Simona Sawhney (Minneapolis: University of Minnesota Press, 1991).

38. Jeff Nunokawa, "Queer Theory: Postmortem," in *After Sex?,* 245–56, here 251. Nunokawa's remarks come in a rich meditation on the way the "sociable" might differ, in small but consequential ways, from the "social" as envisioned in works like Bersani's.

NOTES TO CHAPTER 4

1. Harold Bloom, *The American Religion: The Emergence of the Post-Christian Nation* (New York: Simon and Schuster, 1992), 95.

2. McGarry, *Ghosts of Futures Past,* 155, 157, 157.

3. Bloom, *American Religion,* 101, 99. Or again: "Smith's radical sense of theomorphic patriarchs and anthropomorphic gods is an authentic return to J, or the Yahwist, the Bible's first author" (84).

4. Elizabeth Freeman, *The Wedding Complex: Forms of Belonging in Modern American Culture* (Durham, N.C.: Duke University Press, 2002), 127. She is riffing here on Mary Ryan's *Cradle of the Middle Class: The Family in Oneida County, New York, 1790–1865* (New York: Cambridge University Press, 1981). Much of the work of plural marriage as a bulwark for patriarchy fearing its own decline can be seen too in Marvin S. Hill's *Quest For Refuge: The Mormon Flight from American Pluralism* (Salt Lake City, Utah: Signature Books, 1989), especially 99–126.

5. Bentley's reading underscores how a casting of polygamy as enslavement served to ratify, as freedom itself, what might otherwise appear as still another, if milder, form of enslavement: monogamous marriage for women under conditions of patriarchy. "Polygamy," Bentley writes, "is the bondage that sanctified marriage as freedom" ("Marriage as Treason: Polygamy, Nation, and the Novel," in *The Futures of American Studies,* ed. Donald E. Pease and Robyn Wiegman [Durham, N.C.: Duke University Press, 2002], 341–70). On Mormon polygamy and midcentury sexuality, see also Bruce Burgett, "On the Mormon Question: Race, Sex, and Polygamy in the 1850s and the 1990s," *American Quarterly* 57, no. 1 (March 2005): 75–102. If what Bentley describes here is in some ways the racialization of Mormon intimate practice, that racialization works also in other extensions. Though we will be concerned here vastly more with Smith's early articulations of a polygamous theology than with the vexed institutionalizations of plural marriage in the church later in the century, I would suggest as well—following the lead of scholars in queer and native studies like Bethany Schneider, Mark Rifkin, and Andrea Smith—that Mormonism, which from the first understood itself to be a kind of North American *indigenization* of Christianity, propelled itself by virtue of its attenuations and lateralizing derangements of the dyadic family form into an unstable, tense, and finally for the Mormons, intolerable identification with the native peoples of North

America, whose own arrangements of gender, property, and intimate life (as Schneider astutely reminds us) "distressed white America *because* the kinship structures of that tribal relation stood directly against the heteronormative structures of private property ownership and inheritance necessary to the very foundations of what it means to be a 'fellow-citizen.'" The insistence on a hyperbolically patriarchal kind of plural marriage in later Mormonism—an insistence both authorized and deeply problematized by Smith's own unsystematized pronouncements, as we will see—works, I think, to push back against such anxious proximities, to cut a hard and invidious distinction between Mormon intimate practice and the differently arrayed structures of gender and kinship identified with native peoples and native sexualities. See Daniel Heath Justice, Mark Rifkin, and Bethany Schneider, "Introduction," *GLQ* 16, nos. 1–2 (2010): 5–39, here 17. See also Mark Rifkin's rich theorization of the policing of indigenous intimate forms—and his splendid, nondismissive problematization of "kinship" and "sovereignty" as terms that, when applied to indigenous people, may preclude the recognition of certain sorts of sodality *as* forms of politics—in his *When Did Indians Become Straight?: Kinship, the History of Sexuality, and Native Sovereignty* (New York: Oxford University Press, 2011).

6. See Richard Lyman Bushman's biography, *Joseph Smith: Rough Stone Rolling* (New York: Knopf, 2005); D. Michael Quinn's *Early Mormonism and the Magic World View* (Salt Lake City, Utah: Signature Books, 1998); and Fawn Brodie's seminal *No Man Knows My History: The Life of Joseph Smith, the Mormon Prophet* (New York: Knopf, 1945). Tracking Smith's statements about polygamy itself, as practice and principle, is, as these and other writers make plain, extraordinarily difficult. As Brodie writes, "During the Nauvoo years, filled though they were with lawsuits, arrests, and intrigues among his own people, Joseph found time not only to write the history of his own church, but also to bring Mormon theology to its full flowering." And yet, she goes on, "His teachings were now rarely presented as revelations; there were either introduced in sermons or imparted secretly" (*No Man Knows My History*, 277). This secrecy bedevils efforts to attribute to Smith a coherent "position" with respect to polygamy, which is part of the reason why I turn here to his revelations, not directly concerned with marriage or "sealing" but immensely significant, as I read them, for their vision of the mortal body and its range and capacities. For an especially careful parsing of Smith's statements and practices, and those attributed to him with varying degrees of plausibility, around polygamy, see Todd Compton, *In Sacred Loneliness: The Plural Wives of Joseph Smith* (Salt Late City, Utah: Signature Books, 1997).

7. I am indebted here, again, to McGarry's work in *Ghosts of Futures Past*, as well as to Janet R. Jakobsen and Ann Pelligrini's "Times Like These," their introduction to their 2008 collection *Secularisms* (Durham, N.C.: Duke University Press, 2008), 1–38, and Jared Hickman's suggestive meditations on the inadequacies of secularist framings of modernity in "Globalization and the Gods, or the Political Theology of 'Race,'" *Early American Literature* 45, no. 1 (2010): 145–82.

8. Joseph Smith, *The Essential Joseph Smith: Classics in Mormon Thought*, no. 4 (Salt Lake City, Utah: Signature Books, 1995), 235. Cited hereafter as *EJS*.

9. An excellent history of the legal drama around Mormon polygamy appears in Sarah Barringer Gordon, *The Mormon Question: Polygamy and Constitutional Conflict in Nineteenth-Century America* (Chapel Hill: University of North Carolina Press, 2002).

10. Frederick Douglass, *The Narrative of the Life of Frederick Douglass, An American Slave* ed. Houston A. Baker Jr. (New York: Penguin, 1982), 107. Cited hereafter as *NLFD*. See also Henry Louis Gates Jr., "Introduction," *The Classic Slave Narratives* (New York: Mentor, 1987), ix. Further development of the linking of literacy to freedom appears in Robert B. Stepto's *From behind the Veil: A Study of Afro-American Narrative*, 2nd ed. (Urbana: University of Illinois Press, 1991). Peter Walker's *Moral Choices: Memory, Desire, and Imagination in Nineteenth-Century American Abolition* (Baton Rogue: Louisiana State University Press, 1978), offers a seminal account of Douglass in line with nineteenth-century individualism. For more on autonomy and gender difference, see Valerie Smith, *Self-Discovery and Afro-American Literature* (Cambridge, Mass.: Harvard University Press, 1987); Ann duCille, *The Coupling Convention: Sex, Text, and Tradition in Black Women's Fiction* (New York: Oxford University Press, 1993); and Rafia Zafar, "Franklinian Douglass: The Afro-American as Representative Man," in *Frederick Douglass: New Literary and Historical Essays*, ed. Eric , ed. Sundquist (Cambridge: Cambridge University Press, 1990), 99–118. On slavery and contract, and in particular on the vexed relation of contract to marriage, see Amy Dru Stanley, *From Bondage to Contract: Wage Labor, Marriage, and the Market in the Age of Slave Emancipation* (Cambridge: Cambridge University Press, 1998).

11. For an account of Douglass in concert with Jacobs that works "by emphasizing the two texts' similarities rather than their differences by insisting that differences stemming from the prerogatives of gender . . . do not of necessity set the texts at odds," see Donald B. Gibson, "Harriet Jacobs, Frederick Douglass, and the Slavery Debate," in *Harriet Jacobs and "Incidents in the Life of a Slave Girl": New Critical Essays*, ed. Deborah M. Garfield and Rafia Zafar (Cambridge: Cambridge University Press, 1996), 156–78, here 162.

12. Hortense J. Spillers, *Black, White, and in Color: Essays on American Literature and Culture* (Chicago: University of Chicago Press, 2003), 220. The readings originate in the essay "Mama's Baby, Papa's Maybe: An American Grammar Book," which first appeared in *Diacritics* 17, no. 2 (1987).

13. Spillers, *Black, White, and in Color*, 218.

14. Stanley, *From Bondage to Contract*, 181.

15. See Claudia Tate, *Domestic Allegories of Political Desire: The Black Heroine's Text at the Turn of the Century* (New York: Oxford University Press, 1992), and duCille, *The Coupling Convention*. My approach to Douglass and marriage has been strongly informed by Amy Dru Stanley's work on the vexations of marriage as a special category of contract (*From Bondage to Contract*, especially 175–217) and by Tess Chakkalakal's new work on marriage as a site of pained ambivalence for postemancipation black writing (*Novel Bondage: Slavery, Marriage, and Freedom in Nineteenth-Century America* [Champagne-Urbana: University of Illinois Press, 2011]).

16. Nothing about this logic should be unfamiliar to us, today, in the midst of season after political season of dispute around marriage. The framing of the question of gay

marriage as a the state's ultimate form of acknowledgement, ratification, and recognition—far greater not just bureaucratically or economically but *morally*, in a way that renders all other arrangements with the state supposedly second-class—harks back to deployments of marriage exactly like Douglass's. Michael Warner's is only the most thoroughgoing contestation of the reduction of queer politics to marriage politics, and of the aggrandizement of marriage that takes place there, in *The Trouble with Normal*. A splendid, more recent worrying over the celebration of marriage politics appears in Katherine M Franke's editorial, "Marriage Is a Mixed Blessing," *New York Times*, 23 June 2011, A25.

17. Bloom, *American Religion*, 106.

18. Terryl L. Givens, *The Viper on the Hearth: Mormons, Myths, and the Construction of Heresy* (New York: Oxford University Press, 1997), 82.

19. Bloom, *American Religion*, 104.

20. Joseph Smith, *Doctrine and Covenants* 132, nos. 1–2, in *The Book of Mormon: Another Testament of Jesus Christ, The Doctrine and Covenants of the Church of Jesus Christ of Latter-day Saints, The Pearl of Great Price* (Salt Lake City, Utah: The Church of Jesus Christ of Latter-day Saints, 1981), 266–67. Cited hereafter as *D&C*. *D&C* 132 is the formalization of the revelation written in July of 1843 and published after Smith's death in the *Desert News Extra*, in Salt Lake City, in September of 1852. See *EJS*, 192–99.

21. On the plainspokennesss of Smith's revelations, and especially on their characteristic running together of divine and quotidian purpose, see Richard Lyman Bushman's "The 'Little Narrow Prison' of Language: The Rhetoric of Revelation," in *Believing History: Latter-day Saint Essays* (New York: Columbia University Press, 2004), 248–61. For Bushman, the effectiveness of Smith's mode lies in the way "The lives of plain people are caught in the same rhetorical space where God's voice speaks of coming calamities and the beginning of the marvelous work and a wonder" (257).

22. *The Book of Mormon*, with its manic genealogies, is finally a narrative that shifts the scene of sacred drama from the Holy Land to North America, to which the descendants of Lehi flee before the Babylonian destruction of Jerusalem. Lehi's sons, Laman and Nephi, do battle in America in a millennial war that results in the eventual extinguishing of the virtuous Nephites by the cursed, dark-skinned Lamanites, whom the text identifies with the indigenous people of America. (In this, Smith follows a fairly conventional early nineteenth-century reading of Native Americans as remnants of the Lost Tribes of Israel.) That a gathering of "those who have complied with the requisitions of the new covenant" should transpire in *Missouri*, then, simply rearticulates the complex indigenization instantiated by *The Book of Mormon*, wherein the indigenous people of America are read both as cursed in their racialization *and* as the final inheritors of millennial promise in the American world. But there is more to the matter than this vast truncation of *The Book of Mormon* suggests, and more particularly where polygamy in its relation to natives in America is concerned. Though indigeneity comes to figure less and less prominently as Smith's prophetic career develops, and as he turns to a theorization of the proto-divinity of humankind and of the necessity of polygamy, still many of those later revelations—about the plurality of gods, the righteousness of plural marriage—stand Mormonism in vivid, tense relation to an

indigeneity that it plainly emulates and expropriates, but from which it seeks also, often denigratingly, to distinguish itself. On the complexity of *The Book of Mormon*'s relation to indigeneity, I am most especially indebted to Jared Hickman, who takes up the work in the register of multigenerational racialist epic and of what he names an "Amerindian apocalypse" (Hickman, "*The Book of Mormon* as Amerindian Apocalypse," mss.). See also Terryl Givens's *The Book of Mormon: A Very Short Introduction* (New York: Oxford University Press, 2009); Armand L. Mauss, *All Abraham's Children: Changing Mormon Conceptions of Race and Lineage* (Urbana: University of Illinois Press, 2003); and Bushman's *Rough Stone Rolling*; though Hickman's remains for me the most theoretically nuanced meditation on race, racialism, indigeneity, and *The Book of Mormon*.

23. Givens, *The Viper on the Hearth*, 89.

24. Givens is especially strong on this point. Reading Mormon leader Orson Pratt and apostle George Q. Cannon on the question of the Christianity of Mormonism, he observes that their "claim that Christendom has persisted almost two thousand years in a state of apostasy is tantamount to declaring Christianity so-called is a misnomer. Harold Bloom is correct in saying Mormonism's hallmark is its deliberate obliviousness to two millennia of Christian tradition" (*The Viper on the Hearth*, 81). Hence his sense of the Mormon restorative project as aimed at "the demystification of Christianity itself" (83).

25. Terryl L. Givens, *People of Paradox: A History of Mormon Culture* (New York: Oxford University Press, 2007), 131, 117–42. For popular accounts of Mormonism that emphasize the extraordinary histories of violence that surround its founding and development—with special attunement to matters like "blood atonement"—see Jon Krakauer, *Under the Banner of Heaven: A Story of Violent Faith* (New York: Anchor Books, 2004), and Mikal Gilmore, *Shot in the Heart* (New York: Anchor Books, 1994).

26. Brodie, *No Man Knows My History*, 294.

27. Brodie, *No Man Knows My History*, 300, 294. Or again: "Mormon theology was never burdened with otherwordliness. . . . There was a fine robustness about it that smelled of the frontier and that rejected an asceticism that was never endemic to America" (*No Man Knows My History*, 187).

28. Quoted in Givens, *People of Paradox*, 45.

29. Brodie, detailing the exchanges around the courting of Nancy Rigdon, rightly reads his letter as a "forthright argument for polygamy" (*No Man Knows My History*, 310).

30. On Whitman's disciples and the religiosity of their regard for him, see especially Michael Warner's introduction to his edition of Whitman's complete poems, *The Portable Walt Whitman* (New York: Penguin, 2003), as well as Robertson, *Worshipping Walt*.

31. Quoted in Givens, *People of Paradox*, 133.

32. Jared Hickman, review of Givens, *People of Paradox*, forthcoming in *Books and Culture: A Christian Review*.

33. Brodie, *No Man Knows My History*, 305.

34. I am especially influenced here by the multifaceted work of D. Michael Quinn, most particularly his *Same-Sex Dynamics among Nineteenth-Century Americans: A Mormon Example* (Urbana: University of Illinois Press, 1996), as well as his "Mormon Women Have

Had the Priesthood since 1843," in *Women and Authority: Re-emerging Mormon Feminism*, ed. Maxine Hanks (Salt Lake City, Utah: Signature Books, 1992), 365–409. For a more recent reading of the underexplicated, nonnormative possibilities of Smith's revelations, and of Mormon theology more generally, see also Taylor G. Petrey, "Toward a Post-Heterosexual Mormon Theology," *Dialogue: A Journal of Mormon Thought* 44 (2011): 106–41. *Women and Authority* takes up, more broadly, the question of Mormon feminism, which has often been rooted in twinned considerations of women's relation to the priesthood, as practiced and endorsed by Smith and others (a matter that broaches different kinds and degrees of priesthood, and differences between priesthood as endowment and office), and in questions about "God the Mother," or, in Linda P. Wilcox's terms, the "idea of a mother in heaven" ("The Mormon Concept of a Mother in Heaven," in *Women and Authority*, 3–21, particularly 3). See also Margaret Merrill Toscano, "Put On Your Strength O Daughters of Zion: Claiming Priesthood and Knowing the Mother," in *Women and Authority*, 411–37. For treatments of these questions tuned more to contemporaneity, see Martha Sonntag Bradley, *Pedestals and Podiums: Utah Women, Religious Authority, and Equal Rights* (Salt Lake City, Utah: Signature Books, 2005), especially "The Uses of History," 1–28. For a more recent, searching consideration of women, priesthood, and plural marriage, see Kathleen Flake, "The Emotional and Priestly Logic of Plural Marriage." Arrington Annual Lecture, Paper 15 (2009), http://digitalcommons.usu.edu/arrington_lecture/15.

35. Part of the story of that migration, too, is a story of *fracture*: of the dividing of the Mormon faith, in the aftermath of Smith's death, into separate sects, often on the basis of painful disagreements about the sanctity of plural marriage. Some of these disagreements appear in a biography of Emma Hale Smith, Joseph's wife, by Linda King Newell and Valeen Tippetts Avery, titled *Mormon Enigma: Emma Hale Smith* (Champaign: University of Illinois Press, 1994).

36. Bloom, *American Religion*, 86.

37. Justice, Rifkin, and Schneider, "Introduction," *GLQ* 16, nos. 1–2 (2010): 17. It is in this sense—the sense of the obliquity of native cultures' intimate structures to the "monogamous heterocouplehood and the privatized single-family household" that comprise the "official national ideal"—that Rifkin, in his *When Did Indians Become Straight?*, encourages us to consider indigenous people as marked by *an insufficient straightness* throughout the American nineteenth century (6).

38. Deborah A. Miranda, "Extermination of the *Joyas*: Gendercide in Spanish California," *GLQ* 16, nos. 1–2 (2010): 253–84.

39. Givens, *The Viper on the Hearth*, 83.

NOTES TO CODA: UNCEREMONIOUSNESS

1. Molly McGarry unfolds exactly this point in her *Ghosts of Futures Past*: "If the confessional is one culturally specific site for producing speech about the self, the Protestant evangelical tent, the revival meeting, and the Spiritualist séance may be among its American corollaries" (157).

2. Foucault, *History of Sexuality*, vol. 1, 148–50. The point here is not that Foucault has no account of racism useful to the American context—he does—or that Americanists ought therefore to dismiss the book as untenable. My claim is simply that the trajectories toward the emergence of modern sexuality are distinct in European and American contexts, and that the career of "race" in nineteenth-century America brings into sharper relief some of those divergences. For a seminal account of race and Foucault's *History of Sexuality*, see Ann Laura Stoler's *Race and the Education of Desire: Foucault's "History of Sexuality" and the Colonial Order of Things* (Durham, N.C.: Duke University Press, 1995). For strong new work that demonstrates how Foucault's thought, and particularly his explorations of biopower, might usefully shape critical race theory, see Nikolas Rose, *The Power of Life Itself: Biomedicine, Power, and Subjectivity in the Twenty-First Century* (Princeton: Princeton University Press, 2007); Puar, *Terrorist Assemblages*; and Lynne Huffer, *Mad for Foucault: Rethinking the Foundations of Queer Theory* (New York: Columbia University Press, 2010).

3. Harriet Jacobs, *Incidents in the Life of a Slave Girl, Written by Herself*, ed. Jean Fagan Yelling (Cambridge, Mass.: Harvard University Press, 1987), 201. Cited hereafter as *ILSG*.

4. See Valerie Smith, *Self-Discovery and Authority in Afro-American Narrative* (Cambridge, Mass.: Harvard University Press, 1987), and P. Gabrielle Foreman, "Manifest in Signs: The Politics of Sex and Representation in *Incidents in the Life of a Slave Girl*," in *Harriet Jacobs and "Incidents in the Life of a Slave Girl": New Critical Essays*, ed. Deborah M. Garfield and Rafia Zafar (New York: Cambridge University Press, 1996), 76–99. I am particularly influenced here by Foreman's account of how Jacobs "locates her astute analysis in the realm of the undertell" (81).

5. Herman Melville, *Moby-Dick, or the Whale*, ed. Harrison Hayford, Hershel Parker, and G. Thomas Tanselle (Chicago: Northwestern University Press and the Newberry Library, 1988), 73. Cited hereafter as *MD*.

6. See Samuel Otter, *Melville's Anatomies* (Berkeley: University of California Press, 1999), 159–71, and Geoffrey Sanborn, *The Sign of the Cannibal: Melville and the Making of a Postcolonial Reader* (Durham, N.C.: Duke University Press, 1998), 119–69.

7. This point follows from Otter's, who writes in *Melville's Anatomies*: "In *Moby-Dick*, touch transforms not only character relations but also racial distinction and syntax" (161).

8. See along these lines Leo Bersani, who writes, "the Ishmael-Queequeg marriage enacts a sensuality that cannot be reduced to the psychology of either heterosexual or homosexual desire" ("Incomparable America," in Bersani, *The Culture of Redemption* [Cambridge, Mass.: Harvard University Press, 1990], 147).

9. Bersani, "Incomparable America," 139.

10. Cesare Casarino, *Modernity at Sea: Melville, Marx, Conrad in Crisis* (Minneapolis: University of Minnesota Press, 2002), 129.

11. Casarino, *Modernity at Sea*, 172.

12. I am indebted here to Otter on touch, Bersani on sexual subjectivity, Casarino on the "igneous body of living labor" (*Modernity at Sea*, 131), and also Jennifer Doyle on "the boring parts" of *Moby-Dick* and their relation to Ishmael's "celebration of manly love"

(*Sex Objects: Art and the Dialectics of Desire* [Minneapolis: University of Minnesota Press, 2006], 5).

13. Casarino, *Modernity at Sea*, 175, 177–78.

14. See on this point David Bradley's essay "Our Crowd, Their Crowd: Race, Reader, and *Moby-Dick*," in *Melville's Evermoving Dawn: Centennial Essays*, ed. John Bryant and Robert Milder (Kent, Ohio: Kent State University Press, 1997), 119–46, especially 144.

15. Frederick Busch, "Introduction," *Billy Budd and Other Stories* (New York: Penguin, 1986), xviii.

16. Reading Elizabeth Keckley, with a nod back to Jacobs, Luciano writes, "Her declared reluctance to speak [of "the direct cause" of her son's birth by an unnamed white assailant] ironically renarrates the form of the family by challenging its timing, pinpointing the sexualized female body as the unspeakable origin of maternal affection." In so doing, Luciano argues, Keckley offers a story in which "the desexualization of the middle-class white maternal body also works to dehistoricize the social origins of this sexual violation by forcing 'lascivious' black women to bear the blame" (*Arranging Grief*, 251, 252).

17. Foreman, "Manifest in Signs," 81.

18. Lauren Berlant, *The Queen of America Goes to Washington City: Essays on Sex and Citizenship* (Durham: Duke University Press, 1997), 231. What I frame here as a kind of dispossession, Berlant describes as "a hybrid experience of intimacy and alienation of a kind fundamental to African American women's experience of national sexuality under slavery" (228).

19. Glenn Hendler, *Public Sentiments: Structures of Feeling in Nineteenth-Century American Literature* (Chapel Hill: University of North Carolina Press, 2001), 7.

20. Spillers, *Black, White, and in Color*, 155.

21. Spillers, *Black, White, and in Color*, 156.

NOTES TO CHAPTER 5

1. Nathaniel Hawthorne, *The Blithedale Romance* (New York: Penguin, 1983), 1–2. This edition reproduces volume 3 (1964) of the *Centenary Edition of the Works of Nathaniel Hawthorne* from the Ohio State University Press. All references are to this edition, and will be cited hereafter as *BR*.

2. Versions of these readings of the novel, given different inflections in different historical and critical moments, are far from uncommon. An overview of them might include such works as Frederick Crews, *The Sins of the Father: Hawthorne's Psychological Themes* (New York: Oxford University Press, 1966); Richard H. Brodhead *Hawthorne, Melville, and the Novel* (Chicago: University of Chicago Press, 1976); Lauren Berlant, "Fantasies of Utopia in *The Blithedale Romance*," *American Literary History* 1 (1989): 30–62 (Berlant's is the argument about the misarticulation of mass and intimate politics in the terms of the other); Brown, *Domestic Individualism*; Richard Millington, *Practicing Romance: Narrative Form and Cultural Engagement in Hawthorne's Fiction* (Princeton: Princeton University Press, 1992); Lori Merish, *Sentimental Materialism: Gender, Commodity*

Culture, and Nineteenth-Century American Literature (Durham, N.C.: Duke University Press, 2000); and Clark Davis, *Hawthorne's Shyness: Ethics, Politics, and the Question of Engagement* (Baltimore, Md.: Johns Hopkins University Press, 2005). A strong, usefully skeptical account of "the general consensus that *Blithedale* has to be read in conservative terms" appears in Robert S. Levine's "Sympathy and Reform in *The Blithedale Romance*" in *The Cambridge Companion to Nathaniel Hawthorne*, ed. Richard H. Millington (New York: Cambridge University Press, 2005), 207–29, here 224.

3. This is the reading of Hawthorne's use of the first-person in *Blithedale* offered in *Hawthorne's Shyness*, 105–17. Clark Davis reads in Coverdale's narrative Hawthorne's deployment of an ethically rich kind of reticence, through which he endeavors to speak with a heightened sense of the limitations of self and its claims. For more on the complexity of the first-person in *Blithedale*, see also Jonathan Auerbach, *The Romance of Failure: First-Person Fictions of Poe, Hawthorne, and James* (New York: Oxford University Press, 1989).

4. On Brook Farm, see *The Brook Farm Book: A Collection of First-Hand Accounts of the Community*, ed. Joel Myerson (New York: Garland Publishing, 1987). On Hawthorne and the possibilities of the "Romance," exemplary works include Joel Porte's *The Romance in America: Studies in Cooper, Poe, Hawthorne, Melville, and James* (Middletown, Conn.: Wesleyan University Press, 1969); Michael Davitt Bell, *Hawthorne and the Historical Romance of New England* (Princeton: Princeton University Press, 1971); Elissa Greenwald, *Realism and the Romance: Nathaniel Hawthorne, Henry James, and American Fiction* (Ann Arbor: University of Michigan Press, 1989); Millington's *Practicing Romance*; and the work collected more recently in *Hawthorne and the Real: Bicentennial Essays*, ed. Millicent Bell (Columbus: Ohio State University Press, 2005).

5. For a recent account of the need for precisely this shift in emphasis—a shift toward questions of sex and away from an identification of Coverdale with Hawthorne—see Michael J. Colacurcio, "Nobody's Protest Novel: Art and Politics in *The Blithedale Romance*," *Nathaniel Hawthorne Review* 34, nos. 1–2 (2008): 1–39. Though I diverge from Colacurcio's reading of the novel as "an oblique but determined protest" against the expansive utopian promises of the midcentury's sexual reformers, who offer the prospect of an enlarged "circle of intimate loves" as "a cure for civilization's prime discontent," still he is exemplary in his attention to the inextricability of sex from what are understood to be the novel's more conventional forms of "politics" (32).

6. Colacurcio, "Nobody's Protest Novel," 25.

7. I follow here in the footsteps of Jordan Alexander Stein, whose splendid essay on queerness and style in *Blithedale* looks "to collect into the history of sexuality versions of queerness that never accede to discourse" ("*The Blithedale Romance*'s Queer Style," 212).

8. See Barbara F. Lefcowitz and Allan B. Lefcowitz, "Some Rents in the Veil: New Light on Priscilla and Zenobia," *Nineteenth-Century Fiction* 21 (1966): 263–75; Berlant, "Fantasies of Utopia in *The Blithedale Romance*"; Robert K. Martin, "Hester Prynne, *C'est Moi*: Nathaniel Hawthorne and the Anxieties of Gender," in *Engendering Men: The Question of Male Feminist Criticism*, ed. Joseph A. Boone and Michael Cadden (New York: Routledge,

1990) 122–39; Benjamin Scott Grossberg, "'The Tender Passion Was Very Rife among Us': Coverdale's Queer Utopia and *The Blithedale Romance*," *Studies in American Fiction* 28, no. 1 (2000): 3–25; and Stein, "*The Blithedale Romance*'s Queer Style." Other accountings of queer possibility in Hawthorne can be found in Christopher Castiglia's "The Marvelous Queer Interiors of *The House of the Seven Gables*," in Millington, *The Cambridge Companion to Nathaniel Hawthorne*, 186–206; John N. Miller, "Eros and Ideology: At the Heart of Hawthorne's Blithedale," *Nineteenth-Century Literature* 55, no. 1 (2000): 1–21; and David Greven, *Men beyond Desire: Manhood, Sex, and Violation in American Literature* (New York: Palgrave, 2005).

9. Levine, "Sympathy and Reform in *The Blithedale Romance*," 211.

10. Berlant, "Fantasies of Utopia in *The Blithedale Romance*," 36.

11. See Hawthorne's *The Life of Franklin Pierce*. Of course, not all critics read the novel as inconstestably anti-utopian. Nina Baym offered an early dissent in "*The Blithedale Romance*: A Radical Reading," *Journal of English and Germanic Philology* 67 (1968): 545–69. Other critics find ampler possibilities, too, in the voices of characters other than Miles: Zenobia, for instance, or (in Russ Castronovo's account), the farmer Silas Foster. See, for instance, Joel Pfister on "the social construction of femininity" in *Blithedale* in his work *The Production of Personal Life: Class, Gender, and the Psychological in Hawthorne's Fiction* (Stanford, Ca.: Stanford University Press, 1991), 80, 80–103, and Russ Castronovo, *Necro-Citizenship: Death, Eroticism, and the Public Sphere in the Nineteenth-Century United States* (Durham, N.C.: Duke University Press, 2001), 137–42. Robert S. Levine astutely interrogates the tradition of reading *Blithedale* as committedly anti-reformist, going so far as to suggest that *Blithedale* "is one of the boldest reform texts of the 1850s" ("Sympathy and Reform in *The Blithedale Romance*," 225). I am less convinced than Levine that the novel is the performance of an attempt to "contain" radical sympathies Hawthorne nevertheless entertains about politics, though I very much appreciate Levine's reading of the novel as an adumbration, rather than assertion, of political possibilities. My reading takes politics, as such, to be more vehicle in the narrative, chiefly for the displacement of specifically erotic anxieties, than tenor.

12. Levine, "Sympathy and Reform in *The Blithedale Romance*," 224.

13. Davis, *Hawthorne's Shyness*, 108.

14. Davis, *Hawthorne's Shyness*, 109–10. In Davis's reading, it is precisely Hawthorne's commitment to a kind of removal from the tumult of contestatory politics that allows him a stronger purchase on the undergirding questions of political and ethical life. Accounts of Hawthorne as reticent or disengaged and therefore apolitical in this way miss the point, in Davis's account, of the ultimately critical, ethico-political nature of Hawthorne's strategic reticence.

15. This approach to Hawthorne recalls, along with Foucault's admonitions in *The Order of Things*, Christopher Nealon's point, made in reference to Toni Morrison's reading of Willa Cather in *Playing in the Dark*, that "the moral life of fiction lies in how authors may celebrate or mistrust what their imaginations bring them, not in what they imagine" (*Foundlings*, 88).

16. On the Veiled Lady, and mesmeric entertainments, and their propriety—which would of course be of such intense interest to Henry James in *The Bostonians*—see, for a start, Samuel Chase Coale, *Mesmerism and Hawthorne: Mediums of American Romance* (Tuscaloosa: University of Alabama Press, 1998), as well as Taylor Stoeher, *Hawthorne's Mad Scientists: Pseudoscience and Social Science in Nineteenth-Century Life and Letters* (Hamden, Conn.: Archon Books, 1978).

17. A range of critics have noted Coverdale's especially scopophilic relation to Zenobia and how it answers to the more manifestly patriarchal forms of authority claimed in the novel by figures like Hollingsworth and Westervelt. (See especially Merish's *Sentimental Materialism* on this point, as well as Levine's "Sympathy and Reform in *The Blithedale Romance*.") Such misogyny qualifies, but does not in the end wholly obviate, Coverdale's "critique," if that is the word, of the corporeal politics of sentimental femininity. His investment in the sex of femininity is at once manifestly self-serving—he likes to imagine that a liberated femininity coincides nicely with a femininity made sexually available to him and to his imagination—but his account here is not, for that, *identical* to a reduction of Zenobia, or of womanhood more generally, to the body. The wearing of bodies under the strictures of what he calls the "feminine system" seems to him, here, to express a more general binding and diminishment of women, and of the ampler possibilities for feminine life, and he was hardly alone, at the midcentury, in making that connection. Echoes of it can be heard in Fanny Wright, of course, but also in the work of Margaret Fuller, whose presence so haunts Hawthorne's imagination in *Blithedale*.

18. Levine writes, "Coverdale obsesses on Zenobia's bare shoulder, hot-house flower, and sensual body, but his looking is often elicited by Zenobia's deliberate design" ("Sympathy and Reform in *The Blithedale Romance*," 217). But Coverdale's habitual depiction of his own impulses as originating in the bodies and consciousnesses of others complicates Levine's contention. One surely wants to grant the point about the power Zenobia wields, particularly over Coverdale; but it is wise to note as well that the imputation of calculated "design" in Zenobia's demeanor threatens to under-read Coverdale's tendencies, pronounced and, I am suggesting, enormously consequential, toward self-exonerating projection.

19. See Barker-Benfield, *The Horrors of the Half-Known Life*, as well as Smith-Rosenberg's *Disorderly Conduct*. As Robert K. Martin puts it, "Thus nineteenth-century theories of separate spheres simultaneously provoked, while they sought to control, the possibility of same-sex desires and hence the collapse of sharp gender distinctions" ("Hester Prynne, *C'est Moi*," 137). Related points appear as well in Helen Lekfowitz Horowitz's *Rereading Sex: Battles over Sexual Knowledge and Repression in Nineteenth-Century America* (New York: Vintage, 2002). The civic deformations entailed by this strict separation of genders also preoccupy Ann Douglas throughout *The Feminization of American Culture* (New York: Knopf, 1978).

20. For more on bachelorhood and the tradition of bachelor writing in which Washington Irving figures so prominently, see Michael Warner, "Irving's Posterity," *ELH* 67, no. 3 (2000): 773–99; and Traister, "The Wandering Bachelor."

21. On onanism as a post-Enlightenment affliction, and particularly a disease of the ungoverned imagination, see Laqueur's *Solitary Sex*. See also the essays collected in Bennett and Rosario's *Solitary Pleasures*. For an excellent consideration of the masturbator as among the earliest iterations of modern sexual identity as such—"modern" sexual identity as tracked and specified by a theorist like Foucault—see Eve Kosofsky Sedgwick's essay "Jane Austen and the Masturbating Girl" in *Tendencies* (Durham, N.C.: Duke University Press, 1993), 109–29.

22. This line anchors the reading of same-sex desire, its flourishing and its policing, in Benjamin Scott Grossberg's essay "The Tender Passion Was Very Rife among Us."

23. In a riff on projection, misrecogntion, self-loathing redescribed as virtue, and sadism redescribed as compassion, Nietzsche writes, "For with the priests *everything* becomes more dangerous, not only cures and remedies, but also arrogance, revenge, acuteness, profligacy, love, lust to rule, virtue, disease—but it is only fair to add that it was on the soil of this *essentially dangerous* form of human existence, the priestly form, that man first became *an interesting animal*, that only here did the human soul in a higher sense acquire *depth* and become *evil*." See the first essay, section 6, of *The Genealogy of Morals*, in *"The Genealogy of Morals" and "Ecce Homo,"* ed. Walter Kaufmann, trans. Walter Kaufmann and R. J. Hollingdale (New York: Vintage, 1967), 32–33.

24. For more on Fourier in *Blithedale*, see especially Berlant's "Fantasies of Utopia in *The Blithedale Romance*." For an especially fine account of Fourier in his relation to American bohemianism and sex-radicalism in midcentury America, see Moon, "Solitude, Singularity, Seriality."

25. Martin, "Hester Prynne, *C'est Moi*," 132.

26. In this reading I depart from Robert K. Martin's strong account of sex, gender, and anxiety in the novel. "Gender confusion," he writes, "occasions for Hawthorne the deepest anxiety. For the rules of gender, arbitrary as they are, remain the foundation of male power and female subordination; Hawthorne hardly dares imagine the consequences. Hence his plot moves to foreclose the very possibilities that the multiple relationships among his characters have opened up" ("Hester Prynne, *C'est Moi*," 137). Once more, this is a reading that seems to me to mistake Hawthorne for Coverdale, whose anxieties do indeed struggle to foreclose what his desires have opened up. I have tried to present *Blithedale* here as a novel that is in essence *about* precisely that anxiety—that is in all an exacting study of the forms such anxiety takes and the foreclosures it struggles to produce, with whatever dishonesty or violence—rather than an uncritical enactment of it.

27. For the definitive treatment of Hawthorne's Puritan tales, see Michael J. Colacurcio, *The Province of Piety: Moral History in Hawthorne's Early Tales* (Durham, N.C.: Duke University Press, 1995).

28. On orphanhood as a nationalist project, see Leo Bersani, "Incomparable America"; on the relation of style in *Moby-Dick* to orphanhood and nationalism, see Peter Coviello, *Intimacy in America*.

29. On freedom and terror in Twain's novel, see especially Toni Morrison's introduction to *Adventures of Huckleberry Finn* (New York: Oxford University Press, 1996), xxxi–xli.

NOTES TO CHAPTER 6

1. Henry James, *The Wings of the Dove* (1902; New York: Vintage, 1986), 175. Cited hereafter as *WD*.

2. Eve Kosofsky Sedgwick, for instance, artfully describes *Wings* as "a novel where the supposed glory of the unspoken things that continually 'hang fire' seems stretched to fineness of sublimity" ("Is the Rectum Straight?: Identification and Identity in *The Wings of the Dove*," in *Tendencies* [Durham, N.C.: Duke University Press, 1993], 76).

3. On James and his relation to the Wilde trials, see Sedgwick's suggestive asides, in her *Wings of the Dove* essay; on James's fascination with the Wilde trials, in *Tendencies*, 76–78, as well as Stacey Margolis's comments at the outset of her chapter on *The Sacred Fount* in *The Public Life of Privacy in Nineteenth-Century American Literature* (Durham, N.C.: Duke University Press, 2005), 169–95, here 173. For a strong account of sexual naming, Wilde, and James's "The Turn of the Screw," see Neill Matheson, "Talking Horrors: James, Euphemism, and the Specter of Wilde," *American Literature* 71, no. 4 (1999), 709–50.

4. Two especially fine parsings of late Jamesian style that have been crucial to me are Ruth Bernard Yeazell's *Language and Knowledge in the Late Novels of Henry James* (Chicago: University of Chicago Press, 1976) and Sharon Cameron's *Thinking in Henry James* (Chicago: University of Chicago Press, 1989). See also Leo Bersani in *A Future for Astyanax: Character and Desire in Literature* (New York: Columbia University Press, 1984) and his more recent parsing, with Adam Phillips, in *Intimacies* (Chicago: University of Chicago Press, 2008). And for an exemplary account of "the interruptions of intelligibility" manifest in James's style, "its systematic challenging of the presumption that desire can be, or ought to be, represented," see Kevin Ohi's "'The novel is older, and so are the young': On the Queerness of Style," *The Henry James Review* 27, no. 2 (2006): 140–55, here 141.

5. On the trials, see Cohen, *Talk on the Wilde Side*; for an accounting of the period that emphasizes the emergence of this mode of resistant identity, see especially Katz, *Love Stories*.

6. Jagose, *Inconsequence*, 57, 65.

7. Tessa Hadley, *Henry James and the Imagination of Pleasure* (Cambridge: Cambridge University Press, 2002), 1. She goes on, "For all the variations in emphasis and tone, new ways of explicitly addressing the homoerotic in his writing have made themselves quickly at home in our awareness." Hadley, who in her work takes up what she calls "that great release of ripe worldliness in the late novels," is only one of the strongest among many critics—Leo Bersani, Eve Kosofsky Sedgwick, Ross Posnock, Hugh Stevens, Wendy Graham—who have aimed to free us from the familiar inherited versions of James as, in her words, either "unsexual" or "squeamishly appalled and fascinated by sex" (4, 2). See Bersani, *A Future for Astyanax*; Sedgwick, *Epistemology of the Closet*; Ross Posnock, *The Trials of Curiosity: Henry James, William James, and the Challenge of Modernity* (New York: Oxford University Press, 1991); Hugh Stevens, *Henry James and Sexuality* (Cambridge: Cambridge University Press, 1998); and Wendy Graham, *Henry James's Thwarted Love* (Stanford, Ca.: Stanford University

Press, 1999). Many of these readings can be said to follow from Mark Seltzer's opening of James to a mode of criticism explicitly rooted in Foucault, in his *Henry James and the Art of Power* (Ithaca, N.Y.: Cornell University Press, 1984).

8. "When Philip Rahv in 1945 and Lionel Trilling in 1953 brought *The Bostonians* back into print and official critical approval," Habegger writes, "they rested their case to a great extent on some large claims for Basil Ransom as a conservative hero challenging a culture of triumphant vulgarity and intrusiveness" (*Henry James and the "Woman Business"* [New York: Cambridge University Press, 1989], 189–90). Habegger does not dismiss these visions of the novel so much as recast them and, without dismissing James's own critical ambivalence about Basil, goes a long way in showing how such claims about James's misogyny might be made to stick. My sense of the novel's misogyny as hysterical follows especially from Claire Kahane's important essay, "Hysteria, Feminism, and the Case of *The Bostonians*," in *Feminism and Psychoanalysis*, ed. Richard Feinstein and Judith Roof (Ithaca, N.Y.: Cornell University Press, 1989), 280–97.

9. Henry James, *The Bostonians* (New York: Vintage, 2000), 301. Cited hereafter as *B*. My own reading builds on the resistance to offhandedly homophobic accounts of the novel pioneered by Judith Fetterley in *The Resisting Reader: A Feminist Approach to Fiction* (Bloomington: Indiana University Press, 1978), 101–15, as well as on elaborations of this premise, and on the possibility of an other-than-dismissive interchange between the narrative and Olive Chancellor, in Joseph Litvak's *Caught in the Act: Theatricality in the Nineteenth-Century English Novel* (Berkeley: University of California Press, 1992); in Valerie Rohy's *Impossible Women: Lesbian Figures and American Fiction* (Ithaca, N.Y.: Cornell University Press, 1990); and in Jagose's *Inconsequence*.

10. Sedgwick, "A Poem Is Being Written," *Tendencies*, 206. Thinking of female anal eroticism she writes, "What we have located, then, is a really quite large vacant space in our culture that presents a kind of lovely laboratory for the testing out of a Foucauldian hypothesis, if for whatever reason we were interested in looking at it that way" (206). My sense is that in *The Bostonians* James presents Olive with a like vacancy, one that results from the inadequacy, with respect to the force and extent of her desire, of the homosocial model of female intimacy, and the inadmissibility (because of their pathologizing intent, as well as what Olive would understand more plainly as their *vulgarity*) of any emergent sexological models.

11. On "the emergent" in *The Bostonians*, and for a reading of the novel "in the context of its immediate future," see Jennifer L. Fleissner *Women, Compulsion, Modernity* (Chicago: University of Chicago Press, 2004), 158. My understanding of the novel as especially attentive to intuited futures borrows from Fleissner's strong account of "the emergent" in *The Bostonians*, and in particular of "its ability to mark the ongoing presence of an as yet unrealized future within the confines of the historical instance."

12. Bersani and Phillips, *Intimacies*, 25. Cited hereafter as *I*.

13. The letter refers to Verena's "natural talent for public speaking," which sets her in a compensatory sort of relation to Olive, who has "no talent for appearing in public . . . [but] a dream that her friend and she together (one by the use of her money and the other by her eloquence) may, working side by side, really revolutionize the condition of women." See

The Complete Notebooks of Henry James, ed. Leon Edel and Lyall H. Powers (New York: Oxford University Press, 1987), 18–20.

14. Henry James, *"The Turn of the Screw" and "The Aspern Papers,"* ed. Anthony Curtis (New York: Penguin, 1984), 41.

15. Jagose provides a sharp account of interiors in the novel as the site of, Olive hopes, a kind of shelter for her singular intimacy with Verena. Basil, she observes, is forever entering interior spaces into which he is either not invited or where he is not particularly welcome; that interior thus proves, much to Olive's pain, porous, but is still precious to her: "Despite . . . its constant vulnerability to intrusion, and its failure to claw to itself the sustenances and sanctions of marriage, the domestic architecture of Olive's home enables the production and maintenance of a homosocial intimacy" with Verena (Jagose, *Inconsequence*, 75). Though she underreads a bit the degree to which that interior signifies, too, Olive's *wealth*—signifies, that is, the force and weight of her status, which is one strong card she has to play in her battle with Basil—still Jagose is acute on the salience of rich interior space as a kind of bulwark, however permeable, against the invasions of heterosexual privilege.

16. In this critique of the identificatory politics of sympathy, we might find another strain of the novel's oft-remarked indebtedness to *The Blithedale Romance*. The terms of this critique recall Glenn Hendler's trenchant commentary in *Public Sentiments*, where he underscores how the promises as well as the vexations of sentimental politics turn on a "fantasy of experiential equivalence," leaving scholars of sentimentality "to focus either on its potential to build bridges between people or its colonizing proclivity to collapse them" (*Public Sentiments*, 7, 8). For more on the critique of sympathy in Hawthorne, see Levine's "Sympathy and Reform in *The Blithedale Romance*," 207–29.

17. Sedgwick writes especially sensitively about the arrangements of worldliness—of knowing, insufficient knowledge, and sex—in *The Bostonians*. See her comments in *Epistemology of the Closet*, 97–98.

18. Jagose, *Inconsequence*, 67.

19. For influential versions of such critiques, see Nancy Armstrong, *Desire and Domestic Fiction: A Political History of the Novel* (New York: Oxford University Press, 1900), or, in a different key and with respect to the American canon, John Carlos Rowe, *At Emerson's Tomb: The Politics of Classic American Literature* (New York: Columbia University Press, 1997).

20. Judith Butler, *Gender Trouble: Feminism and the Subversion of Identity* (New York: Routledge, 1990), 57–72. See also Butler's *Bodies That Matter: On the Discursive Limits of Sex* (New York: Routledge, 1993), 233–36.

21. Quoted in Deitcher, *Dear Friends*, 110.

22. Jagose, *Inconsequence*, 65.

23. Olive is of course hardly the novel's only purveyor of acute, and particularly erotic, misrecognition. Nor, even, is Verena, upon whose own self-misperceptions the whole plot of the novel turns. (She leaves Olive for Basil, deciding that her own calling resides not in reform and reformers but in loving Basil.) There is Basil himself. Forever claiming to

himself that what he desires in women is a sort of bright-spirited docility—a cheerful acquiescence to their roles as angels of the home and denizens of a very strictly delineated private sphere—Basil emerges nevertheless as a man who, quite like Miles Coverdale, finds himself erotically captivated not by timorous modesty but, precisely, *publicity* in women (his actress girlfriend in New York, the nearly famous Verena). It is the *violation* of strictly demarcated gendered propriety that most excites and beguiles him, not least because in the chance to "'squelch' all that at a stroke" (*B*, 306)—to render public women private— he finds a vividly eroticized kind of triumphalism, a virilizing conquest he persistently describes to himself and Verena as "love."

24. Fleissner, *Women, Compulsion, Modernity*, 151.

25. Marcus, *Between Women*, 203, 202. Though I find Olive Chancellor to be a figure less safely housed by the marriages Marcus describes as viable and accepted, at least in England and at least within some networks, still her reading of female marriage, especially in her chapter "The Genealogy of Marriage" (193–226), has been crucial to my sense of Olive's dilemma.

26. Jameson, *The Political Unconscious*, 102.

27. On the exigencies of a specifically male world of romantic friendship in nineteenth-century America, see Nissen, *Manly Love*, esp. 11–53.

28. Henry James, *Hawthorne*, in *Henry James: Literary Criticism*, vol. 1, ed. Leon Edel (New York: Library of America, 1984), 352.

29. See for instance Judith Halberstam's work in *In a Queer Time and Place*, or Carla Freccero's more deconstructively attuned *Queer/Early/Modern*. James's ill fit inside such narratives suggests to me, again, the pitfalls of a too-easy analogy between temporal and sexual propriety. Such analogies can induce us to forget that not all those who desire errantly refuse to hew to the most traditional frameworks of temporality. This may cause them pain—as it plainly does Olive Chancellor in *The Bostonians*—but it does not make them not, or somehow insufficiently, queer.

30. In a way that might remind us of Kenneth Warren's readings in *Black and White Strangers*, James addresses a central American racial dilemma without talking about race per se. I am suggesting that thinking about Olive, about untimely queer women, is for the novel a way of thinking about former slaves. See *Black and White Strangers: Race and American Literary Realism* (Chicago: University of Chicago Press, 1995).

31. Stadler writes, "there is certainly a note of triumph, and a conferral of authority, when the novel leaves Olive, a queer figure, still *inside* a modern institution of culture and still discursively, physically, and mentally involved in its operations and social relations" (*Troubling Minds: The Cultural Politics of Genius in the United States, 1840–1890* [Minneapolis: University of Minnesota Press, 2006], 137–38).

NOTES TO CODA: THE TURN

1. James, *Selected Letters of Henry James to Edmund Gosse, 1882–1915: A Literary Friendship*, ed. Rayburn S. Moore (Baton Rouge: Louisiana State University Press, 1988), 126.

2. Ed Cohen describes that interplay masterfully in *Talk on the Wilde Side*.

3. I am thinking here of Castiglia's argument, throughout his *Interior States*, that "imaginative fiction is the archive of the socially possible, an archive of alternatives to the historically or sociologically 'real'" (13), and of McGarry's work, in *Ghosts of Futures Past*, on sex, secularism, and the lost futures of what were nonsecular imaginings of habitable sexual possibility in across nineteenth-century America.

4. "There is no question that the appearance in nineteenth-century psychiatry, jurisprudence, and literature of a whole series of discourses on the species and subspecies of homosexuality, inversion, pederasty, and 'psychic hermaphrodism' made possible a strong advance of social controls into this area of 'perversity'; but it also made possible the formation of a 'reverse' discourse: homosexuality began to speak in its own behalf, to demand that its legitimacy or 'naturality' be acknowledged, often in the same vocabulary, using the same categories by which it was medically disqualified" (Foucault, *History of Sexuality*, vol. 1, 101). On Symonds's investments in German sexology, see again Michael Robertson's chapter on Symonds in *Worshipping Walt*.

5. A fine, concise critique of the progressive account of queer history in the twentieth century appears in the introduction to Nealon's *Foundlings*, especially 2–13.

6. Kevin Ohi, "The novel is older, and so are the young," 141.

7. Adam Phillips, *Terrors and Experts* (Cambridge, Mass.: Harvard University Press, 1995), 19.

8. Sedgwick first develops this notion of the Gothic in *The Coherence of Gothic Conventions* (New York: Arno, 1980), and sharpens its sexual dimensions in *Between Men*. See also Shoshana Felman, "Turning the Screw of Interpretation," *Yale French Studies* 55/56 (1977): 94–207.

9. Ellis Hanson, "Screwing with Children in Henry James," *GLQ* 9, no. 3 (2003): 367–91, here 371.

10. Henry James, *"The Turn of the Screw" and "The Aspern Papers,"* ed. Anthony Curtis (New York: Penguin, 1984), 35. Cited hereafter as *TS*.

11. For more on the tale and Freud, particularly the Freud of the case studies, see David Wagenknecht, "Here's Looking at You, Peter Quint," *American Imago* 55 (1998): 423—58.

12. Phillips, *Terrors and Experts*, 19.

13. Edmund Wilson's article, "The Ambiguity of Henry James," which made its initial appearance in 1934, appears in revised form in *The Triple Thinkers: Twelve Essays on Literature Subjects* (New York: Farrar, Straus, and Giroux, 1976), 88–132. For the interpretive battles around the tale, pitting Freudians against anti-Freudians, see *A Casebook on Henry James's "The Turn of the Screw,"* ed. Gerald Willen, 2nd. ed. (New York: Thomas Y. Crowell Co, 1969).

14. Quoted in Phillips, *Terrors and Experts*, 66.

15. Matheson, "Talking Horrors," 711.

16. Hanson, "Screwing with Children," 369.

17. Felman, "Turning the Screw of Interpretation," 193, 192, 164. On the play of the word "grasp," see 161–71.

18. Foucault, *The History of Sexuality*, vol. 1, 112.

19. Sigmund Freud, "A Case of Hysteria," in *The Standard Edition of the Complete Psychological Works of Sigmund Freud*, vol. 7, trans. and ed. James Strachey (London: Hogarth Press, 1953), 77–78.

20. Felman, 197. For an especially fine account of the blurring of the identities of female patient and male physician, and of the panics that blurring instills, see Neil Hertz, "Dora's Secrets, Freud's Techniques," in *The End of the Line* (New York: Columbia University Press, 1985), 135–54.

21. Freud, *Standard Edition*, vol. 7, 203.

22. For two famous iterations of Bersani's vision of desire as self-shattering see, first, *The Freudian Body* (New York: Columbia University Press, 1986), and his subsequent essay "Is the Rectum a Grave?" in *AIDS: Cultural Analysis, Cultural Activism*, ed. Douglas Crimp (Cambridge, Mass.: MIT Press, 1988), 197–222.

23. Freud, *Standard Edition*, vol. 7, 145.

24. I am thinking of Freud's intellectual exasperation, in the third of the three essays, at the fact of the clitoris, which piece of physical morphology presents him with immense conceptual difficulties in his effort to sequester the sexuality he had theorized in the first two essays back into the drive toward reproduction. See especially *The Standard Edition*, vol. 7, 220–21, where he worries over what happens to young women in puberty whose "clitoridal zone refuses to abandon its excitability." It is a moment in Freud's corpus that recalls forcefully Foucault's observation about "the difference between the physiology of reproduction and the medical theories of sexuality" that developed in the nineteenth century. Of that "incongruity" he will say of the latter, which Freud in this instance plainly exemplifies, "Their feeble content from the standpoint of elementary rationality, not to mention scientificity, earns them a place apart in the history of knowledge" (Foucault, *History of Sexuality*, vol. 1, 55, 54).

25. Sedgwick, *Epistemology of the Closet*, 53; Luciano, "Touching, Clinging, Haunting, Worlding"; José Esteban Muñoz, "The Sense of Watching Tony Sleep," 149–50; Elizabeth Freeman, "Still After," in *After Sex?*, 27–33, here 32. We might think, too, in the register of Muñoz's comments, of Jasbir K. Puar's theorization of "assemblage": "We cannot know assemblages in advance," she writes, "thus taunting the temporal suffocation plaguing identity politics" (*Terrorist Assemblages*, 222). Indeed, I take much of the force of her critique of "homonationalism" to reside in the ways it arms us to resist the forced equivalencies, expressed in an *already-knownness*, that have come to invest "queer" as it circulates in the global marketplace and, in Puar's astringent reading, in queer critique itself.

26. Thinking of queer in the register of the "always already," as the name of an interior structural incoherence, seems to me, in other words, another kind of universalism,

another way of knowing in advance *precisely what sex is.* That the content of this sex is always a negativity that escapes codification of any imaginable sort does not alter the style of determinism—call it a structural determinism—in which it emerges.

27. The phrase "a touch across time" comes from Dinshaw's *Getting Medieval*, 21. Love's work—in a chapter titled "The Demands of Queer History" that sets Dinshaw's work on historical identification and desire alongside that of a range of queer theorists of temporality (Christopher Nealon, Valerie Traub, Carla Freccero)—emphasizes "the pain that is at the heart of lesbian and gay historiography" (*Feeling Backward*, 42).

28. "The project of this book," Sedgwick writes, "will be to show how issues of modern homo/ heterosexual definition are structured, not by the supersession of one model and the consequent withering away of another, but instead by the relations enabled by the unrationalized coexistence of different models during the times they do coexist" (*Epistemology*, 44–48, here 47).

29. The matter is not that cultivated anachronism cannot be incisive or productive as a queer historiographic strategy. Valerie Rohy, for instance, does especially strong work under just that rubric in *Anachronism and Its Others*. But the cultivation of anachronism as the antidote to a "historicism" that is imagined as hostile and phobic—the sense that "the historical argument mirrors the fundamental logic of sexual discipline" (130), say— seems to me to misrepresent, in the first instance, the plurality of the field's historicisms, and to rewrite what are differences of emphasis and interest as conflictual oppositions, forms of incompatible sexual politics.

30. In these formulations, particularly about the friction of historical exchange, I am especially influenced by Elizabeth Freeman's work. See her *Time Binds*.

31. Warner, *Trouble with Normal*, 139, 115–16.

32. Warner, *Trouble with Normal*, 75.

33. Sedgwick, *Epistemology of the Closet*, 25, 26, 24.

34. Stockton, *Queer Child*, 39.

Index

About the Author

Peter Coviello is Professor of English at Bowdoin College, where he has directed the programs in Gay and Lesbian Studies and Africana Studies. He is the author of *Intimacy in America: Dreams of Affiliation in Antebellum Literature* and the editor of Walt Whitman's *Memoranda During the War.*